PASTORAL THEOLOGY
FROM A GLOBAL PERSPECTIVE

Pastoral Theology from a Global Perspective

A Case Study Approach

HENRY S. WILSON

TAKATSO MOFOKENG

JUDO POERWOWIDAGDO

ROBERT A. EVANS

ALICE FRAZER EVANS

ORBIS BOOKS

Maryknoll, New York 10545

The Catholic Foreign Mission Society of America (Maryknoll) recruits and trains people for overseas missionary service. Through Orbis Books, Maryknoll aims to foster the international dialogue that is essential to mission. The books published, however, reflect the opinions of their authors and are not meant to represent the official position of the society.

Published by Orbis Books, Maryknoll, NY 10545-0308
Manufactured in the United States of America

Library of Congress Cataloging-in-Publication Data

Pastoral theology from a global perspective : a case study approach /
   Henry S. Wilson . . . [et al.].
      p.   cm.
   Includes bibliographical references.
   ISBN 1-57075-079-3 (alk. paper)
   Pastoral theology.   2. Pastoral counseling.   3. Church and
social problems.   4. Social justice.   5. Women in Christianity.
BV4011.P3457   1996
253'.09—dc20
                                     96-24882
                                     CIP

CONTENTS

ACKNOWLEDGMENTS

This labor of love represents a commitment to pastoral ministry by a remarkable collection of people from around the world. The authors are deeply indebted to the communities and individuals who offered their stories for publication. Their powerful images of hope and sorrow, triumph and trial, are gifts to the global church.

While the authors acknowledge and live by the enduring resources of prayer, Bible study, and the examples of those who have gone before us, we especially raise up in these chapters the often surprising resource of Christ speaking to us through one another. This volume witnesses to a contemporary and continuing Road to Emmaus. Our commission to those who read these stories of faith and hear the voices of the storytellers is to take them seriously, to seek to understand their challenges, and through God's grace, to learn from them. We hope these stories will inspire readers to reflect on and share their own journeys of faith with others they meet "on the way."

Colleagues in ministries as far apart as Australia, India, Peru, the Philippines, and Zimbabwe helped the authors of the commentaries better understand the context of the following stories presented as case studies. The dialogue between colleagues and the liberating power of new insights also heightened the authors' awareness of the common issues and common bonds shared by those who serve the church in pastoral ministry.

The authors thank the staff of Orbis Books, especially editors Robert Ellsberg and Sue Perry, for their continued commitment to the biblical themes of liberation and justice. These themes challenge and motivate the institutions which sustain our ministries. We also express deep appreciation to those friends and staff members who assumed the challenging and critical work of information gathering, production, editing and proofreading: Maralyn R. Lipner of Plowshares Institute; Carolyn McComish of the World Council of Churches; and Margaret Owen of the World Alliance of Reformed Churches.

INTRODUCTION

A surprising, almost revelatory pattern began to emerge on the chalkboard. As the pastors and lay leaders from Africa added their insights to those listed by small groups from Asia, Latin America, Europe, and North America, someone declared, "Look at how many problems and challenges we share!"

On that warm afternoon in August 1994 in Bossey, Switzerland, some thirty colleagues from around the world—participants in a consultation sponsored by the World Council of Churches and the World Alliance of Reformed Churches— shared important discoveries about how to be practical theologians. Their findings were strikingly similar: not only the primary problems of ministry in very diverse settings, but also the biblical and theological resources which were suggested to address these problems. Strong hope began to rise with the realization that perspectives on pastoral theology held by theologians from the South and the North might be on a collaborative rather than a collision course.

Some central themes for pastoral ministry in the twenty-first century were identified by this fellowship of pastoral servants; they shape the structure of this book. Not only are local pastors and lay leaders called to care for human needs, a traditional and universally accepted theme of pastoral ministry, they are also faced with global issues of economic justice and ecological harmony; empowering marginalized peoples; the role of women in church and society; and reconciliation and peacemaking.

This creative dialogue between laity and clergy, women and men, young and old, from different continents, races, ethnic backgrounds, and theological perspectives not only revealed common problems but generated a vision for pastoral theology. Pastors and lay leaders counsel and love their parishioners through problems that they all assume are personal and local, when they are in fact systemic and global. While church leaders are called to accompany brothers and sisters through these problems, it is frequently impossible for them to resolve the dilemmas if they continue to perceive them only as products of local realities. With the recognition of common global themes comes the opportunity to liberate pastors and lay leaders from their burdens of isolation.

Pastoral theology has often been limited to or dominated by an approach to the discipline that focuses on contextual pastoral care and counseling. The authors, all of whom participated in the Bossey consultation, propose that pastoral theology

1

can encompass much more. While awareness of the specific context of a personal, family, or congregational problem is essential for understanding, these persons, families, and congregations are also vitally linked to the human community and the church universal. Viewing pastoral concerns globally invites Christian sisters and brothers from around the world who are struggling with similar problems to share their wisdom and insights.

The Brazilian educator, Paulo Freire, has said, "Don't ask a fish about water." Pastoral counselors are also captives of their context and are often quite unaware of the social and cultural forces which shape their understanding of ministry and the gospel. The fresh perspectives of those outside this context may well be a source of God's grace breaking through unrecognized barriers of subjectivity.[1] Global part- ners in ministry can become a vital community of support for local church leaders by offering one another rich resources of years of experience, deep insights, wise advice, and fresh perspectives.

Rather than raising up North/South or East/West ideological confrontations, global pastoral theology offers a path to reconciliation, renewal, and mutual growth. A woman pastor in India ("Should a Woman Lead the Church?") can find solidarity with a Christian lay woman in Peru ("Support for Rosa") as they seek recognition of their dignity and their ministries. A fishing community in the Philippines ("Another Face of Tourism") shares a common cause with Hispanic shepherds in the United States ("Green Pastures") in their search for ecological justice. Pastors serving an Australian Aboriginal Islander community and a Nigerian village are bonded by threats to traditional ways of life. Sharing learnings could bring critical new perspectives and renewal to their ministries.

TEXT AND CONTEXT

There are no simple, single answers to universal and systemic pastoral problems. No ready-made medicines can heal the wounds of individuals or societies. Being a pastoral theologian is about being a "reflective practitioner."[2] A central goal of theological education and pastoral formation should be to enable lay and ordained pastors to reflect continually on their ministry and the persons they serve. Pastoral Christian thinking is best pursued when the text is put in dynamic relation with the context. The Bible and confession must be in dialogue with empirical facts and the experiences of ministry.

When the conjunction between text and context occurs, often in surprising new ways, the Word breaks in, and pastoral reality is illumined. Pastors, parishioners, and communities discover healing in sharing their stories and in the confirmation of God's action in their lives. Poor rural farmers in Haiti ("The Fate of Té Bouké') and village residents in war-torn Uganda ("Who Are the Victims?") journey with fraternal workers who are accompanying them in their struggle. A North American church commission ("Visit to a Shrimp Farm") focusing on sustainable development confronts an impending ecological crisis in Honduras, while an Angolan missionary faces a cultural crisis in his own country ("The Power of Tradition"). All will be informed and perhaps transformed by God's grace through dialogue about theology and economics and through the encounter between gospel and culture.

Church leaders must be prepared for unforeseen situations and community conflicts. Reconciliation and restoration call for one who accompanies others to "be in their feet." This kind of empathy is more grounded, more rooted, more contextual, and ultimately more biblical than the image of "walking in their shoes." Jesus walked with people and addressed their questions with parables from their everyday lives. According to biblical accounts, Jesus was a practical theologian who told stories, asked hard questions, and rarely gave long sermons or "patent medicine." A primary challenge to seminaries, Bible schools, and Christian educators is to prepare church leaders to be practical theologians—pastors and lay leaders who can feel people's pain, learn from their life stories, ask insightful questions, and be open to receive God's grace even when it comes in surprising ways.

Joseph Hough and John Cobb affirm in *Christian Identity and Theological Education* that "there are significant movements today toward an inclusive use of 'practical theology.'"[3] Johann Metz calls for practical theology to be accepted as foundational theology. His argument is not that pastoral theology should become the basic type of theology; rather, he sees practical theology as "critical reflection on the Church's practice in view of the dangerous memory of the passion of Jesus. Church practice is evaluated in light of its role in the public world."[4] Every believer is called to be a comprehensive "practical Christian thinker."[5]

In an address to a group of overseas visitors from Europe and North America, a Christian lay leader from Kenya said, "I understand that you pray for us regularly. You should know that we seldom pray for you!" The speaker responded to the startled looks on the faces of his guests by continuing, "because you don't share your problems with us, and we don't really know how to pray for you." When members of the Christian community become vulnerable to one another by sharing stories about problems and failures as well as about successes, and by exchanging cases which expose needs for hope and healing, they also become open to receiving illumination and sustainable solidarity.

The five authors are privileged to spend much of our ministries in dialogue with Christians all over the world. We have been transformed and profoundly enriched by these global, ecumenical, and spiritual encounters. This book is filled with stories of pastoral ministry from individuals and communities throughout the world who invite readers to share some of their experiences at "a fraction of the cost." The goal of this volume of stories in the form of case studies is to allow members of the global community of faith to build new bridges of understanding, act in greater solidarity, and pray for and with one another with new depths of empathy and compassion. To get "into other people's feet," to be enlightened by the Holy Spirit through the testimony of fellow travelers a world away, can be empowering as well as exciting. We hope our readers will become partners in our journey to become more faithful and effective practical theologians who are empowered by a global perspective.

ORDER AND CONTENT

The fifteen case studies in this volume come from thirteen countries and almost all regions in the world. The cases have been organized into sections which focus on five systemic global issues. All the cases are true and deal with real issues; none has been fabricated. However, the names of the persons and places have been disguised to protect the privacy and the anonymity of the individuals involved. Although most of these cases seem to present a single problem, they all raise numerous and complex issues well beyond the sections into which they are categorized. These components make them good cases for study because they present situations similar to those faced by pastoral theologians throughout the world.

The overview at the beginning of each section will help readers see the common threads linking the three cases in each section. Although these cases deal with different issues in different countries and settings, they raise common central issues or concerns. The overviews are not direct commentaries on the cases themselves; they are intended to offer the author's perspective and an analysis of the topic under discussion.

A commentary written by one of the five authors follows each case study. Most of the commentaries include a discussion of the case context, an assessment of issues, and the author's suggestions or guidelines for resolution. The commentaries are by no means intended to be exhaustive or definitive. They are observations by theologically trained authors who are experienced in using case studies in teaching pastoral theology in classes, seminars, and workshops. In many instances the authors crossed international boundaries by commenting on cases set in geographic contexts unfamiliar to them. This approach challenged the authors to learn about the context from others, often the case writer, while freeing the commentators to offer insights informed by their own world views. These commentaries are not substitutes for the creative thinking, analysis, and decision making of readers who bring their own wisdom and insights to the discussion. Because some of the commentaries advocate particular perspectives, a case facilitator may decide to hold a discussion of a case on one occasion and on another occasion moderate a discussion of the commentary which may be equally lively.

LEARNING FROM CASE STUDIES

It should be clear from the commentaries that many issues faced in pastoral ministry have no one correct answer. In fact, a simplistic approach or the application of ready-made medicine can often make a serious situation worse. Unfortunately, many programs of theological education and ministerial formation have not prepared pastors or lay leaders to deal wisely or effectively with complex conflicts. One way for them to become better equipped is to be in honest dialogue with other pastors and lay leaders who are grappling with similar issues. This approach calls for a constructive forum in which to hear different perspectives, reflect theologically, and share experiences and biblical resources which illumine the issues. The teaching notes which immediately follow each case study are designed to facilitate such a discussion.

There are many ways to teach a case study. The teaching notes were intentionally written in different styles to reflect the different approaches of the authors. These differences should encourage readers and facilitators to find the style most suited to the discussion participants and their context. In spite of these differences, however, there is one thesis common to all the teaching notes. While the authors take a position on many issues raised in the commentaries, they assume that the most important goals of teaching notes are to raise consciousness and facilitate an open discussion of issues and alternatives; the goals are not to arrive at a consensus or come to a particular conclusion. The most effective case discussions are those in which participants can share honestly, ask real questions, and listen carefully to the insights of others. A good case facilitator is a good moderator and guide who studies the terrain, points the way, insures a safe travel environment, and then joins the participants on the journey.

One traditional format for studying a problem-oriented case is to set clear goals, identify the setting or context of the case if it is relevant, discuss the primary persons or actors, identify and discuss the issues, analyze the strengths and weaknesses of possible alternatives, and share insights about resources that may facilitate creative responses to the case dilemma(s). This tested approach is followed in several of the teaching notes, but it is not a prescribed formula for all case discussions. There are many creative ways to help a group enter into constructive dialogue.

In parts of the world where a more authoritative style of teaching is the norm, one of the greatest challenges for a case facilitator will be to convince participants that the answer is not in the back of the book—that the leader will not lecture or supply an answer but is actually depending on participants to bring forward their observations, understandings, and alternative resolutions. The cases will help with this task; they all present dilemmas, and readers want to know what will happen. Most of the cases call for decisions and actions that will have consequences for the future of individuals, families, and even whole communities. The urgency and importance of these decisions draw readers into the case and invite them to respond. Additional encouragement for discussion participants will come from adequate time to read or hear the case in advance, time to think about the issues, and even time to write down their thoughts about what advice they would give to the central characters in the case. Participants need to be urged to voice their opinions but also to be prepared to defend them with data from the case and clear theological reasoning.

Other guidelines for leading an engaging and productive discussion are to study the case carefully, plan specific goals in advance, follow a teaching plan or note, and anticipate how much time will be needed for each set of questions. All the designs suggested by the prepared teaching notes take a minimum of one hour for an effective discussion. More time is usually needed for groups larger than fifteen or twenty people. A chalkboard or newsprint is very useful for recording a few words of each participant's contributions in order to validate the contributions, make connections between ideas, and give order to the discussion. The discussion guide should affirm the different points of view, encourage those who have difficulty expressing themselves, and be careful not to side with one person or viewpoint. One of the greatest learnings for participants and for the guide is awareness of the different perspectives which even a small group of people may have about the same data.

There are many other suggestions experienced case teachers might offer. However, the most important guideline may be that the best facilitators are those who are prepared to learn from the wisdom and insights of the group. Just as a goal of this book is to empower church leaders by seeing pastoral theology from a global perspective, the goal of a case discussion is to empower members of a community of faith to learn from each other and to be open to hear God speaking between and among them.

These cases have helped and empowered the authors to understand the problems and the issues churches around the world confront in pastoral ministry. We hope that this book will become a catalyst so that others will share their problems and thus share empowerment.

NOTES

1. Alice Frazer Evans, Robert A. Evans and William B. Kennedy, eds., *Pedagogies for the Non-Poor*, Maryknoll, NY: Orbis Books, 1987.

2. Joseph C. Hough, John B. Cobb, Jr., *Christian Identity and Theological Education*, Chico, CA: Scholars Press, 1985, p. 90.

3. Ibid.

4. Ibid., p. 91.

5. Ibid., p. 81.

PART I

EMPOWERING MARGINALIZED PEOPLES

Billionaire philanthropist George Soros stated in a recent interview with *Time* magazine that "Our civilization is built upon the pursuit of self-interest, not on any preoccupation with the interests of others."[1] Although the pursuit of self-interest may indeed temporarily raise an individual's or a community's standard of living, the accumulated effect of the pursuit of self-interest by individuals and communities is deprivation and despair for a large section of humanity. That over one billion people on Earth today live in extreme poverty and hunger, and that more than three-fourths of the Earth's population is condemned to share only 15 percent of the Earth's resources are statistics well known to many. Such economic deprivation often leads to social, cultural, and political marginalization just as marginalization often leads to economic deprivation. Marginalized people are those who have been pushed to the fringes of society, socially, culturally, politically, economically, morally, and religiously.

When one or several areas of community life are affected because of various kinds of marginalization, the possibilities are strong that individuals and/or communities will be relegated to a dehumanized situation. Statistics sometimes fail to remind us that they refer to real people with hopes and aspirations for a better humanity. Around the globe marginalized people, and some who are committed to change their situation, continue to struggle against overwhelming odds. In such struggles the empowerment of the people is a vital component in challenging the various factors that have marginalized people and in rectifying the circumstances.

The empowerment of marginalized people has two components. On the one hand, those who are marginalized have to regain their usurped power and dignity in order to organize their lives in the best possible way. Several barriers—

psychological, social, political, economic—have to be overcome through appropriate education, conscientization, programs of solidarity, and acts of liberation. On the other hand, those who are the custodians of power need to be motivated to share their accumulated power, privilege, and resources for the greater good. They, too, need education to liberate themselves from their captivity by greed, wealth, and readiness to use brute force to protect their interests. One of the criteria that may be applied in evaluating human systems is to find out whether such systems are life-affirming or life-diminishing for the majority of people in the society. In an unjust and conflicted situation it is crucial to be aware that both the marginalized and their oppressors live in a dehumanized situation that fails to uphold the dignity and sanctity of life.

The three cases in this section deal with communities of people who have been marginalized in their own societies—Aborigines in Australia, Dalits in India, and Hispanic-Americans in North America. Their interests were pushed to the periphery by other communities that have acquired socioeconomic and political power. For decades these people have been struggling for their rights and privileges. Looking into the history of some of the unjust historical roots and exposing them are both essential in fighting against discrimination toward any indigenous or marginalized people. Even though some positive achievements have been made in lifting the oppression, it is only in recent years that their cause has been seriously taken up by international organizations such as the United Nations and the World Council of Churches.

Within Christian circles it may be useful to recollect that Jesus himself experienced marginalization and that the early Christian community was made up of people who had been marginalized from the dominant political and religious community of their time. According to John Meier, Jesus experienced marginality as a poor, self-educated layman from rural Galilee, recognized as a prophet and teacher primarily by the simple folks who followed him. According to the religious authorities of his time, he preached disturbing doctrines which were dangerously anti-establishment. He lacked a power base in the capital and was therefore an insignificant person.[2] Jesus knew firsthand the pain, agony, and suffering of being a marginalized person.

The Bible makes several references to marginalized people. They are not taken seriously by the people who control political and economic power except for the purpose of exploitation. Jesus condemned such a distorted human societal condition and directed his followers not to compromise with the evil order. Regaining human dignity for all through repentance, accountability, forgiveness, reconciliation, and loving relations is the vision upheld in the Bible. Therefore, to be true to the vision and the message of the Bible, the emancipation of the marginalized should include a comprehensive sociopolitical and religious empowerment so that they are able to assume responsibility for their own well-being without becoming the targets of continual paternalism.[3]

The early Christian community was originally treated as a sect and was not afforded any privileges. However, it was not reticent about having in its fold the poor, the neglected, and other marginalized people. It was clear that its mission was to proclaim the wholeness of life to every human being, made possible through Jesus Christ, and to work toward building a new human fellowship on that basis. So the church was from the very beginning a community for others, especially for the marginalized. Martin Walton states, "The thrust of claiming that the church is only the church when it is a church for others is to indicate that the poor and the marginalized are not marginal or coincidental, but central to the life of the church."[4] Involvement with the marginalized in their struggle for dignified humanity is not an ancillary ministry matter to the church but an essential mandate for its existence. Because the Christian community is a minority in certain regions and locations, it needs to carry out this task in collaboration and cooperation with other religious and secular bodies.

Only one case in this section, "By the Sword," deals directly with the role of the church, religions, and spirituality. However, it is important to recognize that religion and spirituality do play an important role in the emancipation and liberation of both marginalized people and their adversaries. Spiritual and religious resources can sometimes be more challenging and motivating forces than ideologies, as they may present themselves as nonthreatening to the parties in conflict. Even today religious myths, stories, rites, and rituals have a significant place in the lives of many people—the rich and the poor, the educated and uneducated, the urban and rural. Of course, one can cite several incidents of such sources being misused to continue to oppress religiously motivated people and keep them in bondage, but if the same resources are interpreted and utilized in liberatory ways, they are a great asset, especially in communities more oriented to religiosity and spirituality as their cultural norm.

This essay begins with a quotation which states that historically self-interest has been a predominant characteristic of human beings and communities. At the same time, almost all religious teachings (which in many cases emerged independently) include strong pleas against self-centeredness based on excessive self-interest. Religious commandments also encourage adherents to think of the good of others and call for self-sacrifice in certain circumstances. Such a thrust has been incorporated into secular political ideologies with their own rationales, but in both religious and secular spheres there is ample evidence to demonstrate that these noble teachings are not necessarily followed by believers at all times and in all circumstances. This departure from central teachings has led to a consolidation of power to protect personal interests and to the discriminatory societies found in all the human communities of the globe.

While circumstances vary significantly, several basic steps are necessary to emancipate those who have become victims of marginalization. First, there should be general awareness and recognition of the crisis in all societies regarding marginalization, victimization, and impoverishment of certain sections of the population. This crisis, once recognized, needs to be properly understood through appropriate analysis of the situation, so the impact of negative forces can be moderated and communities of solidarity built. Finally, it is the involvement of marginalized people in the liberatory struggle for concrete results that ushers in emancipation and empowerment. Needless to say, the process mentioned here does not materialize overnight nor does it proceed without creating further uncertainties, conflicts, and tensions. But liberatory struggles need to continue until the marginalized community involved in the struggle reaches its own destiny.

Awareness of the crisis is a key step. In many instances oppressed and oppressors can continue in their existing life situations as though they were part of a plan to be adhered to without questioning: the status quo is preserved. But if any community is prepared to listen to the views and demands of all the sections of its people, it will not fail to discern soon the discrimination, oppression, and marginalization that exist in each human community. From then on, the theological and ideological vision for a holistic human community should enable each community to strive toward the goal of committing itself to eradicating the existing discrimination and marginalization of people.

In order to work toward this vision of holistic human community, a thorough analysis needs to be undertaken of the various historical factors that have been responsible for the existing social order and those that continue to perpetuate it. Several tools developed by social scientists and others are available for this purpose, but engaging in social analysis should be undertaken with the utmost care and with a proper evaluation of the undergirding theological, ideological, and sociological emphases and biases.

The identification of the crisis and the realistic evaluation through social analysis will not proceed much further until a community of solidarity is formed to resist and overcome the forces of oppression. A proper pedagogy for liberation from stereotypical thinking is of the utmost importance to inculcate any hope for change. Such pedagogy is needed for all the parties concerned: the marginalized, the power holders in the society, the state bureaucracy, the religious leadership, and so on to create a network of solidarity. Such solidarity between class, race, profession, religion, gender, and age is crucial as every group has power and influence to help or hinder. It is important that the solidarity thus created between various parties grows through mutual challenge, reconciliation, and covenanting to hasten a common just future.

In the final analysis the actual involvement of the marginalized people themselves and others in solidarity is a crucial factor in empowering and facilitating liberation. The three cases in this section point to such incidents of involvement. There is no universal pattern for how that involvement is triggered. A concerned individual within the marginalized community, or an outsider—even one belonging to the oppressing group—could be a catalyst for change which might emerge as a communitarian movement through action and a process of reflection. Whatever the initial step, success in the struggle depends on the number of people who can join the struggle and the facilities that are available for empowerment of all the sections of the people. The success rate in every stage is a crucial motivator. The cases end with just such crucial decision-making moments for future action.

Two of the cases, "Green Pastures" and "Pipeline to the Future?" involve the role of the state and state officials. Even though the state may be collaborating with the oppressors as the cases indicate, the mobilization of state power through the intervention of committed and progressive people within its fold is always a great asset in the struggle for empowerment and liberation. The state can be either a good facilitator for change or a hindrance. The sources of injustice may be enshrined in the policies and institutions of the state. In such cases any mobilization for struggle by and for the cause of the marginalized people may lead to more suppression and oppression. The fight for a political solution, which could be mustered within the country and from international solidarity, is crucial.

In the cases that follow we do not hear very much about the connection between the local struggle and global networks or global nongovernmental organizations. Yet it is increasingly the situation that local oppression has strong links to international operations managed from a foreign country. Therefore at certain stages in the struggle for justice, there is a need to turn to persons or agencies that can lend and mobilize support internationally. In the struggle for empowerment and liberation of the local community, discerning global connections and implications is also significant.

NOTES

1. *Time International*, July 10, 1995, p. 39.

2. John Meier, *A Marginal Jew: Rethinking the Historical Jesus*, New York, NY: Doubleday, 1991, p. 9.

3. Theodore Walker, Jr., *Empower the People: Social Ethics for the African-American Church*, Maryknoll, NY: Orbis Books, 1991, pp. 23ff.

4. Martin Walton, *Marginal Communities: The Ethical Enterprise of the Followers of Jesus*, Kampen: Kok Pharos Publishing House, 1994, p. 237.

PIPELINE TO THE FUTURE?

Case

Sitiveni Vanua stood in the shade of a gum tree as the people of the Aboriginal island community gathered on their festival ground. On this warm afternoon they were hearing a report from a tribal elder and two representatives from the Australian Transnational Corporation, which operated a zinc mine on the mainland.

The mining company was seeking support from the Aboriginal community for a pipeline that would cross their tribal lands and extend into the bay for direct delivery of mined zinc onto waiting barges. The entrance of the barges into the shallow bay would necessitate building a deep water port near the Aboriginal community.

Friday Stockman, a tribal elder and member of the community council who had been invited to visit the mine site and discuss the plans with company personnel, spoke first. "We need to be free from the chains of government aid. I have just returned from visiting the mine. This pipeline, a new harbor, and maybe jobs will bring new life to our community."

The company public relations representative and then an engineer spoke. As they continued to promote the pipeline, Sitiveni heard a member of the community whisper hoarsely to a friend, "They will kill our turtles and dugong (manatees) and poison our fish with their leaking pipes." The crowd listened politely, but Sitiveni could feel their restlessness. He wondered what he would say if called on to give his opinion of the pipeline and development project.

Siti had worked beside the island people for more than a year. He understood their quiet ways and their struggle to survive as a community, although his own island community was in the Pacific. The struggle had intensified since the Islander and Aborigine fishermen were now competing with international fishing trawlers, that sometimes plowed the bay all night.

Siti left his own community as a boy to be educated in a mission school and then received several years of higher education through scholarship programs. His commissioning as a community organizer by the Aboriginal and Islander Congress of the Uniting Church had brought him to the island. Although Siti had initially agreed to stay for only a year, a special bond with the island people and an empathy with their struggle to cope with an insistent encroaching modernization had moved him to stay on despite prospects for a better salary and housing as an urban organizer.

As custodians of this region for 40,000 years, Aborigine people had been increasingly marginalized by the white European settlers who had violated their sacred sites and disparaged their way of life. Yet, as strongly as he felt about the need for the community to preserve its life in the face of constant bombardment from outside, Siti wondered how he would feel if he were an unemployed islander with nothing to do but hunt and fish and, in one's spare time, drink and dance.

He knew that those who chose to leave the island for towns on the mainland found themselves ill-equipped to deal with the loneliness, alienation, and fast-paced pressures of the urban centers. Far too many ended up living in squalid shacks on the fringes of European society. And rather than giving long-term support, government subsidies drained both the young and the old people of initiative to succeed on their own. Convinced of the need for the community to stay together on its own land for its survival, Siti wondered if there was any way this pipeline proposal could bring empowerment rather than ruin?

Siti's attention was drawn to the enthusiastic presentation by Mark Spencer, the Transnational public relations representative. "Island people must find alternative forms of employment to fishing. There is presently enough seafood for your daily diet. But there is too little to be commercially viable. The new harbor would provide employment during construction and then for servicing the barges and loading materials." Mark held up to the audience a beautiful architect's drawing of the proposed port with an artist's impression of new shops, a new school, and a health clinic. His closing words were, "This is the promise of prosperity for this previously isolated island community."

Friday spoke again. He had initially expressed reservations about the pipeline, but since his visit to the mine he was one of its greatest supporters. "Our people have suffered by being robbed of our land and then being made dependent on government handouts. This development project gives us a chance to share in the benefits from the land and regain our dignity as an island community."

The gathered community then began offering their responses to the presentations. Gumbuli, an elder and a member of the community council, spoke first. "This is too close to our sacred sites both on land and in the sea. The company only wants to do this as the cheap option. Let them take the zinc away overland. The very presence of Europeans in large numbers will threaten our traditional way of life. The law protects us from their entering our lands and destroying our sacred sites. Let us reject this seduction and send the white men away. That is how we will have our dignity and power."

Grandmother Ailsa then expressed her concern that a great danger to the community's survival was not keeping the young men and women on the island. "For us old people this is not an isolated place but our home and the center of our life, but now more young people leave us every year to find work, and few ever return. This drift away from our country will destroy our people. If the white men can bring jobs, perhaps we should allow them to come."

Another grandmother spoke respectfully to the old woman, "It wasn't the need for work that took my son away but his wanting to travel to the bigger towns. Others are taken to Townsville to be put in prison there. We don't need this mine to improve our life on this island."

Gumbuli spoke again. "White people cannot control the wind and the sea. If the pipeline leaks into the sea or a barge is wrecked in a storm, this would destroy our fishing and breeding grounds forever. Even without the chemicals entering our waters, dredging for the harbor would destroy the breeding grounds of the turtles and dugong that have lived in peace in our mother the sea since Dreamtime. If our mother dies, we die. The white men have lied to us before, and 'development' is a new lie that will destroy us and our culture."

Thomas Conley, the Transnational engineer quickly assured the crowd that "expert research scientists are developing the most effective materials to insure the safety of our equipment and prevent any possible environmental accidents. The advanced technology being applied to this pipeline and the harbor provide excellent security against any rupture or spill. Isolation will not protect the tribal values. It will only further impoverish people until all your children will leave the island in order to survive. The way to new power is full participation in Australia's future, and this is the pipeline to the future."

Siti was convinced that these consultants did not appreciate the perspective of the island people, but he also saw that both the community and the island church that he served were divided on the issue of the pipeline. He knew that the traditional approach was for the community to reach consensus on major decisions, so the talk would go on into the night. However, those who thought their views were not being heard might leave before the decision was made.

Siti felt the glances of several people around him as they looked for his response to the educated words of the engineer. As Siti searched for the right words, he realized he was struggling with understanding how the church could hear "the cry of the people" and stand with the poor and marginalized. He also wondered whose ideas would inform the church's understanding of "development" and "progress."

Teaching Note

Siti Vanua, as a pastoral agent serving an Aboriginal island community, struggles with how to facilitate a pastoral strategy that would be empowering for the community in the debate over a development proposal. Questions of marginalized peoples' land rights and protection of religious sites give this case global implications for a comprehensive approach to pastoral care. (Please refer to the commentary for a discussion of the term "marginalized." Persons within separate cultural communities do not necessarily consider themselves marginalized. Their world view may place them at the center rather than the periphery. Defining a group as marginalized is more frequently a perspective of those within a dominant culture describing those who are different from themselves.)

I. This teaching note is designed to reach the following goals:

A. Explore different meanings of the term "development" for dominant and "marginalized" cultures in a society.

B. Examine different peoples' relationship to the land and the implications of relationship to the land for one's identity and dignity.

C. Analyze approaches to pastoral care which support individual, communal, and systemic empowerment in the pipeline case and in readers' arenas of pastoral ministry.

II. Context of the Case

What are the causes of the conflict over the pipeline proposal in the Aboriginal community? How has the historical treatment of Aborigine people in Australia affected the climate of the development discussion? In what ways do discussion participants' understandings of the relationship between the dominant white culture and indigenous peoples in other parts of the world inform this situation?

III. Group Dialogue

To generate a lively discussion of the meaning of "development," divide the group into three sections and assign one of the following three roles to each group:

A. Those people in the Aborigine community who agree with Elder Gumbuli that the pipeline should be rejected;

B. Aborigine people who follow the perspectives of Elder Stockman and Grandmother Ailsa and accept the pipeline;

C. Australian Whites or persons of European descent who represent Transnational Corporation and are aligned with the views of Mark and Thomas in their support of the pipeline and improvement of the port.

Ask members of the groups to discuss their feelings and concerns about development. From their perspective, what are the assets and liabilities of the development of mineral resources in Australia and development of the port? After approximately ten minutes, ask each group to select a spokesperson who will argue that group's views beginning with a two-minute statement of position and a brief rebuttal in response to the other groups' positions. The case leader should moderate the discussion. Allow a few minutes to "de-role" each representative before asking the observers how they felt about the discussion and what they learned about the meaning and implications of development for a nation and for marginalized people.

IV. Issues

Assist the participants in identifying questions and insights about basic issues raised in the case. Points raised could include:

A. Criteria for development that respect ecological integrity;

B. Sources for human dignity and the connection between dignity and the value of labor and group identity;

C. The relationship of Aboriginal people to land and why land is considered sacred;

D. The meaning of empowerment and what it implies for those who are dominant and for those who are marginalized.

V. Strategies for Pastoral Care

Encourage the discussion group to consolidate their insights by identifying specific pastoral approaches for clergy and lay leaders to aid in empowering people, especially those who are considered marginalized by the dominant culture. Request concrete proposals of pastoral responses that are addressed to individuals, to communal concerns, and to systemic issues raised by the case. How do these recommendations address some of the issues raised earlier in the discussion? How are these recommendations supported by biblical and theological rationale? Do the demands of justice have special importance for marginalized peoples?

Ask participants to identify which strategies might apply to the communities in which they minister. What level of functional priority are these approaches given by the institutional church?

VI. Closing

Offer participants the opportunity to write out or offer a sentence prayer in gratitude for their learnings, both personal and institutional, from the case discussion and from marginalized communities with which they have worked.

Commentary

". . . and what does the Lord require of you, but to do justice, to love kindness, and to walk humbly with your God?" (Mic. 6:8) This biblical mandate may well be in Siti's mind as he struggles with the immediate problem of how to respond with pastoral integrity to the pipeline development proposal confronting the island community. In order to be both effective and responsible, Siti's response needs to be comprehensive in terms of a pastoral care strategy which includes individual, communal, and systemic components.

Whether this divided community says "yes" or "no" to the pipeline, there will be important *individual* pastoral work to do. Elders Stockman and Gumbuli who are on different sides of the dispute; the two grandmothers with divergent concerns about the youth; the unemployed youth of the island and those already relocated in the cities or the prisons; and the mining company representatives are all within the sphere of pastoral concern for the church. Nonetheless, pastoral concerns inevitably transcend the care of individuals; in this situation there are also *communal* care issues interpreted by some as those of identity and even survival.

In addition, pastoral care in a global perspective regularly contains underlying *systemic* concerns, as it does in this dilemma, involving the criteria for human development and the integrity of creation and of ecological systems. Competent pastoral care demands that pastoral agents, whether lay or clergy, think and act with a multilevel, multicultural, integrated approach. Those now engaged in pastoral ministry who did not have the benefit of inclusive and globalized training, have had to learn it in the field. Readers may be able to employ this case as an effective catalyst for learning about ministry which calls for cross-cultural dialogue and empowering marginalized people.

CONTEXT

For more than 40,000 years, Aboriginal and Islander peoples of what is described in current political history as the Australian continent have considered themselves to be the custodians of this land. Their role was to be good stewards of this gift passed on to them by their ancestors. Scholars and interpreters of Aboriginal culture suggest that "Dreamtime" is a term used to refer to the time, long ago, when Aborigine spirit ancestors created the world and their society.

"Sacred sites" are those places where special ceremonies or events in their mythological stories or "dreaming" occurred.

It is a historically acknowledged fact that the colonial settlers of Australia dispossessed the Aborigine and Islander people of their native lands in a series of brutal and often genocidal invasions. This process was accomplished by disregarding legitimate rights of access to land and sea. Also ignored was the special relationship to the land and sea that shaped the identity of the Aboriginal people. Leaders of the Aboriginal and Islander communities frequently proclaim that there are continued violations of their traditional values and sacred sites of land and sea. The suffering the indigenous people have borne through dispossession and death has shaped the contemporary relationship between the dominant white European culture and that of the descendants of the original inhabitants. Being uprooted from traditional locations and the subsequent loss of identity are the legacies of colonial occupation for many indigenous individuals and communities. They experience loss of self-esteem and loss of human dignity, and they share feelings of inferiority with many displaced indigenous peoples around the world.

From the colonial period to the present, both secular and religious advocates of the rights of Aborigine people have tried to speak out. Siti has been given his pastoral assignment by the Uniting Church in Australia under the auspices of the Uniting Aboriginal and Islander Christian Congress. The congress has promoted a pastoral policy that understands the indigenous people of faith to be part of the Body of Christ, the church. In supporting Siti's ministry with Aboriginal people, the Uniting Church recognized that this part of the Body of Christ was oppressed and needed special care. Siti's role is not only to minister to his assigned community but to struggle with how to interpret the way in which God hears the "cry of the people" and what it means for the church to stand in solidarity with poor and marginalized people. In choosing to continue to serve the island community, Siti affirms a theological stance. He appears to be living out concretely God's preferential option for the poor as confirmed in Luke 4:18–19: "The Spirit of the Lord ... anointed me ... to bring good news to the poor ... release to the captives ... the oppressed go free" (NRSV). The biblical mandate may be clear to Siti; the problem is implementation. What do these directives mean for pastoral care of the poor and nonpoor? Why do the majority of church members in the dominant culture fail to act concretely on this strong biblical mandate for solidarity? How can Siti's pastoral strategy empower the poor and also call for a theologically inspired relinquishing of power by the nonpoor?

To ignore or underestimate the importance of the context of invasion, dispossession, and oppression in any society with a colonial history could distort the pastoral analysis. A significant threat posed by the pipeline is its potential to violate the land and sacred sites on the land and in the water near where the pipeline would enter the shallow bay and where the proposed port would be built. The Rev. Djiniyini Gondarra, an Australian Aborigine pastor, theologian, and congress officer, has spoken frequently about the pastoral significance of government or industry development proposals. Gondarra suggests that when religious tribal leaders say that this mountain or that land is their dreaming, they mean the land holds sacred knowledge, wisdom, and moral teaching given to the Aborigine by the Spirit of the Creator.[1] The connection with the land is a bond to the creator and to creation.

Some of the most effective pastoral agents are able to so empathize with those with whom they minister that they see a situation "through their eyes." As a Pacific Islander whose surname, Vanua, means "land" in Fijian, Siti has bonds to the land and sea similar to those of the Australian island community. However, the mining company representatives, members of the Euro-Australian society, and many readers of this case, may find it more difficult to understand the relationship of Aborigine people to their land. In contemporary market-oriented societies, land is a commodity to be bought and sold. The right to private property is promoted and protected by most legal systems. Global populations are becoming increasingly urbanized, and few urban people view land as sacred. Most people are also uncomfortable when zealots proclaim that all creation belongs to God alone and that human beings are only temporary stewards of the land, responsible as communities for maintaining the integrity of creation and passing on this gift to their children.

Many urban people view the attachment which indigenous people have to the land as impractical, sentimental, and even superstitious. However, the attachment of native peoples to the land is comparable to biblical perspectives such as that held by Naboth (I Kings 21) who refused, at the cost of his life, to sell or trade his land to King Ahad because this piece of land was his "ancestral inheritance." While it is true that many people from farm communities say they love the land, some analysts suggest the love is for a way of life rather than for a parcel of land. Understanding different views of the land is a critical component in Siti's development of an effective pastoral strategy.

HUMAN DIGNITY

A pastoral perspective consistent with Micah's call for justice includes the protection and enhancement of the human dignity of all persons in the case but gives special attention to the most vulnerable. The human worth and dignity of the islanders is theologically undergirded by their status as children of God. The case suggests that a factor in sustaining their dignity is their maintenance of traditional values and patterns of life.

Siti may need to raise with the community, the corporation representatives, and the Uniting Church questions about the intrinsic meaning of human work. Why is a person normally counted as part of the work force only if he or she is salaried or produces a product or service that can be assigned a price in a cash economy? Why are fishing, hunting, and gathering to sustain one's family and community not valued equally with being salaried? In a comparable form of economic discrimination, the domestic labor of women, which globally sustains most rural economies, to say nothing of family life and values, leads women to be identified, like the youth in the island community, as unemployed rather than differently employed. Labor that is respected and considered meaningful by a society brings a sense of dignity and fulfillment.

An ancillary question is whether the proposed new jobs at the harbor, if they become a reality, will enhance the self-esteem of the salaried workers. Or will the labor in this economic opportunity only further alienate the workers from their tribal identity? What type of labor, or education, or service will reinforce rather than undermine the human worth and dignity already assured by creation as children of God? The intrinsic value and meaning of work is a pastoral issue for the public relations officer, engineer, barge captain, or mining executive as much as it is for members of the Aboriginal community.

The perspective of being isolated or even marginalized begs the question: isolated from what? and marginalized by whom? Aboriginal or island communities are not isolated from their land, mother sea, sacred sites, or God. Neither are they marginal to the nutritional and spiritual resources of a flora and fauna with which and from which they have lived for generations in a relationship of dignity and integrity in most instances. Aborigine people are frequently distant from the cities, transportation routes, and markets of white communities. However, this distance should not carry a negative connotation. The implications are clear that the cultural identity and issues of ecological integrity must be given as serious attention as economics.

It is also important not to romanticize indigenous peoples and traditional lifestyles for their own sake. Members of Aboriginal communities, like those of dominant cultures, have littered and abused the rural and urban sites they occupy. The culture of dependency and substance abuse that plagues indigenous communities world-wide are not only a result of colonization but also the responsibility of those who cooperate with the deculturalization process of the dominant culture and economy. Some indigenous people tend to obstruct rather than support their own leadership or succumb to internal polarization that has the potential of disrupting the island community described in the case.

EMPOWERMENT

Human dignity often depends on the relationship between communities and individuals, and relationships can be distorted by inequality of power. Power, like conflict, is a natural and unavoidable factor in human relationships. From the power of God to the powerlessness of Christ's redemption, biblical and theological traditions have addressed power in different ways. However, there has been a consistent theme of God's special concern and even identification with the power-less as reflected dramatically in Mary's "Magnificat" (Luke 1:46–55), in which Mary acknowledges that God has "brought down the powerful . . . and lifted up the lowly." Empowerment appears to be most effectively realized through the initiative and on the conditions determined by those who acknowledge that in some dimensions of their lives they have been unjustly discriminated against. Seeking the liberation from oppression promised by God in the gospel, pastoral agents are called to facilitate processes in which those who are oppressed participate as fully as possible.

Siti worries about how to respond if asked to express his views about the pipeline. For Siti to side with either position on the pipeline will almost certainly alienate him from a portion of the church and the community. To offer his opinion may also reduce the potential of a ministry of reconciliation and healing that will be needed no matter what decision is reached. Siti's initial role may be to urge further investigation of the development proposal. This pastoral approach contextually honors themes of justice and dignity and supports sustainable empowerment of the islanders. The community may need the opportunity to study, reflect on, and pray about the meaning of progress and the prevailing approach to development which often neglects both questions of context and sustainability.

Siti may help empower the community by raising basic questions of process. Was the negotiation process sufficiently inclusive with only one elder speaking? Was adequate time allotted to reflect, discuss, and reach a consensus? Was all the information about costs and dangers available? Empowerment may require starting the negotiations over.

A new process of negotiation could include contractual guarantees if the pipeline and harbor improvement are to be permitted by the community, e.g., compensation for access rights; numbers, type, and longevity of employment for community members; clean-up and restoration in case of an accident or ecological damage to the bay; means of monitoring the agreement; and Aboriginal representation on the committee to administer the project. The principles of empowerment—recognition, participation, process agreement, decision making, monitoring, and adjustment—apply to both partners and should help establish a relationship of respect for all stakeholders.

PASTORAL STRATEGIES

Pastors who seek to empower their communities should include individual, communal, and systemic approaches to their ministry. Prophetic declarations may also be required as part of pastoral strategy for the empowerment of those who appear marginalized. Such a declaration is stronger if it embodies the voice of the Christian community rather than the voice of an individual pastoral agent. Prophetic announcements need to be articulated with thorough knowledge of the situation and appropriate biblical and theological support. Siti and the church elders may feel compelled to denounce the pipeline and harbor as threats to the community's identity and spiritual integrity. They may see this action as the only recourse to the seductive powers of a hegemonic market culture. There are times when the church accepts no alternatives or conditions, with prophetic resistance as the only faithful response.

There are other times when pastoral strategies could prepare for "no," "yes," or "maybe" responses to development proposals that have the potential for threatening traditional values. The pipeline proposal means that elders Stockman and Gumbuli and both grandmothers need pastoral visits. One goal of such relation building would be encouraging better communication in order to seek common ground among all the parties for meeting community needs. Youth on the island engaged in different types of work, as well as those who have migrated to the cities or landed in prison, need to be contacted and urged to retain regular contact with the island. The mine representatives may need information about the values and life patterns of the Aboriginal community. Such strategies should be relational, inclusive, and comprehensive.

Pastoral strategies call for building networks. Development proposals similar to the pipeline have been rejected after thorough investigation by other indigenous communities on the grounds that such development will not contribute to an authentic future, sustainable development, or meaningful progress for their people. Constructing networks among these communities recognizes the power of shared experience. The potential for mutual benefit makes exploration of communal pastoral needs an urgent task.

Assisting a community to set its own priorities is a component of empowerment. Building the capacity of a community to reflect on the biblical and traditional values which inform their priorities may come through Bible study, leadership training, programs that promote solidarity for women and youth, and workshops in community conflict resolution. The Presbytery or other church structures can provide support and solidarity for Aboriginal communities from whom they also have much to learn. Pastors may consider mutually beneficial exchange programs among Aboriginal communities and also with suburban and urban European residents to explore the relationship between faith and land. Creative pastoral care requires that old stereotypes be confronted and new relationships developed.

The church with its mission of justice, human dignity, and empowerment has national and global responsibility to address the pipeline case as an illustration of a pressing systemic global issue of pastoral care: empowerment of marginalized people. Empowerment embodies God's preferential option for those treated by many people in dominant cultures and economic systems as disposable. Exclusion of one part of the human family stands over against the vision of the holistic reign of a creator God of justice and compassion. God's redemptive process includes Christ's incarnation among the poor, suffering and death at the hands of the powerful, and resurrection for the sake of the dispossessed and excluded. Those who uproot and reject the dispossessed also reject Christ. Justice, kindness, and humility are the marks of this peaceable and sustainable vision which may be the only authentic pipeline to the future

NOTE

1. Terry Djiniyini Gondarra and Don Carrington, "Commentary to Sacred Sites," in *Human Rights: A Dialogue between the First and Third Worlds,* Maryknoll, NY: Orbis Books, 1988, p. 114.

BY THE SWORD

Case

A dream puzzled Azu, the young Dalit (outcaste) Christian boy. In his dream he had seen himself as a landlord of a big piece of fertile land in Punjab, a state of India. In his dream he had enjoyed full freedom and the juice of the finest sugarcane from his own cane crusher. But when he awoke he was in the animal manger, a bonded laborer, and the landlord was standing beside him about to beat him for sleeping during the day. He felt caught in snares everywhere. Around him were landowners, courageous Sikh people who always carried a sword with them as a sign of bravery and of their religion.

Azu was caught in a dilemma over his faith in Christianity. He thought, "My father is proud that he was baptized by a white missionary, and my mother tells me that the great Gordon Sahib (Andrew Gordon) baptized her. She goes every Sunday to church, but she also goes every Thursday to offer a *roti* (sweet bread prepared in oil) to the Bala Shah (an indigenous god). This means that Christ is only another god like Bala Shah. Even after becoming Christians we are still outcastes and live at the edge of the village. Our residing place is still known as '*thathi*' (a name of ridicule for the place of the Dalits, situated on the western side of the village). We can neither have land nor build a proper house made of bricks and cement."

Suddenly Azu's thoughts turned to Nathu, the boy whose mother was raped by an upper-caste landlord's son. Nathu had run away from the village. One night he came back, killed the young man and his father, and again fled. Nathu was the son of recently converted parents who thought that after accepting Christ as their Savior they would receive protection from all kinds of oppression and injustice. That protection did not happen, so Nathu had thought that it was his duty to stop the injustice in his village. Azu thought, "He is a brave young man. He was baptized by Padre Sahib (the Christian pastor), but now Padre Sahib neither praises Nathu as brave nor visits his mother for fear of the landlords. Instead he branded Nathu a coward. Padre Sahib teaches 'Turn the other cheek' and says that 'a slave of the Lord does not need to fight, for God knows all the suffering of his children, and those who patiently endure will be rewarded.' The Christian message has become a hindrance in the fight against injustice, cruelties, and suffering."

Several days later Azu met a young man his own age. The boy carried a sword and wore a turban of a special color and a uniform type dress. Azu recognized the boy as one of his kin whose parents had accepted Sikhism as their religion. Azu called out to him, "Lachhu!" The boy replied, "I am no longer Lachhu. I am Lachman Singh (lion)." These words fell like a hammer on Azu. He immediately decided, "How brave he is! I shall become like him. I shall change my name from Azu to Azu Singh."

Azu started growing his head hair and beard. The Sikh shrine gave him a turban to wear and a sword to carry. He began learning how to read Punjabi in the shrine school and consequently learning to read the Sikh scriptures. He soon became a good Sikh boy. He was happy to see all kinds of people—rich and poor, Dalits and upper castes—sitting together and eating in the Gurudwara shrine. Azu was now proud to be called a singh. No one was there to object to his carrying a sword. He felt that one day he would become a landlord.

All too soon Azu learned that his new name and new life as a lion could not keep him strong for long in the caste-based society of India. One day, right at the gate of Gurudwara, an upper-caste Sikh, instead of calling Azu "*Sardarje*" (a respectful word for a Sikh), called him "*Churah*" (the lowest grade connotation for a Dalit). Azu realized that even the most modern religion could not liberate him from the agony of being an outcaste.

Once again Azu focused his thoughts on Christianity. He decided to read the Bible himself and learned to read it in Punjabi. While he was reading the Gospel according to Luke, he read Jesus' words, "Let the one having no sword, sell his outer garment and buy one" (Luke 22:36). Those words revolutionized Azu's idea of Christianity. He suddenly felt that Christianity is a religion of bravery. His interest in the Bible increased and he read it again and again. But when he went to the church and heard the conventional reading of the Bible, he was very puzzled. The Church's teachings on forgiveness and the plea to live in constant poverty in order to go to heaven was a dilemma for Azu. He was willing to accept Christianity again but on the condition that it had a place for bravery. Through his reading of the Bible he had accepted Christ as his Lord and revolutionary guru. According to Azu's understanding, Christ as a risen and living Lord liberates people here on earth. Christ wants his followers to be brave and daring. Azu felt that the church in Punjab should not miss that important message of the gospel. Finally, Azu approached the pastor. "Pastor, I want to become a Christian once again and be baptized."

The pastor who listened carefully to Azu's wish had no immediate answer for him. After a brief conversation with Azu, the pastor had several questions and a few serious doubts about Azu's new and self-discovered interpretation of Christianity as it related to Punjab. He did not dampen Azu's enthusiasm and advised him to return after a week. A week later Azu Singh, dressed in his best clothes and with the sword hanging on his shoulder, walked toward the pastor's house expecting to be baptized.

Teaching Note

This is a historical case. The main character, Azu, struggled for fifty years for justice and equality for the Dalit people. Late in life he had personal success and became a land-owning farmer. Throughout his adult life he continued to be a faithful and strong believer in Christ. When he died in 1976 people of all faiths, rich and poor, came to join his funeral. Word spread that "a true Christian has left us." He is now known by the name Asa Mal. This information, however, is not critical to teaching the case. There are still tens of thousands of young people like Azu, caught in desperate poverty and seeking dignity and respect through a faith perspective. Although a brief glossary of terms is noted below, readers may be assisted by additional information on the Sikh religion and on the present condition of Dalits and bonded laborers in India. The commentary section titled "Situation of the Case" offers additional background information.

Christianity: The Christian population is a little less than 3 percent of the total population of India. It is estimated that more than 70 percent of Indian Christians are Dalits and tribal converts.

Churahs: According to the Hindu caste system, they are the "untouchables," considered the lowest in India. In Punjab they are called the "sweeper class." The people of this caste are known as *Isai* if they are Christians, *Mazhalei* if Sikh, and *Balmiki* if Hindu. Besides Christianity, *Churahs* have been converted to Sikhism and Islam.

Dalit: People of this class of "untouchables" have given themselves this name. It means "oppressed" or "broken."

Gurdaspur: A district of Punjab which contains one million Christian converts. They are all Dalits.

Gurudwara: A Sikh place of worship.

Punjab: A state in India situated across the border from Pakistan. Fifty-two percent of the population belongs to the Sikh religion which began in Punjab in the fifteenth century. The rest of the population adheres to Hindu, Christian, or Muslim beliefs.

I. Teaching Goals

A. To better understand the oppressive power of the caste system in India. The institution of caste has a long history, and discrimination based on caste has so penetrated Indian society that it is practiced as a matter of routine.

B. To understand how the institutional church easily adjusts to social norms of society even if these norms are oppressive. Sometimes it is said that two areas of social reality where Indian Christians have unconsciously been indigenous are retaining of the caste system and the custom of dowry. Both are discriminating. These forms of oppression need to be openly discussed.

C. To discern the role of religions, including Christianity, in the context of social injustice. Religion can easily be co-opted by society, especially when religious bodies and hierarchies have vested interest in the status quo.

D. To explore international solidarity that could be extended toward the liberation of oppressed people. While the church is basically a local community, at the same time it is a global fellowship. This global interconnectedness is of great value to a local community in times of struggle, especially when a local group needs solidarity and resources beyond its capacity.

E. To evaluate the theological presuppositions which tend to support the status quo. Theological articulations are closely related to the social biography of a community. If the articulators are from one section of the community, they tend to control the theologizing process according to their needs and interests. Traditionally Dalits were excluded from the process of theologizing in India. It is important that they are not further oppressed by theology that does not lead to their liberation and wholeness.

F. To help discussion participants connect their learnings from this case to their own context.

II. Case Discussion

The case leader may wish to give a "mini-lecture" on the economic and social condition of the Dalits, the specific setting of the case in the Punjab, and the role of the Christian church in this area. An alternative approach would be for the leader to suggest or assign advance reading for additional background information.

Begin the case discussion by asking about Azu, his needs and perspectives, and the significance of other figures in the case. Which previous experiences with the church made an impression on Azu? Consider the importance of his mother, Nathu, and Padre Sahib.

What roles do Dalits play in Indian society? Consider the economic implications of their roles. Are there other reasons why they continue to remain "untouchable"?

Several other issues which may be explored are:

> a theology of conversion and its relation to culture;
>
> the meaning of salvation in different contexts;
>
> submission and victimization of a minority community;
>
> pastoral ministry to persons who are marginalized.

A fruitful discussion may also center on how one does or does not justify the conditions set by Azu for his baptism. Encourage people to share scripture and theological understandings that illuminate their positions. Ask which approaches to Azu's request would help most to empower him. Urge participants to give their rationale for suggestions.

In considering appropriate responses for the Christian pastor, raise these additional questions: Should the church be involved in empowering people to liberate themselves from unjust structures in their society? If so, how? What biblical and theological understandings support the role of the church in seeking social justice? Focus on concrete ways the church could be involved. Specific examples could include legislative or state policy, seeking liberation through conscientization of both Dalits and members of the dominant community, and building networks between the larger community of Dalits and those who champion their cause.

III. Conclusion

Ask participants to identify persons in their own community who are discriminated against. While many societies do not have as stringent a caste system as that in India, there are many other ways people can be excluded. For example, discrimination against people living with AIDS and racism are often as deeply embedded in a society's ethos as the caste system. Ask about ways the church knowingly or unknowingly supports the status quo. What are some concrete ways the church can challenge discrimination?

Commentary

We are living in a period when people are constantly becoming more aware of their identities and roles in society. If the perceived roles and places are denied to them, one of the ways they can achieve them is through mobilizing forces to counter the structures that guard the status quo. Some discriminatory social structures are protected through "structured selfishness" and are defended by institutional lies by the beneficiaries of the structural selfishness.

SITUATION OF THE CASE

Azu found the possibility of liberation from the caste system, especially his status as an "untouchable," in the example of the Sikh boy. A Christian should not be burdened with the caste oppression operative in Hinduism, but in India things do not work that way. Azu's romance with Sikhism came to an end very soon as he found out that feelings about caste were prevalent even among the Sikhs. The only way forward for Azu was to re-enter Christianity and seek liberation from within that religion.

Some historical background is necessary to understand the caste phenomenon in India. Caste and its accompaniment, untouchability, have been deeply entrenched in the Indian psyche and have a long social history. The origins of the caste system can be traced to an early evolution of the division of labor in the pre-Aryan society of the Indian subcontinent. As in societies everywhere, those who are involved in governing the people and the community (rulers), heads of various community functions such as defense (warriors), and taxation and law and order (bureaucracy) are regarded highly in society, compared to those who carry out their livelihood through "mundane" trades and those employed by others (servants, slaves) or employed in menial tasks such as cleaning and sanitation upkeep (low-grade workers). With the arrival of the Aryans around 1500 B.C. and the imposition of untouchability status on the indigenous people, the rigid caste system came to stay and became an important factor in the social life of the Indian people. This system is further consolidated by the religious myth of divine origin of four castes as recorded in the Code of Manu. According to the myth, from the mouth of *Purusha* the Eternal One, came the *Brahmans,* the priestly caste; from his arms came the *kshatriyas*, warriors; from his thighs the *vaishyas*, traders; and from his feet the *sudras*, laborers. The remaining groups were relegated to the ranks of untouchability and became "outcastes." They were outside the fourfold caste system.[1] Once this caste order was promulgated as divinely sanctioned, it could not easily be altered. This view is still held by many Indians but with much less conviction than earlier.

The practice of untouchability has been forbidden by the constitution of the Indian nation, which guarantees equal rights and privileges to all its citizens. By the Order of the Government in 1955, any discriminatory act, including addressing the outcastes by derogatory caste names, was punishable. Some social and economic uplifting through quotas in educational institutions and employment opportunities was also undertaken by the Indian government. Christians were not included in these provisions at the suggestion of their own leaders, who were optimistic in the 1950s about the egalitarian society emerging among Christians. The 1955 order was applicable only to Hindus, but in 1956 Sikhs were also covered. In May 1990 provisions of the order were extended to Buddhists.[2] Outcaste converts to Christianity and Islam are not covered by the 1955 order on the grounds that caste is not a determining factor in the social and religious lives of these religious communities. But the caste system is a deep-seated and very prevalent social practice in Christian communities, and caste will not vanish without determined effort. Christians and Muslims have made several representations to the government of India that they be included under the provisions of 1955.

Even though missionaries, through general and Christian education, contributed to the uplifting of the untouchables, the struggle gained new momentum only when they themselves recognized the need for total liberation and took up the challenge. Until then, their cause was not prominent on the church's agenda. It is the emerging consciousness and liberation struggle among the Dalits that has brought contemporary challenges to the still-prevalent discrimination against them. Today it is common for Indians in church conferences and deliberations in India or abroad to speak about the role and the place of Dalits and their religious and cultural input to emerging theologies in India and elsewhere. Today Dalit and other indigenous theologies bring a much needed addition to hitherto prevailing theologies which bypassed them for centuries.

Dalit means "oppressed," "downtrodden," and "torn asunder." Even though "Dalit" has been in use since the 1930s as a translation for "depressed class" or "untouchable," it is the recent rise of conscientization among the untouchables that has given it a revolutionary content. M. E. Prabhakar notes that "Dalit" implies double oppression—social and economic—of the outcaste, ritually impure untouchables. "Dalit" thus became a symbol of assertive pride and resistance to and rejection of the linked oppression of caste and class. This understanding was popularized in the early 1970s by the Dalit Panthers' party, inspired initially by the American Black Panthers.[3] Dalit literature, Dalit theology, and Dalit solidarity programs have given a tremendous boost to the struggle, which in Azu's day had to be undertaken by individuals and isolated groups with great courage and at great risk.

To understand Azu's struggle we may need some knowledge about the Churahs of Punjab. The Churahs, one of the major low-caste communities in Punjab, were traditionally known as the "scavenger caste." Their duties included "sweeping in private houses and on village lanes, making dung cakes, grazing cattle, and serving as village messengers."[4] Because of their low social rank, many Churahs lived in utter poverty, depending mainly on leftover food and portions of grain harvested through their labor. They rarely received any remuneration in cash, which led to their perpetual indebtedness to landowners and local merchants. Some had to pledge their services for long periods of time, sometimes including the services of family members, in order to secure loans for organizing family obligations and ceremonies, such as marriages and religious or community festivals. In cases when the borrowed amount, including the high interest, was not repaid in time, the period of labor was extended for a lifetime—a type of slavery practiced widely in the past and even today in some areas.

From the 1870s most converts to Christianity in the Punjab were from the Dalit community. It is estimated that one-quarter of all Churahs in the state of Punjab had become Christians by the 1930s,[5] but handling the conversions was not an easy matter for Christians or missionaries. Azu's case highlights one such struggle.

Was Sikhism a solution? The case indicates it was not. Sikhism is a religion inspired by the Hindu *bhaktas* (devotees) and Muslim *Sufis* (mystics). It was founded in the late fifteenth century by Guru Nanak (1469–1539). The majority of Sikhs reside in the state of Punjab.[6] "Sikh" means disciple. Committed Sikhs are expected to let their hair and beards grow (signs of asceticism) and to carry a saber (sign of bravery). The Sikhs consider themselves a chosen race of soldier saints. The religious consequences of Sikhism include the development of a monotheistic religion and breaking away from some of the Hindu social structures, especially the domination of the priestly caste or Brahmans. However, occasionally caste feelings do play a role in the social relations within Sikhism as mentioned in the case.

THEOLOGICAL AND CHURCH DILEMMA

It was not easy for the Western missionaries to enter into the world of the Indian social system, where a major characteristic was the caste system. How different missionary societies and missionaries dealt with the caste factor is an interesting study which we will not discuss here. But one thing was clear: conversion from Hinduism did not completely free Christians from the structures and feelings of the caste system. First, Hindus still related to Christians from the caste point of view. For a Hindu every Christian convert—Brahman, Sudra, or untouchable—became an untouchable socially. Second, converted Christians still held to the memory of their caste status and for the most part related to one another in that way even within the church. What a contradiction! A new community with old values. However, in several areas, new converts experienced change through education, respectful and gainful employment, medical care, participation in worship and religious celebrations, and festivals.

In the case, we read that Azu believed his dream of becoming economically independent through land owning would not materialize through Christianity as it was preached. He reasoned that Christianity was too submissive. According to Azu, liberation was possible only through the exercise of bravery. His opinion was that a certain amount of militancy is demanded on the part of Christians as disclosed in Luke 22:36. He dreamed of a day when that type of spirit would spread through the entire community and when daring individuals like Nathu would become heroes of the community rather than being castigated. The fact that Azu turned to the pastor for baptism may mean that he recognized that the support of a community and institution was essential for his struggle. Unfortunately, the pastor might not see the need for such a struggle.

The pastor faced a threefold dilemma. First, it could be that in the theology of the pastor there was no place for Azu's kind of militancy. Second, the pastor may have been nervous about breaking with the tradition and practice of the church, for example, baptizing Azu in the presence of an alien external symbol such as the sword which Azu carried. Or third, the pastor might have been wondering about Azu's real motive for seeking baptism and membership in the church. Was Azu seeking only some material gain? These are but a few of the questions many missionaries had to face when converts sought baptism. Predominant among the questions was one of motive. Were people seeking baptism for material benefits such as food, job, land, money, or other temporal gains, or were they convinced about the religion? If material gain were the motive, would the new converts be able to face disappointments and withstand persecution? Even today in the missionary outreach of the church, especially in the southern hemisphere, motive is an issue. Sometimes missionaries have to face the accusation that they are converting people because of the promise of material gain.

Another theological issue in this case is the place for popular religiosity within Christianity. Azu's mother went to church on Sunday, and on Thursday she made an offering to her indigenous god, Bala Shah. Apparently she made the offering without any feeling of conflict with her faithfulness to her new religion, Christianity. According to mission history, Western missionaries customarily expected converts to break completely with those past religious beliefs and practices which were contrary to the Christian faith and the practices of their particular church or denomination. But for new converts this separation was not always easy, especially when they continued to live in the environment that had shaped their lives and the life of their community. In the contemporary discussion on Christian mission and witness, the issue of gospel and cultures is a crucial one. Is there a Christian culture which is universally valid? What cultural elements can younger churches or new converts retain? Who decides?

A related issue in mission theology is the question of salvation. Is salvation for human beings offered only through Jesus Christ, or is salvation through other religions possible? There are vast numbers of Christians who argue that salvation is possible only through Jesus Christ. Their belief is based on John 14:6 (Jesus said, "I am the way, the truth, and the life. No one comes to the Father except through me") and other biblical texts. What is implied is that salvation is through Christianity only.[7] Others, based on the parable of the last judgment (Matt. 25:31–46) and other texts, argue that we cannot deny the possibility of salvation for people of different faiths through their own religion.[8] This debate will continue in the years to come now that more and more people are living in multireligious communities, and many religions are engaged in missionary enterprises to propagate their faith in the same way as are Christian churches.

In recent decades a number of churches and Christians have recognized the need to be tolerant in their attitudes toward people of other faiths and, where possible, to engage in inter-religious dialogue for the sake of promoting better understanding among followers of different religions. Among Christians today there is a much humbler acceptance of God's mysterious ways of dealing with humanity, without necessarily giving up Christian teachings on the purpose and goal of human life. Developments in the Roman Catholic Church since Vatican II and various programs of the World Council of Churches, as well as regional and national councils of churches, have contributed to this attitudinal change among churches. Collaboration among Christians and people of other faiths on concerns such as humanitarian reaching out during times of natural disaster, rescuing communities from mass poverty and hunger, or promoting proper attitudes and use of nature are on the increase. Theologies and communitarian experiences coming from marginalized people such as Dalits contribute to this development.

POSSIBLE ALTERNATIVES

Many alternatives may be considered in dealing with the caste issue. These include seeking legal protection, mobilizing the Christian community through proper education, and working with political movements or nongovernmental agencies with similar missions. Azu did not seem to be aware of these possibilities which may be why he tried to address the issue as an individual crusader. The pastor could use the situation to lead Azu in the right direction. If the pastor himself was not adequately informed about these possibilities, he could turn to the committee of his pastorate, other pastors in the area, or knowledgeable lay persons in his community.

I will deal briefly with these three possible alternatives. First, according to the law of India any derogatory remarks or action based on caste is punishable, and there are cases where individuals and groups seek legal protection under that provision. The Christians' plea to extend this provision to Dalit converts to Christianity should be supported without any hesitation on the part of the church leadership. In recent years the church leadership, among whom are several Dalit Christians, has given much support to this request, including having meetings with the president, the prime minister, and key political leaders, to register this matter as a vital issue for the Christian community. Of course, the political domination of the country by upper-caste people and the dependence of the Dalits on the upper-caste people who control trade and commerce make it difficult for lower-caste people to fight for their legal rights without undergoing severe hardship and sacrifices. But it is only by fighting for those rights that greater justice can be achieved for those who have been denied it.

Dalits are also increasingly aware of the close link between caste practice and economic deprivation. The lower the caste, the lower the economic opportunity and prosperity. The "caste-class" oppressive phenomenon has been exposed through research and study, enabling Dalits to enlarge the struggle to a secular liberatory movement as well.

Second, for the Christian Dalit community to seek legal and other protection and assistance available in the society, it must be aware that such protection exists. Centuries of social conditioning, economic deprivation, and illiteracy are all contributing factors in keeping an oppressed community in bondage. In cases where religious structures are closely tied to the social structure, achieving change in the religious structures becomes difficult. Attention should be given to two areas. The Christians should be helped to shed the view of society that has governed their social life prior to their conversion—the caste structure which is supported by the Hindu religion. They have to be informed about the New Testament vision for a holistic community, which defines human interpersonal relationships as different parts belonging to the same body. When one part suffers, everyone suffers (I Cor. 12:12–26). Further, Christians should be equipped to develop a theology that is conducive to their contextual needs. Such equipment will involve facilitating rereading the Bible and assessing the doctrines and theological formulations they received when they entered the Christian community. From such a process they could arrive at an appropriate religious structure which will enable them to be faithful witnesses to the gospel. Azu followed one path of individual search and found an answer which convinced him. But the challenge he had to face is whether he could convince the community on the basis of his own discovery of truth that his understanding of Christianity was valid for his community context. Otherwise, he might end up frustrated in spite of his good intentions. The role of the community is significant in implementing any lasting social change. But in India or in other situations where the Christian community is a minority, the support and collaboration of the larger society is vital.

Third, in situations such as that in India, support from political and nongovernmental organizations is of immense importance. India has a democratic system of government. Every five years elections are held for political offices. Politicians and parties are eager for votes from all sections of the people. Education about utilizing one's vote as an individual and as a community is a significant matter in a democracy. Education is the most direct way to bring change even though it is sometimes a very slow process and demands a rigorous program of conscientization. The nongovernmental organizations that are committed to the empowerment and uplifting of Dalits have done much service in this field of conscientization. But in spite of Christian nurturing in the churches, support from political forces, and services from nongovernmental and charitable trusts, the real movement for the liberation of Dalits forged ahead when Dalits themselves took charge of their struggles, through Dalit solidarity movements and actions. This avenue to change holds true both within the church and in society as a whole.

People like Azu are very important in the process of any change. He had the courage and took the risk and the time for study and reflection primarily for his own well-being, but he did not completely forget the community. In a way, his experiment with being a Sikh devotee made him aware that he could not pretend for long to be someone he was not, and he went forward from his status toward the goal he envisaged without the support of his own community. The case makes it clear that Azu alerted the pastor to the need he felt, and in that sense Azu became a catalyst for change. We can only hope that the pastor was well prepared by his ministerial training and practice to handle such a situation, so that Azu's initiative was not put into cold storage.

While the caste system is unique to the Indian subcontinent, the discrimination it demonstrates has a universal pattern. In various parts of the world, humanity has been subjected to discrimination based on race, tribe, ethnicity, class, and gender. While there are examples of overcoming discrimination, no community can claim to have overcome it completely. Even though this is a historical case, it has contemporary significance and relevance. Through the centuries human nature has not changed very much. Human beings need to remind themselves about the hurt and pain that misuse of power and privilege can create. An example from history, such as the present case, can always shed new light and bring new inspiration.

NOTES

1. John C. B. Webster, *The Dalit Christians: A History*, Delhi: ISPCK, 1992, pp. 2–3.

2. James Massey, ed., *Indigenous People: Dalits*, Delhi: ISPCK, 1994, p. 38.

3. M. E. Prabhakar, "Dalit Theology: Emergence of a Contextual Theology," *Contextual Theological Education*, James Massey, ed., Delhi: ISPCK, 1993, p. 39.

4. Webster,*Dalit Christians*, p. 9.

5. Ibid., p. 39.

6. *The Encyclopedia Britannica*, 15th edition, Chicago, 1989, vol. 27, p. 281.

7. Carl E. Braaten, *No Other Gospel! Christianity Among the World Religions*, Fortress Press, 1992.

8. John Hick and Paul F. Knitter, eds., *The Myth of Christian Uniqueness: Toward a Pluralistic Theology of Religions*, Maryknoll, NY: Orbis Books, 1988.

GREEN PASTURES

Case

Anna and her husband Jose took their seats in the crowded gallery at Tierra Wools. Seated around them were most of the members of Ganados del Valle, a ranching and weaving cooperative of fifty families living and working in the northern part of the state of New Mexico. The anxiety in the room was high. Unless the shepherds could find grazing land immediately, they would be forced to sell or slaughter their flocks. That would mean no wool for the weavers.

The shepherds had a month-to-month arrangement with a nearby Apache tribe for the cooperative's flocks to graze on Apache land. The sheep had been there for two months when the arrangement was suddenly canceled. An Apache representative said the tribe was in litigation with the New Mexico Department of Game and Fish over hunting licenses, and the presence of the cooperative's sheep would be detrimental to their case. It was August, and the sheep needed a place to graze through the end of summer. The State Game Commission had denied the cooperative's request for short-term emergency access to any of the three wildlife areas in the area. Tonight's meeting had been called to consider a proposal by cooperative leaders that members move the herd of one thousand sheep onto the wildlife areas anyway. Doing so was clearly an act of civil disobedience, but the co-op leadership saw no other options.

Anna came to this meeting with a heavy heart. She thought back over all that had happened since Ganados del Valle was formed seven years earlier. At that time she and her husband and their friends had wondered how long they would be able to stay in the rural community where their forebears had settled three hundred years ago. Los Ojos was one of the nation's poorest communities with an annual family income of $8,500 compared to a national average of $16,491. Almost all the new jobs the government had created were minimum-wage service jobs at the hotels and motels that supported the growing tourist trade. Too many of these jobs took people away from their families and communities.

This case was first published in a Church-wide Study Document titled, "Sustainable Development, Reformed Faith, and U.S. International Economic Policy," Louisville, KY: Presbyterian Church (USA), 1994. Used by permission.

Anna had seen things begin to change for the people of Los Ojos when Juanita Orteza, a community organizer, began working with shepherds of small flocks to revitalize the traditional pastoral economy. Ganados del Valle grew out of Juanita's inspiration and the energy and efforts of the community as people began to work together. The cooperative raised Churro sheep, a long-fiber sheep that had been traditionally raised by this community, but which had become nearly extinct. The first members of the cooperative began their work with two spinning wheels and four looms. The members hired a professional weaver who had entrepreneurial experience and trained the weavers in traditional production techniques: quality control, pricing, marketing, wholesaling, and retailing. Although she was a teacher during much of the year, Anna learned to spin one summer and continued to work for the cooperative during the summer months. Her husband Jose had struggled for years as a hay farmer with only a few sheep. He joined the cooperative and began to increase his flock with the help of cooperative herding and training in animal husbandry.

Ten years after the Los Ojos community organized, forty-five people were employed by the cooperative. Members of the cooperative had built a wool-washing plant and a combination feed store, coffee shop, and general store. They had established a revolving loan fund to provide cooperative members with seed money for independent projects and for businesses that grew out of the cooperative. They had recently established a scholarship fund which enabled young people to attend a seven-week summer arts program and provided money for cooperative members to take marketing and management courses. And they were working with a local community college to design an associate's degree in fine arts built around the cooperative's weavers training program.

The cooperative also had a shares program which made it possible for local families to become vested by borrowing ten to fifteen sheep. The family would have six years to return the same number of sheep to the cooperative. During this time, the family would give the cooperative one lamb a year as interest.

A former director of economic development for the state of New Mexico had praised the work of Ganados as an example of the kind of development that was needed in the state. He noted that although retail and service jobs could be created much more cheaply—so the number of jobs was higher more quickly—sustainable development depended on the kind of manufacturing jobs that Ganados had been able to create. He affirmed, "These kinds of jobs create a real and lasting economic base for a community." Anna also saw the jobs providing a new sense of hope and pride throughout the community. Now all this was in jeopardy.

From the very beginning of their work together, the shepherds struggled to find enough grazing land for the community's flocks. The task became increasingly difficult as the state worked to develop its tourist industry, setting aside large tracts of land for hunting and fishing, and exploring the development of ski resorts. The sheep owners had been unable to buy or lease land near Los Ojos because land prices had soared out of reach as the southern Rockies became a more popular place for recreation and second home development. Every year the cooperative approached large landowners about the possibility of leasing grazing land. Usually the land was leased to cattle ranchers as was the case this year. The cooperative had worked hard to find an alternative and had been able to work out the month-to-month arrangement with the neighboring Apache tribe, but the Apaches now needed their land back.

Members of the cooperative had been negotiating for several years with the state Department of Game and Fish about the possibility of using some of the 36,000 acres of the nearby Humphries and Sargent Wildlife Areas for grazing. Every year the state had denied their request. Federal and state agencies, environmentalists, and hunting groups officially opposed any form of domestic grazing as a threat to the land and the wildlife. Cooperative members were told that the sheep would be competing for forage with more than one hundred different species of wildlife. Elk grazed on Humphries and Sargent Wildlife lands, and these elk are part of the lure of New Mexico's $350-million-a-year hunting and fishing economy. There was also a history of overgrazing by some ranchers which had resulted in destruction of wildlife and habitats.

State officials said that wildlife areas, acquired with money from hunting and fishing license fees and from taxes on sports equipment, were for wildlife only. Legally these lands could not be used by domestic animals. "Sheep and elk do not mix," said Herbert Adams, chairman of the State Game Commission. "The purchase of the land is subsidized by the U.S. government, and the subsidy is to be used to provide land for wildlife not livestock. If we allow livestock to graze on the land, we risk losing federal subsidies." Members of Ganados del Valle pointed out that other ranchers had been allowed to graze livestock on these very same wildlife areas and that recently the game department had even put one of the areas out for bids, but their evidence did nothing to change the state commission's decision.

Juanita Orteza had found evidence that under certain circumstances grazing sheep might actually improve the range for wildlife. She and other members of the cooperative found examples in Oregon and other states in which sheep were used to improve grazing for elk. Professor Lyle McNeal of Utah State University also claimed that sheep grazing could benefit wildlife. However, no in-depth scientific research had been done. Juanita and members of Ganados del Valle proposed that the cooperative enter into a joint study with the Department of Game and Fish to see if sheep grazing could improve grazing for elk in the Humphries and Sargent

Wildlife Areas. Juanita even went to Washington, D.C. to present her case to U.S. Fish and Wildlife officials in the hope that the cooperative could obtain emergency access to the wildlife areas. She returned with a promise that the officials would listen to a research proposal "sometime in the future." That would be too late; the cooperative needed grazing land now.

Los Ojos was in one of the last rural areas in northern New Mexico with spectacular scenic views. The success of the cooperative had attracted a great deal of "cultural" tourism: people who were drawn to the authentic pastoral setting, people who were interested in the historic culture, and people who purchased the beautiful wool shawls, rugs, and material produced by the cooperative. Aware of their dependence on a pastoral setting, cooperative members had written demands for the protection of unspoiled and undeveloped land into the Ganados charter. Cooperative members continued to press for stringent subdivision regulations. They had joined with local environmentalists to fight against plans to develop a large ski resort in their immediate area. But on the grazing issue cooperative members and leaders of the environmental movement were divided.

A news release by Fred Jenkins of the Nature Conservancy in New Mexico claimed that "wildlife preserves make up only 3.5 percent of the total acreage in Rio Arriba County in which Los Ojos is located. Therefore it is inaccurate to point to small reserves as somehow taking away or limiting opportunities for sheep grazers." Anna disagreed with the implications of the news report; she knew that wildlife areas, Indian trusts, and federal lands comprised about 30 percent of the Tierra Amarilla Grant. Outside interests held 60 percent of the land, and local residents owned about 10 percent.

Anna's attention was suddenly brought back to the meeting as Martin Romero, a seventy-eight-year-old rancher, began to speak. "I've seen sheep and elk graze together all my life." Other ranchers and herders in the cooperative nodded in agreement. "I'm ready to commit civil disobedience and move my flock onto the state wildlife area," he said. "I have worked too hard to watch our sheep slaughtered or sold." He invited the other members of the cooperative to join him.

Anna was not sure civil disobedience was the route to follow, and she knew Jose was equally hesitant. As she listened to other members of the cooperative speak, Anna thought about what one of the leaders had said. What was happening in their community was only one example of what was happening around the world. Environmentalists and sporting interests were at loggerheads with poor, mostly nonwhite communities over the use of sensitive environments and the conservation of wildlife. Anna believed that indigenous people living in a poor area had a right to use public land or the land they once held in common even when that land had been set aside for preserving wildlife and biodiversity. But was she willing to act on that belief?

Anna also thought about the possible personal cost of civil disobedience. She was a school teacher with a state contract. She was afraid that if the cooperative moved the sheep onto state land, she might lose her job. But her job alone didn't pay enough for her family to live on. They needed the income from the wool. As she heard the strong arguments being raised from different perspectives, Anna realized that she was also afraid that a drastic action such as illegally occupying the sanctuary could divide the cooperative and jeopardize everything they had worked so hard to build.

As a long-standing member of the cooperative and a teacher in the community, Anna knew the people were expecting her to speak.

Teaching Note

A false assumption is pervasive in some economically developing countries that the people of Europe and North America are not confronted by oppression and poverty. But even in the most economically advantaged countries, marginalized communities struggle for dignity and survival. Some of the poorest communities in the United States are located in the Southeast, in Appalachia, and in the Southwest, the area where Los Ojos is situated.

The ancestors of the people of Los Ojos were most likely Spanish conquerors who traveled to the area in 1540 searching for gold. New Mexico, also known as the "Land of Enchantment," is a beautiful state with forests and mountains in the north, desert regions with *mesas* (flat-topped hills) in the south, and vast range lands used for grazing cattle and growing crops in the center.

Like the Apache, Navajo, and Pueblo people who were there before them, most of the Spanish descendants were pushed off their land by conquest. Mexico ceded the land to the United States in 1848, and New Mexico became a state in 1912. Today almost half of the state's land is owned by the federal government, with much of this designated for military purposes and for national parks and forests. It is into one of these national forests that the members of the Ganados del Valle cooperative are considering moving their sheep.

I. Discussion Goals

A. To evaluate a creative model of self-development.

B. To assess the importance of land to sustain any form of development.

C. To consider the interconnectedness of state, federal, and local development approaches.

D. To discern ways to strengthen marginalized communities.

E. To celebrate the ingenuity and determination of many marginalized people.

II. Case Discussion

A. Identify the steps taken by the cooperative to achieve its current level of economic independence. Evaluate which steps are the most critical. Following this exercise, ask participants what criteria they applied to select the "most critical" steps? Did their unstated criteria include protection of the environment, stability and economic independence, openness to involving others in the cooperative, and growing empowerment of the community?

B. Identify the underlying issues behind the crisis for grazing land. Consider land use and distribution, political and economic power, environmental concerns, and historical factors which may affect the situation. Is there evidence of discrimination against the members of the cooperative?

C. Look next at the individuals involved in the decision about grazing land.

What are the primary concerns for Herbert Adams of the state Game Commission and Fred Jenkins of the Nature Conservancy?

Urge participants to get into Anna's "feet." What is she *feeling* about the decision facing the cooperative? What are her primary concerns? What are the advantages of moving the sheep onto federal land? What are the dangers?

D. Ask participants how they would vote if they were members of the cooperative. Allow sufficient time for group members to discuss why they support one of the two positions. Are there any alternatives to civil disobedience? If the cooperative decides to move its sheep onto the preserve, are there ways they could maximize the benefits and minimize the liabilities of this action?

E. Ask participants which person or persons they most identified with when they first read the case. Why? What evidence in the case points to the interconnectedness of the poor and the rich? How do the lives and life styles of the discussion participants touch the lives of Anna and Jose?

F. The United Nations World Commission on Environment and Development defined "sustainable development" as "development that meets the needs of the present without compromising the ability of future generations to meet their own needs." (*Our Common Future*, World Commission on Environment and Development, New York: Oxford University Press, 1987, p. 9.) Which actions by the cooperative meet this definition of sustainability? How are other agencies and individuals in the case attempting to meet this definition? How are they compromising it? How do participants' responses relate to the previous discussion of the ways in which participants' lives and life styles touch those of Anna and Jose?

Commentary

The Lord is my shepherd,
I shall not want.
He makes me lie down in green pastures;
he leads me beside still waters;
he restores my soul.
He leads me in right paths. . . .
I fear no evil
for you are with me.

Psalm 23: 1–3a; 4b (NRSV)

The members of the Los Ojos community are marginalized people seeking to live with dignity and sufficiency. Through the Ganados del Valle ranching and weaving cooperative, they have built a model of development with the potential to move them beyond want to the still waters and green pastures of economic viability and cultural renewal. The community is productive and ecologically concerned and has previously been in a constructive interdependent relationship with elements of the dominant culture and economy. The community also seems to be maintaining its distinctive identity. This process of empowerment is now threatened by lack of access to land upon which to graze the sheep.

The struggle over the survival of the Ganados del Valle Cooperative involves the strong possibility of polarizing the community and alienating former allies such as the New Mexico state government, environmentalists, a sporting group, and a neighboring Apache tribe that also experiences marginalization. To continue to prosper, the cooperative needs to sustain unity within its membership and promote solidarity with religious and secular groups. The sustainability of newly energized communities cannot be taken for granted. Liberation requires continual renewal. The empowerment engendered by the cooperative must be protected and extended to the wider Los Ojos community. The challenge this case poses to clergy is to become aware of pastoral care strategies which can strengthen marginalized communities on the verge of greater stability and independence.

THE CONTEXT

The Southwest of the United States has experienced two major waves of invasion and colonization. Indigenous Americans such as the Apache and Navajo were first ignored and later subdued by Spanish invaders who arrived four hundred years ago. The colonizers were well armed with both weapons and land grants from Spanish monarchs. The second major invasion was by settlers from northern Europe and the eastern United States claiming land for farming and grazing by right of "manifest destiny." During the conflict between the invading settlers and the indigenous people, the U.S. government used the Army to support the settlers and deported or placed on reservations most of the native peoples.

The treaty which ended the Spanish-American War established control by the second set of invaders. Both resident native peoples and descendants of the Spanish invaders were dominated by Northern European settlers. One result of this pattern of invasion, colonization, and domination, in which the church has often been a collaborator, was the marginalization and impoverishment of Native Americans on reservations and of many Spanish-speaking people in rural areas and town ghettos. As cultural identity declined in these communities, abuse of alcohol and drugs increased. Native American and Spanish-speaking communities became marginal to the relative prosperity of settler families and to the more recent wave of affluent residents seeking leisure sports and a warm, dry climate for health reasons or retirement. The rapidly rising cost of land, spurred by the influx of new residents to the Southwest, has made land acquisition almost impossible for most poor people and communities.

Some of the poorest communities in the United States, such as Los Ojos, are located in the Southwest. However, movements for identity, liberation, and solidarity have begun to take root in some of these oppressed areas. A new sense of dignity, pride, and initiative is emerging, often nurtured by pastoral care approaches that encourage the rise of indigenous ideologies. A critical step for many communities has been the application of liberation theologies by Hispanic Americans and Native Americans. Los Ojos may or may not have been influenced by nontraditional ways of understanding the gospel. However, it is clear that members of this very poor community organized not only to survive but also to prosper in relation to the dominant culture. Whether the church has instructed the community is uncertain, but it is clear that this community has lessons for the church. Several fundamental issues have implications for pastoral care; some raised by this case are land access, models for development, and protection of empowerment.

ACCESS TO LAND

Years of advocacy programs on behalf of native peoples in North America have led to the establishment of Indian Land Trusts and other special government and nongovernment programs. With regard to land access, most native peoples are less disadvantaged at the end of the twentieth century than are Spanish-speaking communities. International development studies suggest that after access to clean water, access to land is the most crucial factor in self-sufficiency and long-term stability. Other central components, such as food supply, housing, education, and health, depend on land use for agriculture, residences, schools, and clinics. Pastoral theology that is systemic and holistic must inspire theological reflection on the importance of land for identity and stability.

In this section, "Empowering Marginalized Peoples," each case is concerned in one way or another with land. "Pipeline to the Future" deals with protection of indigenous land rights; "By the Sword" with a dream of land acquisition by an individual; and "Green Pastures" with access to land by a community. In a book on human rights the Brazilian philosopher and theologian Rubem Alves reflects on the pervasive and growing presence of a reality reflected in signs that read:

> WARNING
> Private Property
> No Trespassing
> Violators Will Be Prosecuted.[1]

This view of land, Professor Alves concludes, suggests that "Property is something to be protected and defended as part of one's life; my body, my property, my right, a human right like food, air, freedom—something without which I would not survive."[2] Alves contrasts this dominant understanding about land in North America with a view of native peoples on the same continent: ". . . in former times, Indians had used trails that are still to be found in the woods—sacraments of a world that was not divided by fences." Indigenous people did not have private property because they did not need it. "Their world and their corporeality were grander, their fences were distant horizons, mountains, seas, the stars."[3]

A relationship to the land appears to be pervasively important for human identity and essential for human development. Theologically, the Creator God grants access to land as a gift to be held in stewardship by and for the creatures. A prophetic pastoral theology raises the issue of the stewardship of land, as have the people of Los Ojos. Is the primary purpose of land for the benefit of the majority or for the few who control its access by purchase or legal trusts? The norm is wise use of God's gift of the creation of land. Los Ojos needs access, not ownership, of grazing land, whether it is a wildlife reserve, an Indian Trust, or so-called private property.

The challenge raised by the cooperative is a matter of justice: access to land for the benefit of all. Anna and other members of the cooperative are trying to decide how claiming one's human right of access to land should inform their decision about civil disobedience. Although there are theological reasons why impoverished people should have a right to any land that could ensure their survival, the land in question is already within the public domain. Anna believes that indigenous people living in a poor area have a "right to use public land or the land they once held in common" even when that land has been set aside for other uses. She believes that a community's right to survive takes precedence over national and local legislation. Because there is contradictory evidence about whether sheep make grazing land unfit for elk, the community is not necessarily forcing a choice between human survival and the survival of wildlife. Unless an alternative strategy can be developed, the continuation of the Ganados del Valle Cooperative, the identity of the members as part of a community, and perhaps their very survival may depend on their risking illegal access to public land.

SUSTAINABLE DEVELOPMENT AS EMPOWERMENT

A sign of empowerment in most communities is economic development that is both sustainable and equitable. Economic development is not the only path to security and stability, but it is usually essential to more comprehensive human development, which includes cultural identity and relative independence. The development of a sustainable economy is a complicated process, especially when a microeconomic model confronts a significantly different macroeconomic model, as in this case study.

The ranching and weaving cooperative has been engaged in what has come to be called "people-centered development," a process which holds significant potential for being both economically and ecologically sustainable.[4] This model of economic development stresses equitable distribution of economic opportunity and reward. The "people-focus" refers to wide participation by the members of the community in decision making on economic, social, and cultural concerns. As the members of the cooperative responded to their primary goal of meeting the needs of the people, they began to build democratic structures, accountable relationships, and local control over the resources needed for development. These principles are evident in programs such as flock expansion, the wool-washing plant, the weaving looms, the feed and outlet stores, loan funds, and scholarships. Self-reliance and continuation of a people-centered approach is built into the cooperative's educational and training programs, giving integration and integrity to community life. Members of the community are not only concerned about one another, they are investing in the next generation. It is evident that the participation and sense of dignity which promote Christian personhood are central to this form of development. The church has much to learn from the Ganados del Valle Cooperative.

Ecology is also important to people-centered development. The community members are clear that water and grazing space are finite resources which must be protected from overuse. Concern for careful management of natural resources led to a valuable alliance with local environmentalists. While responsible stewardship of the Earth is a central theme of the church's renewed awareness of the integrity of creation, many congregations and denominations have not yet brought these concerns to bear on their daily lives.

Other areas of the community's approach to development are also instructive for the church. For too many years Western Christian mission imported spirituality and worship from the West; missionaries also supported models of development in poor areas which perpetuated dependency and relied heavily on rapid economic growth through industrialization or mass-market sales of services and raw materials to wealthier nations or communities. While this approach to development was initially successful and brought dramatic short-term economic improvement to some areas, its application to marginalized communities today often increases rather than decreases the disparity between the rich and the poor, draws rural poor to overcrowded urban areas, and holds the potential of permanently depleting natural resources.

The case cites the director of economic development who contrasted the "lasting economic base" brought by the cooperative with the short-term success of retail service jobs. Anna identified most of these new jobs in the state as "minimum-wage service jobs" that "supported the growing tourist trade . . . and took people away from their families and communities." Short-term focus on economic growth does not meet the long-term basic human, cultural, and social needs of marginalized people. The Los Ojos community challenges the church to give priority to development programs—not only those which meet a community's basic needs of food, shelter, education, and health, but those which lead to dignity.

The people-centered approach developed in Los Ojos closely parallels the goals of "The People's Earth Declaration," written by nongovernmental organization (NGO) delegates to the International NGO Forum during the June 1992 United Nations "Earth Summit" in Rio de Janeiro, Brazil. The document notes the "many damaging consequences of a development model grounded in the pursuit of economic growth and consumption to the exclusion of the human and natural interest."[5] This gathering of hundreds of people from the so-called developing world called for the organization of "economic life around decentralized, relatively self-reliant local economies that control and manage their own productive resources, provide all people an equitable share in the control and benefits of productive resources, and have the right to safeguard their own environmental and social standards."[6]

In noting "the sovereign right and ability of the world's people to protect their economic, social, cultural, and environmental interests," the delegates affirmed "the people's right to demand that governments and corporations remain accountable to the public will and interest."[7] This call for government accountability raises a central problem with people-centered development: small community development programs, a micro system, can be disempowered by a macro system, especially when access to resources is beyond the control of the micro organization. The state and federal governments in this case support national or regional "top-down" development through tourism, large-scale ranching, and construction of retirement homes. Without state or federal government support, which could grant temporary entrance for the sheep into the wilderness areas or assistance in locating alternate grazing land, the cooperative's people-centered program is seriously endangered. This small, emerging system needs allies and strategies to hold the government structures accountable for meeting the needs of all the people.

PROTECTING AND EXTENDING EMPOWERMENT

A central issue for Anna is whether or not to engage in civil disobedience. What is the cost? How will the decision affect the unity of the community? What impact would illegal occupation of the land have on those who were sometime allies in the community's struggle for empowerment? Because it is imperative to secure access to grazing land in time to save the flock and the cooperative's wool resource, the problem presents itself as a crisis of survival. The undergirding issue is the cost of protecting and extending the community's empowerment. Anna, a respected member of the community and a teacher who may be vulnerable to a reprisal if she supports illegal activity, is expected to speak and give guidance. Components of a wise decision are already present.

To maintain the *unity* of the community calls for careful strategy. Communication is crucial. Because the entire community needs to discuss the basic issues and generate creative options, the leaders of the cooperative have wisely begun a process of open discussion. It will be important to acknowledge that some people will be more vulnerable than others in the face of a decision to invade the land. This group includes Anna and others employed in government institutions or in community agencies outside of Los Ojos. The cooperative's members are surely aware that the more vulnerable members will need special support through this process. They are also aware that it is important not to polarize the community whether or not civil disobedience is chosen.

As the cooperative has realized from past experience, *interpretation* of the community's needs and actions to the wider New Mexico community is significant. There are several issues that require careful and articulate communication: 1) the conviction that access to land for survival is a right of the whole people, not a privilege of a few; 2) the need for cooperation in research concerning the ecological implications of co-grazing elk and sheep; 3) the importance of protecting a recognized and successful model of development; and 4) the question of whether there has been discrimination against the cooperative since the department has issued grazing leases in the past to large-scale ranchers. On the latter issue, a public challenge issued to the state Department of Game and Fish may contribute not only to the unity and empowerment of the cooperative, but also to the dignity and equality of other marginalized communities.

Solidarity needs to be further developed with other partners if empowerment is to be protected for this Spanish-speaking community and extended to others in the state who feel disempowered. The Apaches, with a hunting license problem, are being placed in a competitive stance with the Los Ojos community, whereas the two communities may be natural allies, both pressing their rights for access to land. The environmental and sporting groups which have previously been partners may not understand the nature of the Ganados del Valle crisis about late summer grazing land. Better understanding of the issues might lead some members to support an act of civil disobedience or to help obtain alternative grazing land. The needs of the Los Ojos community must be understood by their natural and former allies especially at this time. Finally, the Christian family could be mobilized on a justice agenda to support the requests of a vulnerable community.

Important pastoral images in the New Testament which may inform the members of the cooperative include Christ's giving priority to seeking one endangered lost sheep even at the risk of the other ninety-nine (Luke 15:3–6). Jesus' identification with a shepherd's willingness to lay down his life for the sheep may strengthen the appropriateness of the costly sacrifice which may be required of members of the cooperative. Civil disobedience to claim public land may be the only way the members feel they can protect and extend the empowerment of their formerly marginalized community.

The Christian church is challenged by communities such as Los Ojos to make advocacy of marginalized people more central to pastoral concerns in congregational mission strategy and theological education. However, it may be more important for churches to learn from the members of the cooperative than to lead them. The community has shown determination, wisdom, and creativity in developing and implementing a process to realize dignity and self-worth. This has been accomplished from the "underside" of a wider, dominant society which often—consciously or unconsciously—blocks empowerment of self-sufficient micro organizations. The biblical image that may be most appropriate for the church to consider is that of Jesus on the road to Emmaus (Luke 24:13–35). The disciples' eyes were opened to recognize Christ where they least expected to meet him.

NOTES

1. Robert A. Evans and Alice Frazer Evans, *Human Rights: A Dialogue Between the First and Third Worlds,* Maryknoll, NY: Orbis Books, 1983.

2. Ibid., p. 188.

3. Ibid., pp. 188–189.

4. David C. Korten, "People-Centered Development: Alternative for a World in Crisis," Manila, Philippines: People-Centered Development Forum, 1991.

5. "The People's Earth Declaration: A Proactive Agenda for the Future," Rio de Janeiro, Brazil, 1992, p. 1. Contact Green Forum Philippines, Liberty Building, 835 Pasey Road, Makati 1200 Metro Manila, Philippines or Canadian Council for International Cooperation, 1 Nicholas Street, Suite 300, Ottawa, Ontario K1N 7B7, Canada.

6. Ibid., p. 2.

7. Ibid., p. 1.

PART II

THE ROLE OF WOMEN
IN CHURCH AND SOCIETY

Contemporary Christian churches are challenged to distinguish between traditional social patterns that are to be honored as part of a community's intrinsic identity and thus are symbols of self-worth and those traditions that are destructive to some members of the community, most frequently women and girls.

Most societies have historically assigned different roles or duties to women and men. In many traditional societies role designation was socially effective and just, honoring the distinctive gifts each person brought to the wider community. With the onset of what is described as "modernization" and the economic and social changes brought by industrialization, men in societies throughout the world began to leave agricultural communities in search of wage-earning jobs, leaving women at home alone to raise the food crops and educate the children. The supposedly more important wage-earning distinction for men has relegated women to the less important role of child bearer and rearer. This wage earner versus home keeper distinction supports stereotypes of inferiority for women and leads some communities to the decision that the less important, female members of society do not need to be educated or nurtured in the same way as the more important, male members of society.

The social effects of industrialization, as well as deeply embedded practices which assign women to subordinate roles or marginalize them in other ways, have far-reaching negative consequences in many societies. In much of the world the bulk of agricultural labor is provided by women. However, social patterns in many nations exclude women from educational programs that could significantly improve agricultural results. The 1995 Report of the United Nations Development Programme notes that women account for nearly 70 percent of all illiterates and 70 percent of the world's poor.[1] The report indicates that the level of infant mortality is not determined so much by poverty as by the literacy of mothers. Although Sri Lanka has less than two-thirds of Brazil's income per person (on a purchasing power basis), Sri Lanka has a higher rate of literacy; babies are much more likely to survive in Sri Lanka than in Brazil. "Mortality among Indian babies of mothers with primary education is half that of those born to uneducated women."[2] An educated mother better understands hygiene, nutrition, and the importance of immunization. Education also enables women to better realize and employ their innate talents, not only for themselves but for the benefit of their communities. Exclusion of women from education is detrimental to both individuals and societies.

Other cultural practices relating to women which are now seriously debated include marriage of young girls before puberty, often younger than ten or eleven years old, and female circumcision. Many cultures accept the traditional practice of female circumcision as an act of purification that "cuts away unclean flesh," "protects women against rape," "curbs women's sexual appetite," and "discourages premarital affairs."[3] However, people both within and outside those cultures have come to view what they consider to be genital mutilation as a life-long health hazard which can lead to severe hemorrhaging, infections, difficulty in pregnancy, and even death.

Christians must decide when and where they are called to challenge traditional patterns that are not only socially dysfunctional but are also destructive or oppressive for some members of that society and are in conflict with gospel promises of equality in Christ. Local pastors and lay leaders are frequently at the center of these debates.

THE ROLE OF THE CHURCH

Paul's proclamation to the church in Galatia has been understood as a powerful liberating message to Christians throughout history: "There is neither Jew nor Greek, there is neither slave nor free, there is neither male nor female; for you are all one in Christ Jesus" (Gal. 3:28 RSV). The early church struggled with the question of whether circumcision as required by Jewish law was also a defining sign for membership in the Body of Christ. The church ultimately ruled that male circumcision, a primary distinction between Jews and Greeks, was irrelevant to one's unity in Christ. This decision was supported by Peter's powerful vision on the rooftop, which led him to proclaim to the disciples and believers in the household of the Roman centurion Cornelius that "God shows no partiality, but in every nation anyone who fears him and does what is right is acceptable to him" (Acts 10: 34b–35 NRSV).

Although the church fought for many more generations about the issue of slavery, which divided societies as well as nations, this social and economic practice has been declared oppressive and contrary to the gospel. Church bodies throughout the world have come to this conclusion even though slavery appears to have been accepted as normative at the time of Paul's letters. The distinction between male and female, however, and the justice of some traditional relationships between women and men in many societies continue to be debated by the church. And in many instances the church has been a barrier to the acceptance of men and women as equal under God.

Not only did Jesus heal, nurture, and accept women as followers, he repeatedly broke with tradition by affirming the dignity of women as equal with men in the sight of God. God chose Mary Magdalene to be the first evangelist, bringing to the fearful disciples and other discouraged followers the news that Christ had arisen. Women such as Dorcas, Phoebe, Lydia, Priscilla, and Chloe were strong and capable leaders of the early church as recorded in Romans, Acts, and Corinthians. However, contemporary scholarship has revealed that in the following centuries, terms for "human beings" in the scriptures which were not gender specific began to be translated by an increasingly male-led church as "men," "brother," and "son."

Some of the early church "fathers" made strong pronouncements which confirmed a lesser status for women and strengthened patterns of discrimination against women within the church. Tertullian, an influential early church theologian of the third century, interpreted Eve's role in the Genesis story of the "fall of man": "You (woman) are the devil's gateway. You first plucked the forbidden fruit and first deserted the divine law. . . . It was you who so readily destroyed the image of God, man. By virtue of your just desert, that is, death, even the Son of God had to die."[4] Thomas Aquinas, a powerful and historically influential church leader of the thirteenth century, wrote, "As regards the individual nature, woman is defective and misbegotten, for the active force in the male seed tends to the production of perfect likeness in the masculine sex; while the production of woman comes from a defect in the active force or from some material indisposition. . . ."[5]

Such strong pronouncements supported the selective reading of many scriptural verses, raising up as definitive those images which excluded women from leadership roles, for example, and ignoring those which were contrary to this view. Discrimination against women became deeply imbedded in Western culture and was subsequently integrated into the message which the vast majority of Western missionaries carried to the mission fields of Africa, Asia, and Latin America.

In stark contrast, Jesus' model of ministry and Paul's declaration of God's acceptance of all persons challenge practices of domination by one person or persons over others and declare that Christians are free to be united as equals in the Body of Christ. While these gospel images charge Christians of one society to respect the values and traditions of other societies, they also call Christians to a ministry of justice which denounces destructive or oppressive social practices. Much of the global Christian community was united, for example, in its denunciation of South African structures which had legalized the political and economic slavery of people of color through the edicts of apartheid. The World Alliance of Reformed Churches declared as heresy the support of apartheid by the South African Dutch Reformed Church. At what point, then, is the global church called to challenge those culturally or socially defined roles of women or social practices involving women which may be judged as oppressive? The three case studies in this section raise different aspects of this dilemma.

TOOLS FOR CONSTRUCTIVE DIALOGUE

While the case "Support for Rosa" is presented through the perspective of a social worker in Peru, it focuses primarily on Rosa, a courageous and energetic mother of four children who lives in Lima, Peru. Rosa is caught between her commitment to improve the quality of life in her desperately poor community and the need to support the family financially while her husband Manuel is unemployed. Both Rosa and Manuel are also trapped by traditional role expectations which inhibit Manuel from sharing Rosa's burdens. Is the church called to challenge those traditions which increase the hardship of marginalized people, in this case by challenging the continued acceptance of traditional categories of work with children, cooking, or small market sales as "women's work," when the traditional role of women has been expanded to include the role of financial provider? To what extent, if any, is the global church responsible—through its actions or lack of action—for the destructive effects of globalized market economies, particularly on women and children in economically poor countries?

"We Are Also God's People" is set in the African village of Kimeso in Angola. The arrival of Tata Lombo, a new Christian pastor, and the introduction of strong prohibitions against the traditional practice of polygamy, particularly by the church founder, Tata Kiala, divide the congregation and threaten its survival. This case and commentary invite readers to ponder not only the biblical basis for New

Testament support for monogamy but to consider the role and importance of contextual theology, particularly in non-Western societies. Is the new pastor responding to the will of God as revealed in scripture or imposing a synthesis of gospel and Western culture? How can the traditional women in Kimeso, who accept polygamy as a way of life, be reconciled to younger, more educated women, less dependent on men for survival, who criticize this practice?

Participants discussing the situation revealed in "Nothing Really Happened, Did It?" have been divided in their interpretations of how Sophie, a seminary student, should respond to the unexpected and unwanted advances of Paul, another seminarian. The case and commentary raise questions about the consequences of male power in most societies as well as in most Christian churches and about the psychological and theological implications of sexual impropriety or misconduct by church professionals. Readers are challenged to consider the measures that both churches and seminaries should take to ensure that both women and men are able to affirm the gospel promise of equality in the Body of Christ and renunciation of domination over others.

The fact that the role of women in church and society is central to several other cases in this collection indicates the global extent of this theme. "Should a Woman Lead the Church?" calls the Christian community to struggle with the acceptance of ordained women in parish leadership. While "They Still Call Me 'Stinky'" focuses on ministry to people living with AIDS, the case also challenges readers to consider the relationship between the social and economic status of women and the rapid increase of AIDS among women. One reason for the increase is that women are biologically more susceptible to the virus than are men. Perhaps equally important is that women's economic dependence and subordination to men puts them at greater risk. For example, extreme poverty often forces women into commercial sex which "significantly increases their risk of HIV infection."[6] These social realities challenge the church not only to continue its mission of strengthening family structures and the values of fidelity but also to support education and job training programs for poor girls and young women to help keep them from turning to prostitution for survival.

The cases and commentaries in this volume do not make as many declarations as they ask questions. These same questions are being asked by women and men throughout the world. The Fourth United Nations World Conference of Women and the forum for nongovernmental organizations which met in and near Beijing in September 1995 gathered thousands of women who shared stories and suggested strategies to deal with the barriers that maintain their second-class status. The emergence of coalitions of oppressed women who gain strength through their collective voice is a potentially powerful result of these gatherings. Both this stronger voice, and the small voices of individual women subject to oppressive social patterns, call the church to prayerful consideration and prophetic responses which raise up those traditions that build healthy, mutually supportive relationships between women and men and challenge those that do not. Convinced that the response of the global church is crucial to the wholeness of churches and societies, the authors hope that these cases and commentaries will become useful tools for reflection.

NOTES

1. "Different Roads to Development," *The Economist*, August 19, 1995, pp. 35, 36.
2. Ibid., p. 35.
3. Fatuma Hashi, "Halting FGM: What is being done? What can be done," in *Together: A Journal of World Vision*, January–March, 1996, p. 16.
4. Tertullian, *De Cultu Feminarium*, I. 1.1–2.
5. St. Thomas Aquinas, *Summa Theologica*, trans. by Fathers of the English Dominican Province, London, 1921–32. Vol. III, ii, 1.
6. Eric R. Ram, "Community Response to HIV and AIDS: A Global Perspective," in *Together: A Journal of World Vision International*, Vol. 47, July–September, 1995, p. 4.

SUPPORT FOR ROSA

Case

"Rosa, I don't know what I can do, but I'm sure we'll work out something together. I have a staff meeting tomorrow, and I'll ask for their help as well."

As Susana Martinez walked toward the bus stop through the unpaved streets of one of Lima's poorest districts, her words to Rosa Rodriguez echoed in her mind. Susana also vividly recalled the anguished look in Rosa's eyes. Susana dodged the shouting, barefoot children running down the narrow alleys between the simple houses. She walked by the budding medical clinic that Rosa had helped start and took a shortcut through the small "informal economy" market where Rosa sold fruit. Susana smiled and spoke to a number of the women she knew in her role as a social promoter for the *Instituto de Apoyo Communitario* (IAC, Institute of Community Support). Susana, an urban sociologist, was one of twenty young professional people who worked for IAC, a service-oriented, nongovernment organization which sought to address critical urban problems through grassroots programs in Lima's sprawling slums.

Susana had worked with Rosa for nearly two years and continued to be impressed by her dignity, energy, and her remarkable ability to organize people to improve the quality of their lives. Rosa, now twenty-eight, had been born in Lima to parents who had migrated to the city from Ancash in the mountains to the north. They were two of the hundreds of thousands of impoverished rural mountain people who had "invaded" Lima over the past four decades. Rosa's husband, Manuel, was also a child of migrant parents. Their parents lived in the same slum district. Rosa married at fifteen and was pregnant with Eduardo, her oldest boy, at sixteen. The young couple set up house in a new "invasion" of an unoccupied area within the district of San Martin de Porres.

They settled with more than two thousand other families on a barren plot with no roads, water, sewage, or electricity. Manuel, a construction worker, was able to get enough work to pay for basic supplies to begin building their home of brick and cement stucco. They had a small kitchen with a two-burner kerosene stove, two bedrooms, and another small area which served as a living and dining room. It had taken several years to build all the rooms. Now with four children, ages twelve, ten, eight, and five, Rosa said they were cramped, but she had also told Susana how much room they had compared to many of their neighbors. Rosa, like many other urban poor women, began her role in community organization by encouraging her friends and neighbors to march to the city center and demonstrate for the basic services of water and power. Their homes now had cold running water and electricity. However, because of the tremendous deterioration of living conditions, especially for the urban poor, the shantytown dwellers were obliged to face new problems, particularly in nutrition and health.

Susana had met Rosa two years earlier when Rosa came to an information session on community kitchens that Susana was conducting. Rosa had become enthusiastically involved in establishing a community kitchen in her neighborhood and was soon elected the kitchen coordinator. The twenty-two women who ran the kitchen divided their tasks into rotating teams for bookkeeping, developing menus from recipes provided by IAC, buying bulk food from the largest Lima markets, and cooking. Rosa or one of her children picked up a hot, nutritious meal for her entire family every day. Because the food was purchased in bulk, the cost was much less than what Rosa had been paying, and she only needed to work in the kitchen one day a week. Rosa now had other days free. She and her cousin established a stand selling fruit, which Rosa had learned to buy wholesale from the Lima market. She began earning money for the first time in her life.

Within a year of helping to organize the community kitchen, Rosa was elected district vice-president and helped coordinate forty-five kitchens. She became involved in negotiating for government subsidies to help buy the very large and expensive pots needed to establish more kitchens and in lobbying for price controls on basic food items. In her local community Rosa was a strong voice against police corruption and the growing drug trade. The many women who came to her with personal problems constantly demanded her time.

Not long after Rosa was asked to run for office in the local governing council, she quietly asked Susana to come home with her so they could talk. Rosa told Susana that her husband Manuel had not found any work for more than six weeks. He was at home most of the time and wanted her there to care for him and the family. Rosa said that even though Manuel had not mentioned it, he knew that she was too busy to sell as much fruit as she had in the past, and the family needed the money. Rosa was also deeply worried about her son Eduardo. With double sessions, he had school only four hours a day. Rosa was sure she had seen Eduardo running with one of the gangs of young boys who took drugs and robbed the struggling market stands. She didn't think he had taken any drugs, but she was worried about his new friends. Manuel had even hinted that school would not help Eduardo get a job. If there were no salaried jobs, maybe he should start working in the street market. Rosa's ten- and eight-year-old girls took care of the baby and the house. Eduardo was home less and less.

Rosa spoke with quiet dignity. "Susana, I understand the problems of our communities. I have never been happier than I am now because I have found ways of helping my people, but I grieve for my son, and I feel my husband's anger. If I am unable to find some kind of support, I will be forced to resign from my role in the district and will not be able to consider election to the council.

"As you know, our kitchen operates out of our local chapel. The women in our kitchen gather for Bible study with Sister Maria who is very supportive of our work. A priest comes only occasionally to say Mass. I talked to Sister about my problems. She told me how important my work was for the parish. She said she would ask the priest if there were any parish funds to hire me. But Sister insisted that if any arrangement could be worked out, I must spend my time helping our own local community and not get involved beyond that. Yet, Susana, in my prayers and through our Bible study, I feel called to challenge the wider systems that create the poverty in which we live."

Before she continued, Rosa looked out the door to make sure none of the children were near. She then told Susana about the threat she had received. Two young women who had disappeared from the community eight months earlier had returned. From their comments Rosa was sure they had been with the *Sendero Luminosa* (Shining Path). "Susana, those women came to me and said they were watching me. They said that if I take the council seat I will 'pay the consequences.' These people want to destroy all our community has done. I know I must be making a difference, or they would not threaten me. It is now more important than ever that I continue to stand up for my people and not submit to their threats."

The following morning Susana raised her concerns about Rosa with her coworkers at the IAC. She concluded by saying, "Women such as Rosa Rodriguez are critical to the very survival of her community and to the work we are all doing. We've got to find some way to support her through this crisis."

Ramon Gutierrez, Director of IAC, responded. "Susana, if you mean by 'support' some kind of remuneration, you know this would be in direct conflict with our basic principles of grassroots organizing. The introduction of pay for community leaders often leads to division and jealousy and begins to build a bureaucracy. Our goal is to help neighbors, especially community leaders, become self-sufficient and in control of their own programs.

"There is tension in all our communities. With Peru's annual inflation rate at 2,700 percent, the cost of basic necessities is becoming prohibitive for all the low-income families we work with. The International Monetary Fund demanded dramatic reductions in government support of urban development and health programs. On top of that I'm deeply concerned about maintaining our own funding from major supporters abroad now that so many funds are being directed toward Eastern Europe."

Anita, an industrial economist on the IAC team working in support of small businesses, admitted that she often felt guilty about receiving a salary, even though it was very modest, with so many families struggling for survival. "Would it be possible to help Rosa's family with the emergency fund?"

Thomas, the bookkeeper, shook his head. "Those funds are strictly limited to emergencies when people are in the hospital or their homes burn down. Rosa's needs are long-term. Why doesn't she ask the women in her community to give her a stipend?"

Susana responded. "Rosa would never ask her friends. First, they don't have any money, and if they did, they would be using family resources, and that could create serious family tension. Also, many women feel they are working as hard as Rosa. They are not motivated to address the broader issues and are proud of Rosa's role, but I suspect that some are also jealous of her recognition. Though she didn't tell me, I know that Rosa was recently asked to represent her community at an international conference in Colombia."

Several staff members expressed deep concern for Rosa and affirmed the importance of her role in the community, but the pressure of time forced them to move on to other issues. Susana left the meeting feeling confused and frustrated. She had agreed to meet Rosa in late afternoon. The council wanted Rosa to tell them this week whether or not she would accept the nomination.

Teaching Note

I. Goals

This case lends itself to a broad variety of discussion topics. For this reason the leader should determine specific goals in advance and direct the discussion with these goals in mind.

The case does not contain background information on the *Sendero Luminosa* (Shining Path) or the history of "invasions" in Lima. For maximum use of the case, a leader could introduce or assign this background material. A few suggested readings are listed under Part VIII. Many issues concerning the role of women, poverty, sustainable development, global economic patterns, and nongovernmental organizations, however, are universal, and the case can be a useful tool to draw parallels with situations in other countries without additional information.

II. Setting

Build a general picture of life in San Martin de Porres from the case and from other readings. What drove Rosa and Manuel's parents to Lima as migrants from their homes in rural mountain areas? What is the standard of living for Rosa and her family in Lima?

III. Persons

Consider each of the primary persons in the case from two perspectives.

A. Identify who they are, what facts the case reveals about each one.

B. Try to imagine what each person must be feeling at the close of the case. The following suggestions are only illustrations of what participants may say.

1. **Susana:**

   a. *Facts:* an urban sociologist, well-educated, probably upper-middle-class;

   b. *Feelings:* possibly guilt, concern about Rosa, frustration, a sense of determination.

2. **Rosa:**

   a. Energetic, creative, age twenty-eight, married at fifteen, poor, four children, child of rural migrants;

   b. A strong sense of self-worth, feeling fulfilled in the present work, anxious about the future, fear.

3. **Manuel:**

   a. Unemployed, poor, child of rural migrants, creative, industrious, once had goals;

   b. May feel defeated, anxious, a low sense of self-worth, angry, guilty.

C. Briefly identify other persons who may be important to decisions about supporting Rosa: Eduardo, IAC staff members, Sr. Maria.

IV. Issues

Identify the major issues raised by this case. The discussion leader will need to select a primary issue for more in-depth discussion, as this will determine the direction of the discussion on alternatives. If the decision is to focus on the role of women in church and society, for example, then time should be allotted to discuss this issue fully, relating participants' insights to material in the case and possibly to personal life experiences. This focus will raise such issues as the cultural role expectations of men and women, and why women (and children) are more vulnerable to the effects of poverty than are men. If the primary focus is on problems that face the poor and those who seek to serve them, the discussion may center on the factors that contribute to poverty and the approaches of nongovernmental organizations and the church to alleviate suffering.

V. Alternatives

The commentary offers suggestions for addressing Rosa's concerns. Ask participants to raise several alternatives. Consider the implications as well as the strengths and weaknesses of each response. This section of the discussion could be organized around the possible approaches several of the case characters could take.

VI. Resources of Grace

When one thinks of resources of God's grace, images are often of prayer, scripture, or the church. This case suggests a variety of additional ways in which Rosa can experience God's presence. These may include the women in the community kitchen and in the Bible study; Rosa's children and her husband Manuel; Susana and the IAC staff; those who are urging Rosa to run for the council; or her own courage, resourcefulness, and strong determination. These human resources are gifts of God which may bring many different kinds of support to Rosa.

VII. Conclusion

Close by moving the discussion to the participants' social situation. Ask about their relationship to or responsibility for the Rosas of the world. Why and how should individuals and congregations respond to global economic inequalities? Which nongovernmental agencies do discussion participants support and why? Do these agencies offer special programs for women? What are the responses of participants' churches or denominations to the poor, especially poor women who are often the most vulnerable? What theological and social policies guide their denominational approaches to service to the poor? What biblical passages first come to mind when they think of the response of the church or nongovernmental agencies to those who are poor and marginalized?

VIII. For Additional Reading

Christian Faith and the World Economy Today, A Study Document of the World Council of Churches, Geneva, 1992, p. 21.

Christine Gudorf, "Peru: Women's Agendas," *Christianity and Crisis*, November 7, 1989.

"Violence in Peru," *Andean Focus*, Ecumenical Committee on the Andes, Vol. VI, No. 3. August, 1989.

Commentary

The struggle for a decent living is a common problem experienced by millions of people, the majority of whom live in the Third World countries of the South. In the globalized market economy, many small and poor countries in the South experience difficult economic conditions which force them deeper and deeper into debt. Rosa and her family are among these millions, trying to make ends meet and trying to survive the harsh economic reality of their country, Peru. And Peru is just one of many countries in the South that continue to suffer severe economic crisis in the global market economy competition. Many poor countries need international financial and economic aid for their national economic development programs. To receive this kind of financial support many countries are required to make structural adjustments, which usually imply substantial cutbacks in government spending, including support of urban development and health programs, which will, in turn, result in more structural injustice.

THE SITUATION OF THE CASE

Struggle for economic justice anywhere is bound to confront political powers. Economically marginalized people are at the same time socially and politically marginalized. And among the marginalized, women usually suffer the most, because they are also discriminated against and marginalized because of their gender. Women such as Rosa have to work harder and fight harder and suffer more, while at the same time taking heavier risks as well.

Rosa, a twenty-eight-year-old, creative, energetic woman is married to Manuel, an unemployed construction worker. She supports her family of six by selling fruit in the small "informal economy" market and by working once a week in a community kitchen. Their four children are ages twelve, ten, eight, and five. Rosa is a community organizer who has been successful in getting her community of migrant workers in the sprawling slums of Lima to fight for their right to basic services from their government. She and her group were able to bring running water and electricity into their homes and to establish many community kitchens to provide inexpensive family meals. Her success has brought her to a dilemma. On the one hand, she became famous and respected and was nominated for an office in the local governing council. On the other hand, because of her involvement in the community, she spends less and less time with her family. Her dilemma is further complicated because her husband Manuel has not found work in the past six weeks. Manuel expects Rosa to be at home to take care of him and their children, and yet she is the sole income earner. Further, she was threatened by the *Sendero Luminoso* (Shining Path), a guerrilla group fighting in opposition to the national government. The *Sendero* spokesperson does not want Rosa to run for office and dislikes her community activities. However, Rosa is determined to fight and continue the struggle for her community despite these threats.

Susana Martinez, a sociologist working with the Institute de Apoyo Communitaro (IAC), a nongovernment organization (NGO) supporting community works in slum areas, has been a friend and supporter of Rosa and her community activities. Susana realizes that Rosa needs her continued backing, especially at this time, and also needs financial support if she is to continue working for the community and running for office. However, IAC is not able to give Rosa the financial help she needs.

NGOs can be very helpful and supportive in a struggle that involves communities or groups suffering structural injustice. However, many NGOs are also marginalized institutions that have to fight and struggle for their own survival. Rather than risk their existence, struggling NGOs often sacrifice programs and even the people they are trying to help. In this case, Ramon Gutierrez was concerned for two reasons. First, one of the principles of grassroots organizing that IAC has adopted is not to give any kind of remuneration to community leaders. Second, there is no provision in the budget for giving Rosa financial help since the emergency fund was strictly intended for emergency cases, as Thomas, the IAC bookkeeper, explained. Rosa's needs could not be considered an emergency. Although it is not clear from this case if it is true of IAC, many NGOs are also financially dependent on outside sources. Most NGOs in Third-World countries are dependent on financial support from overseas, mainly from the West or countries of the North, which are also the source of many of the problems that plague the countries of the South.

SOME EFFECTS OF GLOBAL INTERDEPENDENCE

Most countries of the South were subjected to colonialism by countries of the North—some for a few decades, others for a few centuries. After their independence, these former colonies became ready markets for the manufactured products and other commodities of the industrially developed countries of the North. They also became the source of cheap natural resources and labor. The countries of the South became economically dependent on the North; loans for national development were given by the industrially developed nations, either directly or through some syndicated banks. The price of natural resources fell on the global market, interest rates on the debts increased, and many poor countries moved into a devastating cycle of additional borrowing simply to pay interest on outstanding loans. However, responsibility for this pattern of growing debt and dependency is not that of Western or Northern capitalist powers alone; responsibility is often shared by corrupt and oppressive political and economic power elites of the South or Third World countries. The loans were not always used wisely or for the benefit of the majority of the people. Third World debt has led to a major global crisis. Debt service ratios in many countries are as high as 35 to 45 percent.

"From the OECD debt table it can be calculated that between 1982 and 1990 the developing countries have remitted to the North *in debt service alone* $1,345 billion (interest and principal) which is $418 billion more than the total resource flow in those years *to* those countries, much of which has anyway [sic] been in the form of new loans."[1] If we compare this situation with the U.S. Marshall Plan, which transferred $14 billion (equivalent to $70 billion in 1991) to rebuild Europe, poor countries have financed six Marshall Plans for rich countries through debt service from 1982 to 1990.[2]

Peru's foreign debt in 1985 was nearly $14 billion. When newly elected President Garcia announced that Peru would pay no more than 10 percent of its export earnings toward this debt, the IMF (International Monetary Fund), which is controlled by the industrially developed countries of the North, "declared Peru to be ineligible for future loans and credits until Garcia adopted more orthodox economic and debt repayment measures."[3] Faced with the loss of most international financial support, the flight of capital funds held by wealthy Peruvians, and continued military action against the *Sendero Luminoso*, the government cut deeper into services for the poorest communities. In many communities such as San Martin de Porres, the only services came from the church and NGOs.

ANALYSIS

The IAC staff has refused to help Rosa financially. There seems to be a contradiction between the policy or basic principles which the IAC staff applied to Rosa and their own practice. It is a basic principle of grassroots organizing that no remuneration should be given to community leaders. This principle was cited by Ramon Gutierrez, director of the IAC, as the reason why the IAC could not give financial support to Rosa personally. Not paying community workers may be a good principle or policy; however, staff of the IAC, who are also working with grassroots people, receive salaries, presumably from the funding source or agencies that support IAC. This seems to be the reason Anita is feeling guilty; she receives a salary from IAC while many families are struggling for survival.

If one looks at the case from the perspective of human needs, a clear question arises. "Is this the only way to deal with the case of Rosa?" To dismiss Susana's request for support of Rosa because of a basic organizational principle not to give any remuneration to community leaders merely begs the question: What about other ways of helping to support Rosa? How can the organization help the children, especially Eduardo, with their school needs, so that Rosa can continue to work for the community? How can the organization help Manuel find work so that he will earn some income, and not "sit around the house all day?" How can the organization offer support for men who feel ashamed about not working or who do not even consider helping to take care of the children at home and share the household chores? What about encouraging Manuel to support Rosa in her campaign for community development instead of expecting his wife to take care of him?

Many suggestions implicit in these questions challenge traditional male and female roles. NGOs and churches that work with poor communities must seriously consider addressing those traditional social patterns which add to the burden of already marginalized members of a society. Because these patterns are usually accepted without question, the task of consciousness raising will take time, patience, intentionality, and great sensitivity. The most enduring changes, however, will not come from the organizations themselves but from grassroots initiatives which challenge an oppressive status quo. Churches and NGOs must be willing to add prophetic support to these initiatives.

If the emergency funds cannot be used to support Rosa, are there other sources for financial help that can be tapped? Other options should be thoroughly explored. What about suggesting that Manuel take over the responsibility for selling fruits and vegetables, thus bringing in income for the family. Rosa needs support to continue to work once a week in the community kitchen. Not only does the kitchen supply a hot meal once a day for her family, it is an important place for Rosa to gain moral support from members of her group. Manuel should be made aware of the success and contribution that Rosa has made to the community. His support would mean that he, too, is helping the community. As a husband he should be proud of Rosa and help her defend herself against the pressure from the *Sendero Luminoso*. He should also be encouraged to join and support the women by getting other men to organize. In this way Rosa can be assured of the support of the whole community, especially of her own family.

PASTORAL STRATEGY

What is the role of the church in such a situation? What is the pastoral function of the church in such a community? One of the basic principles of pastoral strategy is never to let the people feel abandoned. Dismissing any further help for Rosa during such a crucial time amounts to abandoning her. If there is no possibility for IAC to support Rosa financially, have other forms of support been seriously considered? Sometimes, the presence of the pastor or church lay leaders among the people in a struggle can be very encouraging. People who have been struggling and fighting for social, economic, and political justice for many years and have not been able to bring substantial changes can be so frustrated that they become apathetic and lose their fighting spirit, even their hope. Can Sister Maria or the church rekindle these hopes? What is the means or the source for hope in a hopeless situation? It is important for struggling organizations to build a network to share experiences and common problems in order to support each other and each other's programs. The church can lend a helping hand in the formation of networks of community leaders and nongovernmental organizations. Experience has shown that in almost any context no single group can manage many programs on its own. Cooperation and networking are as essential as funding for the success of any program.

SOURCE OF GRACE

The church can become the source of a renewal of hope in people who have been fighting and struggling for human rights, human dignity, and social justice. To perform this function the church must show people its genuine concern and interest in their struggle and manifest these not only through sermons, counseling, advising, and giving moral support, but also through sacrificing time, effort, energy, and funds when necessary (Ref. The Parable of the Good Samaritan, Luke 10:25–37). For those such as Rosa who are confronting dilemmas, comforting words and a prophetic promise may become the source for God's grace to strengthen their will and spirit to work for justice for their communities. "Come to me, all you who are weary and burdened, and I will give you rest. Take my yoke upon you and learn from me, for I am gentle and humble in heart, and you will find rest for your souls" (Matt. 11:28-29 NIV). "Behold, I will create new heavens and a new earth. The former things will not be remembered, nor will they come to mind. But be glad and rejoice forever in what I will create, for I will create Jerusalem to be a delight and its people a joy. I will rejoice over Jerusalem and take delight in my people; the sound of weeping and of crying will be heard in it no more" (Isa. 65:17–19 NIV).

However, these comforting words will not be adequate unless the church is willing to support Rosa in the face of the threat from the *Sendero Luminoso* and is willing to take the risk with her. Should the church take such a risk? The church will encourage and empower Rosa if it is willing to support her nomination to the council. But the question is, should the church be involved directly in such matters? We should be reminded of Jesus's entry into Jerusalem in Matthew 20:17–19. Jesus was aware of the danger and the risk involved, but decided to go anyway, because he was willing to take the risk.

NOTES

1. *Christian Faith and the World Economy Today,* A Study Document from the World Council of Churches, Geneva, 1992, p. 21.

2. Ibid.

3. *The New Encyclopedia Britannica,* Vol. 25, 993, p. 526.

WE ARE ALSO GOD'S PEOPLE

Case

When Kimfuati, a seminarian, returned home on holiday, he could not believe his eyes or his ears. The Christian community at Kimeso village appeared to be disintegrating. An old friend told him that most people were no longer going to church meetings because of a dispute about Elder Tata Kiala's four wives and that Kimfuati would see for himself on the following day.

Kimfuati had just come from Kimalalu Theological School where part of the training had been to reflect theologically on everyday life. Liberation theology had been his favorite course because it developed in him a capacity to reflect critically on praxis.

Kimfuati visited his relatives and the elders in the village who also told him about the situation of the church.

That night when the moon was shining, Kimfuati sat under the mango tree near his home and recalled events that took place before he left for the seminary two years earlier. As soon as he sat down and stared at the church, he realized polygamy must be at the base of the disintegration of the church. The practice had been common in the area. Tata Kiala was a wealthy and respected man who had brought the Christian community into the village. Tata Kiala had four wives. Two of them lived in the same house; another lived in a house next to the main house; the fourth lived in a nearby village. Each wife had children, a total of three sons and nine daughters. The four families knew each other, loved one another, and were linked to the same husband and father. All the wives had responsibilities, and they seemed to share their goods and wealth equally. As Kimfuati observed, everything seemed to be in harmony.

Kimfuati went to bed, but before sleeping he remembered a conversation with Tata Kiala who had told him about the historical development of the church in Kimeso village. Kiala had said, "I always met Christians wherever I went to sell my agricultural products. From these constant contacts, going from door to door, I could invite people to a meeting on the following day. People met under the shadow of the mango tree, and that meeting was the beginning of the worship and Bible study community in the village."

The next morning, a few hours before the church service, Kimfuati had a brief chat with his father, Tata Toko, to ask about his knowledge of the history of the church. Tata Toko added, "The news of the worship community reached Lukika, the nearest mission station. The missionary and his pastors at this mission station came to the village to see the situation for themselves. They were delighted with their visit, and later they sent a pastor to continue the work Kiala had begun and to build a church for this area."

Kimfuati recalled that the first time he had met the new pastor, Pastor Lombo, was when a large delegation from Lukika mission came to officially open the new pastoral post in the village. At first the church at Kimeso flourished, and many local people as well as those from surrounding villages such as Mabaya and Kitadi came to the Sunday worship and Bible study.

While Kimfuati was having his breakfast, he could hear his mother and another woman talking. "Pastor Lombo refused to conduct a funeral service for a child of the third wife of Tata Mvuondo who is a member of the church."

Kimfuati finished his meal and went to the church for Sunday worship. He was welcomed by the pastor who seemed delighted to see him again. The service began and ended with only ten participants. This small number worried Kimfuati who remembered a large and thriving congregation of worshippers in the little church. He decided to go and see the pastor after the service.

The pastor and Kimfuati talked for two hours, and Kimfuati recalled part of their conversation. "Fifteen months after my placement in this village, I decided to examine Tata Kiala's situation," Lombo said. "My intention was to help Tata Kiala so that he could be baptized and be consecrated as a pastor for this area, since I planned to expand my pastoral activities to other remote areas." Lombo explained to Kimfuati that the baptism and consecration were impossible because Kiala was polygamous and did not want to change to conform with Christian ethics. "He moved out of the church and took with him many other sexually sick people," Lombo said.

The conversation ended when the pastor concluded, "Polygamy is sinful according to the scriptures and Christian faith. You know," he said with authority, "we are trying to build the church of God for the people of God. Those who are possessed by the evil spirit of polygamy have gone. The few who remain God knows."

Kimfuati met Tata Kiala a few hours later and heard another side of the story. "You know how this church started in this village. I spent my money and efforts to build it up; now the church has betrayed me. Besides, before I started the church I already had my wives and children. Everything had been going well. Can you imagine what would become of my children, my own flesh and blood, if I abandon them? My faith in God has nothing to do with my wives. Anyway, they love me, and I love them . . . no problem. They also love each other. We are all happy like this. Do you, as a future pastor, think that this way of loving is a sin? Do you understand in what situation Lombo wants to put me? My own blood to be rejected and neglected just like that."

Kimfuati, being part of the community, could understand Kiala's feelings. The next day Kimfuati went to see the pastor about a possible alternative response to and attitude toward Kiala for the sake of the church and the people who were losing their faith.

However, Pastor Lombo raised his voice against Kimfuati. "It is useless for you to insist on this matter, because I am the pastor by vocation and you are just learning theology as a profession. Because I have this vocation, God is using me to act according to what is written in the scriptures. You better finish your studies, start writing books, and become rich," Lombo said.

Teaching Note

Kimfuati, a seminarian who has been away from home studying theology, returns to find a dispute in the village and an almost empty church. He discovers that the once-vibrant church community is split on the question of the compatibility of Christian faith with polygamy, an old African cultural practice which he respects. In his attempt to reconcile the differing parties and heal the split, Kimfuati feels alienated by the pastor who is an outsider and latecomer to the church and community. This case highlights the conflict between traditional social patterns and an interpretation of the gospel.

I. This teaching note focuses on the following goals and objectives:

A. To increase awareness of the importance of the history of a Christian community when working out new patterns of ministry.

B. To develop a wise and faithful missionary strategy for relating an understanding of the gospel message to a people's culture, especially when people have already found a working synthesis between culture and faith that has led to growth of the Christian community.

C. To realize the potential of discerning new truths in new circumstances.

D. To determine ways for pastors and seminarians to relate in a mutually beneficial way. This goal challenges both pastors and students to rise above their positions, either as experienced pastors who feel they have nothing to learn from seminarians, or as seminarians who in the course of their studies are convinced that they have discovered new truths that place them far ahead of their pastors.

II. Context of the Case

Explore the unique way in which the Christian faith came to Kimeso village and flourished. Look at the social relations as well as the power relations in the Christian community and how the origins of the church and these relations are intractably intertwined in determining the future of the Christian community in this village. What does the lack of information about women's perspectives reveal about the context?

III. Actors in the Case

Identify and characterize the main actors in this case. The point of this analysis is to show how their cultural backgrounds are linked to their faith perspectives in such a way that reconciliation becomes very difficult.

What is Tata Kiala's role in the village? Discuss his personal identification with the church. Identify social, political, practical, and psychological factors which have alienated him from the pastor and the church. Discuss his statement: "My faith in God has nothing to do with my wives." Which scriptural references, especially from the Old Testament, support polygamous marriages?

What has shaped Pastor Lombo's understanding of the Christian faith? What was his social role in the community when he first arrived? Identify the components that have alienated him from people in the congregation. On what scriptures does Pastor Lombo draw when he speaks of the "evil spirit of polygamy"? How do you interpret his belief that "God is using me"? Why does he dismiss Kimfuati?

Discuss the factors that have shaped Kimfuati's understanding of the gospel. If Kimfuati's view of the church is based on liberation theology, how does this relate to Pastor Lombo's theological understanding of the "people of God"?

Readers hear from women in the village only through a conversation Kimfuati overhears between his mother and another woman. What are the implications of this conversation? Why did Kimfuati not speak directly to the women and ask their opinion? While Kimfuati does not challenge the traditional practice of polygamy, do readers believe that all of the women in the village support this practice? Why or why not? On which scriptures might women who oppose polygamy draw? How might their understanding of the gospel message differ from that of Pastor Lombo?

IV. Issues

While this case raises many issues, those which may help participants reach the identified goals may include the following:

A. A dogmatic approach to culture versus a dogmatic approach to truth in the gospel.

B. The relationship between concern for human beings and the pursuit of spiritual purity.

C. The importance of placing the gospel in a local context.

D. How committed Christians distinguish between the will of God as revealed in scripture and a synthesis of gospel and culture.

V. Reconciliation and Resources of Grace

Search the group for theological resources that will heal the spirit and preserve family life without sacrificing the truth of the gospel.

Help discussion participants discover pastoral patterns and strategies that will help keep the door open and the dialogue alive until solutions are found. Consider ways in which the congregation in Kimeso could hear the voices of all concerned.

Discuss how the church community could build enough trust to ask if there are some relationships in which love is distorted and some partners suffocated, silenced, or instrumentalized. How could older voices be helped to make room for younger voices and the voices of women?

Are there ways a third party, such as Kimfuati, could reconcile the parties in conflict without sacrificing basic tenets of Christian faith on the one hand, or destroying families and the fabric of the society on the other hand?

Explore ways for pastors and seminarians to acknowledge and draw on one another's gifts and abilities as they work together for reconciliation.

Commentary

THE CONTEXT

This case takes place in the African village of Kimeso in Angola, probably during the civil war. During crisis periods in every society, conservatism assumes the upper hand. Conservatism becomes even stronger in an African village that is normally conservative in many respects. Tradition and culture are frequently invoked to protect the nation by enforcing unity. Most of the Kimeso villagers were not born Christian and have very little contact with other cultures, especially those that are liberal. They live a traditional life and are guided by African traditions and culture. Traditionally, religion maintains the status quo of power and social relations.

In such a traditional setting, the position of each member in society is clearly determined, and roles are neatly spelled out. Men are the most powerful; they determine the place and roles of women and children. They use culture and tradition to secure their own positions and to obtain the collaboration of women and children. In these communities men are the sole interpreters as well as enforcers of culture and tradition. Women have no role in the public sphere. They cannot participate publicly in debates on issues that affect the nation or the village. A woman daring to speak would be seen as representing bad management on the part of her husband. The place for women is at home, and their roles are to serve the men, bring up the children, and pass on to the children traditions of the families into which they married.

Marriage is a highly placed institution in Africa. In rural villages such as Kimeso, every woman prepares for marriage and expects it to take place sooner rather than later. During her upbringing, she is taught all the skills of looking after a man and bringing up children. She is consistently reminded that she should be ready when the right man comes around. Every man is also expected to marry and is taught all there is to know about marriage at the traditional school. If men and women do not marry by a certain age, people in the village ask what is wrong with them. Women, especially, are under severe pressure to marry, even though they are not permitted to search aggressively for a suitable man. That pressure leads to some women marrying men who may not be their choice. In countries such as Angola, torn apart by years of civil war, the overwhelming excess of women also poses a problem when they are under pressure to marry. In some cases, women marry into polygamous situations to escape being spinsters. In other cases, women marry polygamously a wealthy or powerful man to have a share of that wealth and power. Whether they ever attain that position is an open question. What is satisfying is that they have someone to look after and protect them. In a traditional society such as Kimeso, there is no honor or pleasure in remaining unmarried.

The people of Kimeso practiced African traditional religion before becoming Christians. Many are still traditional worshippers. Those who converted to Christianity had started to work slowly through the relationship between their traditional culture and religion on the one hand and the Christian gospel on the other. They worked on the contradictions between their old religion and the new one. They also had to translate their new faith into social, economic, and political life. Since they had no Christians to assist them, they had to rely on themselves. Working out the implications of the new faith for their everyday lives and social relations is not an easy task. In most cases the task of doing so is the prerogative of men despite the fact that they constitute a minority in the church. As at home and in society at large, women's position in the church is also, on the whole, a subservient one.

In villages such as Kimeso, all Christians still adhere to cultural practices and traditional patterns of life. In most instances, villagers struggle to read the Bible and ask themselves its implications for their everyday lives. One group of Christians will regard one traditional practice as contrary to their new faith while another does not. That disagreement can lead to discussion and, at times, to tension. With good leadership, the community will find a solution that does not alienate anyone. A good solution can strengthen the community in its faith. At times, under unwise leadership, the community members fight among themselves and ultimately the church breaks up. Many African Independent Churches have their origins in such poorly managed disagreements.

When this case took place, the community was still working out the implications of the Christian faith without intervention or disturbance from well-established Christians from another culture. Church members had resolved some of their problems in ways peculiar to their village and their cultural setting. One traditional practice with which they had made peace was a polygamous form of marriage. When the first pastor from outside their village arrived, the community was already satisfied that there was no contradiction between Christian faith and polygamy. They did not know what lay in store for them with the arrival of Pastor Lombo.

THE ISSUES

Kimfuati, a student of theology in training for the ministry, returns home on vacation to find a dispute in the village, an unhappy Christian community, and an almost empty church. While making the rounds and meeting his relatives who are members of this church, founding members of the church, and the pastor, he discovers that the once-vibrant church community is split from top to bottom on the question of the compatibility of Christian faith and polygamy, a cultural marriage practice well established in Angola prior to the arrival of Christianity. One can assume that not only the men but also the women of Kimeso are affected by this split and have a share in it. They are also divided along age lines on this issue. Most older women do not see what the problem is, while the younger women, who are generally more educated and therefore less dependent on men for survival, are critical of polygamy. It is, however, still the case in such an African society that the senior women's position is the one that is the official women's position. The women may not be very vocal in public and in the presence of powerful men, but they, too, are expected to make a choice and take a side. This painful situation is totally unacceptable to Kimfuati, and he resolves to do something about it.

The problems of the church are not just objective issues. They are personified by important personalities in the community, namely Tata Kiala and Pastor Lombo. Tata Kiala is a well-respected senior member of the church who is also one of its most influential founding members. In fact, according to him, he started the church. He is very pious and views this male-dominated church as virtually his own. He expects it to bless his way of life and enhance its quality in the same way traditional religion would do. Tata Kiala must be wealthy since he can afford to marry four wives and raise a big family. Not every man does so. He clearly believes in the legitimacy of African tradition and culture and upholds them at home, in society, and in the church. He has surrounded himself with men of his social and economic status who hold similar beliefs. He is so powerful that those who do not agree with his marriage pattern (and such men would be very few in Kimeso), would not have enough courage to criticize him in public.

When Tata Kiala worked hard to start the church, he was already happily married to four wives. He sees no contradiction between his Christian faith and his polygamous marriages. Neither do most members of the church, especially the men. He has a happy family wherein love and mutual assistance abound. His entire family is well looked after, and none of his wives and children has expressed any complaint. The absence of complaints may not be too difficult to explain. As an elderly man, he is married to older women who are still close to African tradition as it relates to marriage and who have accepted that the benefits of such a marriage outweigh its disadvantages.

The first man to criticize Tata Kiala publicly, most probably after talking to him privately in the manner that befits a good pastor, is the new pastor, Lombo. What has turned out to be a problem for the new pastor, who was trained in a conservative seminary, is not Tata Kiala's "ownership" of the church—he can live with that—but Tata Kiala's polygamous marriages. To Pastor Lombo this form of marriage is diametrically opposed to the central teaching of the Christian faith as universally perceived. Polygamy should not be tolerated in the Angolan church just as it is unheard of in a European or American church. In his training, he was not taught much about the contextuality of church theology and dogma, or that there are issues that have to be weighed against the particular context in which the church finds itself. What makes matters worse is that Pastor Lombo is from a different area of Angola and from a different culture. When Tata Kiala and other Christians of Kimeso were working through an integration of the gospel and their culture, he was not there. The church he comes from might have been involved in working out its own integration with a different outcome. Pastor Lombo has remained a cultural outsider even though he was acceptable as a pastor. As an outsider, he is now seen by many members of the church at Kimeso to be imposing not the gospel, but the results of his own synthesis, or that of his village church.

Pastor Lombo, who came to shepherd and lead this church, strongly believes that he has been called by God to do God's will. He strongly believes that part of that will of God is to solve the marriage situation of Tata Kiala, because polygamy is a sin.

Both these men believe in the righteousness of their positions. Tata Kiala believes that if there is love in his extended family, there can be no problems. Besides, he looks after his wives and children. Abandoning his flesh and blood would be a truly unforgivable sin. For Pastor Lombo the issues are also very clear, and he has no doubts. "Polygamy is sinful, according to scriptures and Christian faith." "God is using me to act according to what is written in the scriptures," and it does not matter whether the church falls apart or not. If it does, that may even be a necessary act of purification.

FINDING A SOLUTION

It is important for anyone who searches for a solution to this problem to understand the history of this particular Christian community, how it came into being and how it survived and grew without a foreign pastor or missionary. That history produced leadership and loyalties that have to be respected in a search for solutions to contradictions, especially in cases where the new pastor would like to introduce innovations. Tata Kiala is a central figure in the emergence of this community. He personally brought many people to Christ and pastored them before the arrival of the new pastor. It may be that he was directly responsible for the coming of this pastor. He also led the search for resolution of contradictions between the Christian faith and African traditions and cultural practices. He should be persuaded and not confronted, because both he and the pastor are bound by the same faith and hope. That common faith is the basis for friendly dialogue, exchange of ideas, and prayer. Confronting him will only drive a wedge through the Christian community.

Every new leader of a church should also learn the traditions and the culture of the Christian community that is being served. There should be no sense of superiority and arrogance on the part of the trained pastor from another culture. He or she has to develop respect for the members of the community. It is incumbent on a cultural foreigner to be respectful and exercise patience in all efforts and activities through which innovations are being made. Hurrying through contradictions and disagreements will not be helpful. People should be given time to work through things and to make their ideas and feelings known. Guardianship over the truth and knowledge of the essence of Christianity on the part of the pastor will not help. Instead, such knowledge may become a stumbling block to the growth of the faith and understanding of congregants.

One of the most unhelpful—even dangerous—claims is Pastor Lombo's statement, "God has sent me." No one can say at what point and in which issue God is definitely on his or her side. No one has claim to God's grace. An attitude of humility and prayer are needed in all pastoral situations.

Tata Kiala could also claim that in his reading and understanding of the Old Testament, polygamy is not a sin. He could easily find examples of patriarchs who were polygamous and who are referred to in the New Testament as heroes of faith (Heb. 11). He could also claim that even Paul did not condemn it. Paul only recommended that church leaders should be monogamously married.

In confrontations in which biblical texts are used as missiles to shoot at one another, no one will emerge the winner. Even if one side marshals more texts than the other and wins the textual contest, the matter will not disappear. A different approach is needed, an approach in which a common starting point is sought and found.

People should not be sacrificed in favor of doctrinal purity or belief, because without people there is no Christian community and therefore no doctrine at all in that particular village. Tata Kiala has a strong case when he asks about the cohesion and welfare of his children. In his understanding of the Christian faith, love and peace are central to any and every family, and he can claim without contradiction from fellow Christians that there is love and peace in his family. St. Paul taught that love is the greatest of all commandments (I Cor. 13:13). Love is actually the basis of Christology, the reason for the coming of Jesus to redeem the world. Jesus' entire life and work are actualizations of the love that God has for all of creation and people in particular. His redemptive death and resurrection are the highest expressions of love for the other (John 3:16). It is love that has to serve as the basis of relationships as well as the canopy over all activities among believers at home and in the community. Included in love is freedom and equality of power. Without freedom, love would be distorted. Love would become domination or paternalism, in which one partner suffocates and is silenced and instrumentalized. Any relationship between men and women built on a foundation of love with freedom and equality unfolds under a canopy in which the partners are open to a continual search for improvement of their relationship. This type of relationship should be encouraged instead of sacrificed on the altar of either cultural or theological dogmatic rigidity.

It should be borne in mind that doctrine cannot be imposed. It arises within a particular context in response to local challenges and in the light of a study of the Bible and the guidance of the Spirit of God. A doctrine that is central to one culture may not be central to another. A lot of wisdom is needed in the process of discernment of what the truth is for a particular situation and time. Since the issue of polygamy is still being discussed by members of the Angolan church who are of different ages and cultural development, no dogmatic position of a different context should be imposed.

NOTHING REALLY HAPPENED, DID IT?

Case

Sophie shut the car door and breathed a deep sigh to release some of her emotion. She had expected more from her pastor, much more. As she left the church parking lot and turned onto the busy highway, she wondered if she would receive the same response from the seminary. Would the board hear her pain, believe her story, and take action against Paul, the man she had thought was a friend?

Two years ago Sophie Lowe decided to enter seminary. It was a frightening decision—classes, books, exams, papers. Even more frightening were the responses of other people when she told them she wanted to enter the ministry. Her family said, "What will you do with the children?" and "It will be impossible to manage all that!" Her friends just smiled, nodded, and responded, "What does that mean?" "Ugh!" She prayed about her decision for almost a year. She felt God's presence growing stronger. She could no longer avoid the issue. She enrolled part-time in Evangelical Seminary. Her husband was skeptical about how the family would manage; her two children were too young to understand, but she took the risk.

School was going well. Sophie's grades were excellent, and though it was hard juggling studying, children, and husband, she was feeling very fulfilled with her decision—her ministry. This term she was enrolled in many interesting classes. She met Paul Carr in Christian Theology. He was nice, very friendly. He had joined Sophie and some other friends for lunch a few times. Sophie's friend, Ruth Perez, had told her that Paul was about to become a new father. His wife was having complications with the pregnancy and was confined to complete bed rest for the last three months. It was a stressful time for them. Paul was juggling a part-time job, school, and the pregnancy. Sophie wondered how he was handling all of it.

Ruth told Sophie that Paul was also facing other issues. He was not affiliated with a denomination. He had worked in several churches during his first two years in seminary, all different denominations. He could not find where he fitted. Graduation was six months away, and he was not sure what would happen at that time. Ruth said that it was odd that someone would feel called into ministry, enter a denominational seminary, and yet in two and a half years never affiliate with a particular church.

A few days after Sophie's and Ruth's conversation, Paul approached them on the lawn of the campus. The three of them engaged in idle conversation. Paul then turned to Sophie and said, "Could we talk sometime about the issues raised in Theology today?" "Sure," Sophie said.

The next day during a class break Paul asked Sophie if they could talk. They agreed to meet right after class. Paul waited for her in the hall. "I have a quiet place downstairs for us to talk." Sophie followed Paul into a part of the building she did not know existed. Paul tried several locked doors which Sophie assumed were to offices. He then found an open room and invited Sophie inside. Paul quickly closed and locked the door. The room was not an office but guest quarters for seminary visitors. Paul led Sophie to the bed and said, "I am really glad that you wanted to meet with me." He suggested that they have sex. He insisted that she remain seated on the bed while he tried to convince her that she wanted sex with him. She recalled the words he used and his persuasive tone and realized it took more than half an hour to talk him out of his intentions. She was in shock as she left the room and walked to her next class. Paul was in that class and tried to talk to her there. She told him to leave her alone.

For days she could not believe what had happened. "What should I do?" she asked her husband Michael. "Should I talk to the seminary or what?" she asked Ruth. Both Michael and Ruth supported her and helped her think about the implications of what had happened. She realized she must do something. In six months Paul would graduate and might become a pastor in a church somewhere. What if this happened to someone else? What if he succeeded? What if it had already happened?

Sophie went to the dean of students and told him the story. He responded, "We do not have a sexual harassment policy in place. I am not sure there is a response the seminary can make to a situation such as this. Let me check and see how this matter might be handled." The meeting felt cold.

A few days later Sophie received a note describing a preliminary procedure. She should describe the incident in writing and submit it to the associate dean. Paul would be given an opportunity to respond to the accusation. They would then each meet separately with a board of three men: the president of the seminary, the dean of students, and the associate dean. The board would hear each story and then decide the next step.

Sophie's anxiety grew. Could anything be done? Could she retell the story to the three men? She talked with her husband and with Ruth. Then she decided to talk with her pastor. She made an appointment with the Reverend Faye, her pastor for the past four years. Her husband, Michael, volunteered to go with her. "I will be fine," she said. She went to the appointment expecting support and compassion. The response he gave was, "Nothing really happened, did it?" and "Well, I guess you've learned a good lesson. Never go into a room with a man you do not know."

As Sophie pulled into her driveway, she remembered the note about the board of three men. She was requested to let them know by tomorrow at 3 P.M. Could she tell the story again? Could she handle their response? Maybe she should cancel the meeting.

Teaching Note

The primary goal of this teaching note is to raise awareness in laity and clergy of the serious implications of sexual misconduct by church professionals. Additional goals are to see sexual misconduct as a form of women's oppression (96 percent of all sexual abuse is against women and children), to discuss concrete ways to address clergy misconduct, and to energize participants to become educated about clergy sexual misconduct.

The commentary cites evidence that men and women can best hear and understand some things from persons of their own gender. Men and women will read this case from different perspectives. Consequently, the case leader should take special care that a "safe place" is established so that both men and women are able to speak honestly about their reactions to the case. It is equally important that a group discussing this case is composed of both women and men.

CASE DISCUSSION

I. Immediate Response

Begin the case discussion by asking members of the group their immediate reaction to Pastor Faye's question, "Nothing really happened, did it?"

What does he mean by "nothing"? What are the implications of his question? What did Sophie think happened? What factors may have influenced their different perspectives?

II. Primary Persons

What do readers know about Sophie? For example, what is known about her home life or her decision to attend seminary?

Ask participants to put themselves in Sophie's position. Why did she avoid Paul after their encounter? What did she experience when she first spoke to the dean? To her husband? To Pastor Faye? What emotions is she experiencing at the close of the case?

What do readers know about Paul?

Who is responsible for the encounter between Sophie and Paul? Encourage participants to support their positions from evidence in the case.

III. Central Issues

What concerns are behind Sophie's original intent to report the encounter to seminary authorities? Why might clergy sexual misconduct have more serious consequences than abuse by a lay person? In the course of this discussion, it may be helpful for the case leader to share with the group some of the statistics about clergy misconduct presented in the commentary. Have participants discuss their reaction to the finding by Dr. Peter Rutter that "96 percent of sexual exploitation by professionals occurs between a man in power and a woman under his care."

What factors influence Sophie's hesitation about attending the hearing offered by the dean?

IV. Just and Healing Responses

A. Response to Sophie:

What are the most important concerns that need to be addressed for Sophie?

B. Response to Paul:

What responses would be most helpful to Paul? What reasons support the suggestions that are made?

C. Response to Seminary Authorities:

Form small groups composed of both men and women. Ask each group to develop a set of five to seven criteria for a seminary process to respond to sexual misconduct. For example, one criterion might be to take all complaints seriously. One might be that any group or authoritative body hearing a complaint should be composed of both women and men who are knowledgeable about clergy sexual misconduct. Another might be that any process should include preventive measures such as education of seminarians about the effects of clergy misconduct.

In order to avoid a tedious "report back" process, have each group write its criteria on a sheet of newsprint, post these for the other groups to read, and have participants ask questions of the groups for any necessary clarification. In plenary build the steps of a responsible approach for the seminary based on selected criteria.

V. Conclusion

One goal of the case discussion is to encourage participants to learn more about clergy sexual misconduct. A possible next step could be to make resources for further study available to the discussion participants. These resources could include copies of denominational policies on clergy sexual misconduct, books from the list of sources cited in the commentary end notes, or the commentary itself for reading and a subsequent discussion.

Commentary

We must no longer be children, tossed to and fro and blown about by every wind of doctrine, by people's trickery, by their craftiness in deceitful scheming. But speaking the truth in love, we must grow up in every way into him who is the head, into Christ from whom the whole body, joined and knit together, every ligament with which it is equipped, as each part is working properly, promotes the body's growth in building itself up in love. (Eph. 4:14–16 NRSV)

Some people who discuss this case agree fully with Pastor Faye's response to Sophie. They believe that because Paul did not ultimately force Sophie into having sexual intercourse, then "nothing really happened." These readers also feel that by exposing Paul, Sophie could ruin his career as a pastor. They suggest that Sophie's most caring response would be either to forget the incident or find out how she or their friends might help Paul deal better with the stress and pressures he is enduring. They also note that Paul is not yet ordained, is not in a pastoral relationship with Sophie, does not have any position of leadership or authority over her, and had not approached her for sex or been rejected by her prior to this incident. If any of these factors applied, one or all might provide a basis for charges of sexual misconduct, but in fact, as the dean implies, they do not apply.

Other people, however, are outraged by the pastor's and the dean's responses. They are convinced that Paul intentionally tried to manipulate Sophie into having an intimate relationship which would have been in violation of his marriage vows and hers. He used force by locking the door. No one could have heard Sophie call out from the secluded basement area. She believes that her ability to convince Paul to let her go was all that kept "something" from happening. These readers also point out that Sophie is deeply concerned about Paul's future in the ministry. They wonder with Sophie if Paul tried to force himself on her, would he attempt to do the same in a counseling or pastoral relationship with another woman who was not able to control the situation. They ask if rejection of Paul's advances is another woman's responsibility, or does Sophie have responsibility to speak the truth in love and share her concerns with those who are responsible for affirming Paul's readiness for ministry.

The strong disagreement about the case points to the ambiguity many people have about sexual issues and about the special roles and responsibilities of clergy and those in training for the ministry.

THE ROLE OF POWER IN SOCIETY AND CHURCH

Established social patterns make it difficult for some readers to believe that Paul's actions are serious enough to be reported to seminary authorities. In many families and cultures men are encouraged to see women as objects of conquest; young men attain the status of manhood by succeeding sexually. It is a woman's responsibility to reject unwelcome advances. This pattern is strongest in societies where men assume a dominant role and exert their power over women in multiple ways.

In the same societies, women are taught to be polite and to build nurturing, supportive relationships which accept or tolerate men's behavior. Attitudes or stances of submission to persons in authority and readiness to forgive, particularly in church-related communities, are raised as important values for women. Women are not infrequently reminded of Paul's admonition for wives to be "subject" to their husbands (Eph. 5:22) from speakers who forget to mention the context which calls all Christians to be "subject to one another out of reverence to Christ" (Eph. 5:21).

Several aspects of viewing male dominance and female submission as normative are directly related to this case. One aspect deals with the assumptions that often accompany a woman's charges of sexual misconduct. In a male-dominated society, police force, judicial system, or church it is not unusual for a woman who is raped or harassed to be suspected of enticing the aggressor or being somehow responsible for the aggressor's actions. She is asked why she was in such a place. What was she wearing? What did she say to encourage the man? Sophie, why did you go into that room with Paul? Pastor Faye's conclusion that Sophie learned she should not enter a room with a stranger seems to imply that Sophie was somehow responsible for Paul's advances.

Charges of sexual misconduct are especially difficult to deal with in the church. Sophie expresses great concern that Paul will soon "become a pastor in a church somewhere." Several sources document that 96 percent of the victims of sexual abuse and exploitation in the church are women and children and "between 10 and 20 percent of clergy offend against the integrity of the pastoral relationship and the vulnerability of those entrusted to their care by crossing the boundary from religious service to sexual activity."[1] However, when women risk making public charges against a male pastor, "the woman victim loses the most and, as things stand in most denominations, the pastor loses least." Cooper-White continues by noting,

Typically, when such a relationship or multiple relationships are uncovered, he gets a slap on the wrist, a lot of sympathy and is referred to a counselor. The parish is left to cope with feelings of betrayal and rage—most often directed at the woman as seductress. . . . The family of the woman involved is generally broken up and the burden of blame placed on her. She loses her reputation, her parish, sometimes her job, and even her whole life in the community.[2]

The statistics in this commentary come from North American and European studies. One researcher notes that because of the "code of silence" which clergy and other professionals keep, statistical research in the field of professional sexual misconduct "is still in its infancy."[3] The pressure for much of the research has come from women who have been abused. It appears that even less research has been conducted in the South. However, women in Africa, Asia, and Latin America have confided that the lack of information is not because there is no sexual misconduct in their churches; it is in part because women have not felt empowered or been willing to risk coming forward to share their experiences.

POWER IMBALANCE AND VIOLATION OF TRUST

"If there is a root cause for sexual abuse and exploitation, gender power imbalance, especially as it plays out in the church, must be considered a primary factor."[4] While there are certainly incidents of women clergy who engage in sexual misconduct, considerable research suggests that "96 percent of sexual exploitation by professionals occurs between a man in power and a woman under his care."[5] Male clergy not only have the social status of males, but trusting parishioners grant them significant authority as spiritual guides, teachers, mentors, and counselors. The "man of God" who interprets the Word, administers the Eucharist, and points the way toward salvation has powerful influence over those under his care.

While sexual violation of trust mirrors a cultural power imbalance between men and women, violation of the sacred trust in a pastoral relationship is a particularly destructive form of this oppressive social reality.[6] Many women who have been abused by clergy report that they have not only lost their parish community, but their trust has been so violated that they cannot go to any church.[7] Parishioners who find their trust betrayed by those whom they believe represent God also feel betrayed by God.

Our sexuality is a gift of God; sexual intimacy is a good and powerful way for people committed to one another to express their love. But inappropriate sexual intimacy, particularly in unequal relationships, is destructive to the people involved and destructive to the wholeness of the Body of Christ. "Growing up in every way into Christ" calls clergy to be worthy of the extraordinary trust given to them. While there are strong cultural forces, such as gender, age, status, or authority, which give some members of a society power over others, Christians are called not to be conformed to the world, but to be transformed to prove "what is good or acceptable" (Rom. 12:2).

Sophie is deeply concerned that if Paul is not clear about appropriate sexual boundaries now, his sexual advances could have devastating effects when he has additional power as an ordained clergyman and counselor to whom vulnerable parishioners come for hope and healing. However, Sophie felt that her concerns were coldly received by the dean and that her pastor assigned blame to her for the incident. She seems justifiably concerned about appearing before a panel of three men.

SOPHIE'S DECISION

Should Sophie forget about the incident with Paul? Should she try to speak to him confidentially, hoping he will see his error? Should Sophie cancel her meeting with the board or go forward with her decision to share her story?

One possibility is for Sophie to dismiss the incident, assuming that Paul's actions stemmed from a misunderstanding or an inappropriate expression of his own pain and loneliness. However, this response may be the least helpful to Paul. He appears to have thought ahead about his encounter with Sophie; he located an isolated part of the building and took her there under the guise of "talking about theology." Paul's planning suggests that their meeting was neither spontaneous nor based on a misunderstanding. His studied approach also suggests that Sophie may not be the first person to whom he has proposed a sexual encounter. Researchers suggest that once sexual misconduct has been exposed, it is common for additional victims to be discovered.

"Although women are the obvious victims of forbidden-zone exploitation, men in power also victimize themselves through destructive expressions of sexuality, leaving untouched the wounds that lie hidden beneath their inappropriate sexual behavior."[8] A pastor who wrote an anonymous article detailing the painful process toward healing noted,

> When, like I did, a professional violates the sacred boundary [between priest and parishioner], he or she is in deep personal crisis. When a priest risks

family and life's work and financial security for a sexual encounter, it is a cry for help. Hand-slapping, moralizing, and ignoring may seem to be in order. They are in essence like correcting the grammar on your teenager's suicide note. Listen to the desperation that is behind the action.[9]

"Look the other way" says that the encounter was not serious, that Paul's advances were misunderstood or even acceptable. Confronting his behavior in an appropriate way, by people who are able to respond more substantially than "hand slapping" or "moralizing," could be the most caring response that either Sophie or the seminary community could offer.

Alarmed by the scope of clergy sexual misconduct and the high rate of repeat behavior, some denominational bodies have sought better understanding of the types of people who overstep appropriate boundaries in order to help determine the most appropriate responses. Based on psychological studies and actual cases, the Office for Church Life and Leadership of the United Church of Christ has identified "five types of persons who can abuse."[10] These range from an "Individual in Crisis" (e.g., death, divorce, or job loss), who, through counseling, "may be able to comprehend the damage they have caused and avoid future misconduct," and an "Uninformed Naive Person with Blurry Boundaries," who may be able "to learn new behavior with extensive counseling," to a "Person with a Sexual Compulsive Disorder" or one with a "Character Disorder," who may be "very resistant to treatment." The denominational study suggests that it is "never appropriate to have someone with one of these disorders in a position of pastoral leadership."[11] If Paul does not have an opportunity to deal with his sexuality while he is still under care of the seminary, he may have many years of destructive behavior to himself and those under his ministerial care.

Some would argue, however, that if Sophie does come forward with her account, she could be affected more than Paul. When a family, congregation, or community feels the pain from exposure of negative behavior of a trusted family, church, or community member, the blame often falls on the one who tells rather than on the one who initiated the situation. This response is one way of denying that a trusted person has erred; it is also a primary reason why many women and some men who have been abused through sexual misconduct refuse to come forward.

There are no witnesses. If Sophie comes forward with her story, it is possible that Paul will lie by denying his behavior; he may even suggest that Sophie initiated the encounter. If he accepts responsibility, his marriage could be threatened, and he may even be forced out of the seminary program. If Sophie is believed, she may feel guilty for exposing Paul. If she is not believed, she not only will feel rejected but humiliated by the implication that she has lied. For these reasons the seminary needs to deal fairly and directly with the situation and provide safeguards so that those students and faculty who come forward with a charge of misconduct are not made to suffer and that students and faculty are not charged inappropriately. The process of healing for both Sophie and Paul must be dealt with carefully and sensitively. Clearly established procedures and the provision of strong supportive counseling, which reflect both justice and concern for all parties, can be a part of the healing process.

ROLE AND RESPONSIBILITY OF THE SEMINARY

One approach for the seminary would be for both students and faculty to participate in the public development of concise, clear policies and procedures to address situations of sexual misconduct between students, between faculty members, and between faculty and students. Many communities are much more likely to understand, accept, and honor policies if members have openly discussed and adopted them. This type of open process may also be the healthiest way for denominational bodies to educate clergy and laity and to begin to break the code of silence about clergy sexual misconduct. This open approach does not imply that hearings or charges should be brought into a public arena. Seminaries and churches need to be sensitive to their cultural contexts and to the needs of all parties concerned when deciding how to respond to complaints. But to ignore or to deny the possibility of sexual misconduct by clergy can be destructive to all parties involved. Because sensitive, caring clergy are often deeply involved with vulnerable and hurting people, pastors must be particularly alert to the temptation to cross appropriate boundaries. Education for clergy about warning signs of approaching those boundaries and awareness of the serious consequences of misconduct are critical steps toward prevention of sexual misconduct.

A specific component of the church or seminary's approach to sexually related complaints should deal with the gender of those who handle complaints. Following a traumatic experience with a male student, Sophie felt awkward in her meeting with the male dean, who acknowledged that the seminary had not established procedures for sexual misconduct, and she felt rebuffed by a male pastor who did not understand her. One of her greatest concerns at the close of the case is the prospect of facing three men who may also reject her. Several knowledgeable sources suggest that, especially with situations of sexual misconduct, it is important to have a team of men and women because men and women "respond differently when encountering the profound and often painful truths they must during the process of opening things up. Sometimes people can only hear things they need to from a person of the same sex."[12] Gender balance on the review board would help both Sophie and Paul. For the truth to be told, justice addressed, and healing to begin, both parties must feel heard by people who are able to listen and respond appropriately. Since the seminary has not yet established a balanced team to hear complaints, Sophie may want to seek out a woman of authority and sensitivity who could accompany her to the hearing.

Church and seminary policies on issues of sexual misconduct should include a clear process for filing a complaint and guidelines for the most appropriate way to share the complaint with the one who is accused. The response of the person accused should also be shared with the one who made the complaint. Persons or groups developing policies should seriously consider the extent to which all information gathered and shared by those involved is held in confidence. A panel of trusted and trained male and female faculty and students or clergy and laity should work together to determine as fairly as possible the seriousness of the complaint and the appropriate responses, guided by God's call to compassion, justice, repentance, and protection of the most vulnerable people. The response may involve counseling that is mandated and supported by the church or seminary. The goal of the panel or committee should not be to punish but ultimately to restore the accused person as well as the victim to fellowship with God and full communion with the church, even when forgiveness and reconciliation do not include returning to pastoral authority one who has abused the trust of the church.

The church is called to deal openly and sensitively with the failings of its members, whether they are male or female, clergy or lay persons. Church bodies, including seminaries, need to develop clear and fair procedures to hear and respond to charges of clergy misconduct. They also need to establish thoughtful, well-researched educational programs for clergy and seminary students and careful strategies to prevent clergy misconduct or behavior that can be misinterpreted or misunderstood. These approaches will better equip the church to move beyond damage control regarding sexual misconduct and toward enabling men and women to work together with increased mutual trust as they seek to build up the Body of Christ and witness to God's unending love and faithfulness.

NOTES

1. Marie M. Fortune and James N. Poling, *Sexual Abuse by Clergy: A Crisis for the Church*, JCPC Monograph No 6., Decatur, GA: Journal of Pastoral Care Publications, 1994, p. i.

2. Pamela Cooper-White, "Soul Stealing: Power Relations in Pastoral Sexual Abuse," *The Christian Century*, February 20, 1991, pp. 196–197.

3. Peter Rutter, M.D., *Sex in the Forbidden Zone: When Men in Power—Therapists, Doctors, Clergy, Teachers, and Others—Betray Women's Trust*, Los Angeles: Jeremy P. Tarcher, 1989, p. 34.

4. Nancy Myer Hopkins, ed., *Clergy Sexual Misconduct: A Systems Perspective*, Washington, D.C.: The Alban Institute, 1993, p. 1.

5. Rutter, *Sex in the Forbidden Zone*, p. 20.

6. Ibid., p. 2.

7. Marie M. Fortune, *Is Nothing Sacred? When Sex Invades the Pastoral Relationship*, San Francisco: HarperCollins, 1989.

8. Rutter, *Sex in the Forbidden Zone*, p. 20.

9. "Sexual Addiction," in *Pastoral Psychological Journal*, Vol. 39, No. 4, 1991, New York: Human Sciences Press; cited in Nancy Myer Hopkins, ed., *Clergy Sexual Misconduct: A Systems Perspective*, Washington, D.C.: The Alban Institute, p. 51.

10. "Pastoral Misconduct: Dealing with Allegations of Sexual Contact or Harassment within the Pastoral Relationship," Office for Church Life and Leadership, United Church of Christ, 700 Prospect Ave., Cleveland, Ohio 44115, p. 11.

11. Ibid., pp. 12–13.

12. Hopkins, *Clergy Sexual Misconduct*, p. 3.

ADDITIONAL RESOURCE

Karen Lebacqz and Ronald G. Barton, *Sex in the Parish*, Louisville, KY: Westminster John Knox Press, 1991.

PART III

ECONOMIC JUSTICE AND ECOLOGICAL HARMONY

Rangwezi Nengwekhulu, a respected South African political scientist and economic analyst recently commented, "The greatest challenges facing the Third World countries today are economic justice, development of and protection of participatory democratic culture, and attainment of ecological harmony." One could add that the First World also faces these challenges. Very few informed and critical observers of economic, political, and ecological trends in the world will disagree with Nengwekhulu on his projected agenda for the Third World countries, individually and collectively. Even those who disagree with him would concede that some mistakes have been and are still being made in the implementation of one or another aspect of the lofty economic plans that were devised. It is not important how many scientists agree or disagree with his statement. What is important is why they agree with it. What is the observable and concrete state of democratic, economic, and ecological affairs in the Third World today and what are the causes?

GLOBAL MARKET ECONOMY—
THE NEW FREE ENTERPRISE GOSPEL

The collapse of the Soviet empire in Eastern Europe and the demise of the state-led socialist economic project in those countries have left Western capitalism as virtually the sole surviving visible economic mode of production. In this atmosphere of uncertainty and confusion, capitalists speak triumphantly about the messianic capacity of the free enterprise system to liberate the latent talents and ingenuity of all people in the world, guiding them to heal the world's economic ills. Proponents of Western capitalism are engaged in a heightened campaign to propagate the globalization of economic thought and plans by all macroeconomists and governments. The establishment of new economic blocs in North and South America and in Europe are shining examples.

The dominant features of those plans are already apparent to many people and organizations in the world, including activists, churches, and organizations that have advocated an alternative to the dominant economic model. Implementation of Western capitalism has already had a visible and immeasurable impact on Third World peoples and countries. Many economists, sociologists, health workers, politicians, churches, and nongovernment organizations that have the welfare of people and nature at heart are vigorously discussing the impact. The shrimp farm consisting of 5,000 acres of ponds in Honduras intended to supply shrimp for the American market ("Visit to a Shrimp Farm") and hotels erected on Philippine beaches near prime fishing waters and intended to attract tourists from wealthy nations of the world ("Another Face of Tourism") clearly show the impact of global trade relations.

The world economy is characterized by inequality and domination. Western economic powers, led by North American and European multinational banks and other financial agencies such as the World Bank and the International Monetary Fund, are engaged in unilateral economic plans. In many cases these plans appear to be forced onto weak and desperate governments without sufficient consultation or discussions that involve the people who are intended to implement and benefit from such plans. Poor farmers in the Philippines are losing small plots of productive land on which they grow rice and bananas to industries that do not produce the basic foodstuffs needed by local people. On the northeastern coast of South Africa a large section of marshlands has been lost to a company that intends to establish an iron-smelting plant that might destroy one of the biggest breeding places in that country for rare birds.

With a focus on accelerated development, unfamiliar international models of development are often introduced without sufficient regard to their impact on local cultures and religions. The people of Zimbabwe and Zambia are enduring extreme suffering as a result of the structural adjustment of their economies that was made a condition for loans. Even the people of the First World who become the beneficiaries of interest on loans and stock dividends are not consulted when those plans and economic models are conceived. World economic planning is the preserve of a minority of people in the First World who develop partnerships with a minority of Third World economists, industrialists, and politicians whom poor people see as more and more alienated from their people and blinded by greed to the basic needs of their countries. Too often multinational companies dominate the economic landscape of small countries and weaken and eventually contribute to the collapse of local businesses. Small private and cooperative enterprises with meager resources find it very difficult, if not impossible, to compete against economic giants which have inexhaustible financial resources and are armed with the most modern forms of technology, access to raw materials, and expertise. Multinational companies form networks in which the existence of one leads to the emergence of another. All spheres of the economy appear to be taken over, as is suggested in the following cases. Large-scale fishing contributes to the emergence of a hotel industry, tourism, and prostitution. Shrimp production leads to stimulation of a chemical industry.

In this global economy, the consumption patterns of First World people and countries are an overriding issue. More often than not, their need for consumer goods, luxury items, and pleasures such as exotic travel are satisfied at the expense of the basic needs of poor and weak people of Third World countries. It is common knowledge, for instance, that the U.S. population consumes two-thirds of the world's energy. Production patterns of Third World countries are distorted in the process. These countries produce cash crops to earn foreign currency instead of producing food to feed their children. Ghana produces cocoa for the European market while the children of Accra lack rice and corn. Farmers in Zimbabwe produce export tobacco at the expense of maize production. Zimbabwe must import maize from Argentina and South Africa to feed its people.

POLITICAL IMPACT

The political situation in the world today reflects a paradox that gives credence to the claim that, in this period of the ever-growing spread of democracy, the greatest challenge that democrats in the world face is the erosion of democracy. The recent spate of impeachments of former presidents of some countries and of court cases in which some highly placed government officials in countries of Europe, South America, and Asia are being charged with corruption, are clear evidence of the erosion of democracy. One of the former presidents of South Korea has been sent to prison. The commander of NATO in Belgium was indicted for corruption while he was a member of the Belgian cabinet. The argument that such impeachments reflect the inherent capacity and capability of liberal democracy to correct itself does not take away anything from the fact that democracy is eroding.

Instead, it supports it. The general situation in the developing countries also gives massive support to this claim. It is abundantly clear that military and other forms of dictatorship in Africa, Asia, and South America are rapidly disappearing and giving way to democratically elected governments. There is ample evidence that simultaneously that same democracy is being eroded at an alarming scale in several countries. In many cases, economic interests and greed are at the base of this new development. Many weaker governments are not able to protect the economic interests of their people because they are being coerced by powerful governments working together with multinational companies to repeal laws restricting operations of outside interests. In some instances, Third World governments collude with multinational companies in the erosion of democracy. Corruption sets in when some local officials are bribed to ignore the rule of law. Local officials are sometimes offered shares in companies in exchange for bending the law. Some police officers are bribed to threaten, or in extreme cases even eliminate, those who are opposed to the destructive practices of some companies.

SOCIOECONOMIC IMPACT

The immediate impact of multinational companies with highly developed technology is the mass production of consumer items that are generally intended for First World markets. In the process employment of local populations is stimulated. The expansionism of such companies necessitates the acquisition of more land. The introduction of foreign land ownership systems and the abandonment of communal ownership of land become imperative. The power of foreign corporations and government agencies becomes visible. Weaker governments adopt land policies that would be opposed by local populations and are detrimental to food production. Many peasants lose their land and are forced to join the ever-expanding reservoir of unemployed people or are pushed onto barren hillsides as were the people of Té Bouké ("The Fate of Té Bouké"). They often lose the capacity to feed themselves and their families. Those who remain on the land are forced to overproduce, which weakens the topsoil; erosion follows when the rains come. The introduction of high technology also leads to large-scale unemployment. In most cases, the local labor force is not unionized and is vulnerable to powerful industries. Workers lack protection from exploitation, inhumane working conditions, and long working hours. In many cases, toxic chemicals that are prohibited in First World countries are freely used, and the health of workers is not insured by their governments. Workers' life spans are thereby considerably shortened. Many high-tech companies divide local communities by distributing income and wealth unequally, favoring those who are corruptible.

The land dispossession that results from the insatiable need for land of powerful companies leads to displacement of populations, disintegration of families, and dislocation of communities. The overall effects contribute to the destruction of people's cultures and religiosity, the disintegration of the social fiber, moral degradation, and the introduction of foreign moral norms and immoral practices. Although large businesses bring an injection of low wages through the employment of a few local people, there is serious evidence that most of these operations destroy people and their futures.

ECOLOGICAL IMPACT

The introduction of highly developed forms of technology that maximize production of commodity goods initially results in very high returns and an increase in available jobs and income for the local people. In the process, accelerated production leads to the depletion of natural resources. The case studies based in Haiti, in Honduras, and in the Philippines all reveal the serious effects of abuse of natural resources. The use of chemicals to help nature along is only a temporary measure. In the long run, nature loses its capacity to support life and survive. This is clear in the large-scale deforestation and accompanying erosion of agricultural lands in many Third World countries where overproduction has been rife. Long periods of drought are attributed to the large-scale destruction of rain forests in tropical areas of the world. In some parts of the world drinking water is also poisoned, and people suffer from illnesses that were never found in those areas before. In other areas where there is a fishing industry that does not take the concerns of nature preservation seriously, fish species can be decimated. Poisoning of large portions of the sea and the resulting death of sea life also occur.

THE CHURCH, NONGOVERNMENT ORGANIZATIONS, AND PEOPLE OF GOOD WILL

The negative impact of the operations of large foreign companies in Third World countries constitutes gross injustice to the present and future generations of defenseless people and nature. This injustice raises several challenges to the church, other organizations, and people of good will everywhere. The most fundamental challenge is to believe that there are people in every one of the situations discussed who are not content and who are trying to bring about change. Rolando in

"Another Face of Tourism" and the Daltons and the *animators* in "The Fate of Té Bouké" are such trustworthy people. They form the vital connection and starting point of all solidarity activity of the church. The church has to affirm their efforts and stand beside them with an eagerness to listen and to learn about their concerns and how they intend to solve their predicaments.

The church's purpose should also be to assist in the development of local leadership rather than take the initiative from the people. Tom and Marion Dalton should not take over the leadership of Té Bouké. In a situation where the democratic culture has been eroded, it is the task of the church to concentrate on resuscitating that culture by introducing it into all the church activities with the communities and their leaders. People must be re-empowered in order for them to deal with their problems and find answers through discussions and debates. People who come from outside armed with skills and know-how are tempted to take over the leadership from the local people and dictate their own understanding of the situation as well as their solutions. They will need God's grace to serve with humility and respect for the intelligence and efforts of the victims of political power and economic greed. But that does not mean that outsiders should hide their own opinions and feelings about the situations confronting them and the people they have come to serve. In all their efforts they should respect local cultures and spirituality and aim at helping the local people to achieve independence of thought, initiative, and basic resources crucial to their local economies.

Another challenge to the church and nongovernment organizations is to employ their global networks to address issues of economic injustice and serious disruption of ecological harmony. While the operations of multinational corporations in poor countries have very negative, even disastrous, effects, these corporations also provide more funds for economic development than all foreign governments. The church is called not only to serve the poor but to confront and challenge the nonpoor and those in power to direct funds and energy to the common good. Advocates such as Rolando, the Daltons, or members of the church delegation that visited Honduras should raise their voices and share their stories through the potentially powerful networks of church leaders and other international bodies committed to justice. The most enduring benefits of the 1992 Global Forum in Rio de Janeiro will not come from the documents signed but from the exchange of information and the networks of mutual support between nongovernment organizations committed to sustainable development.

These voices can challenge the nonpoor to learn about the connections between their overconsumption and lives in the Third World. One message to share with multinationals is that an investment in people is an investment in the long-term stability of communities and nations, while a narrow focus on short-term profits can destroy communities and destabilize the countries in which companies work. However, moral imperatives are ultimately more powerful than arguments for self-interest. Investment in maintaining strong, independent communities and in programs such as reforestation and soil conservation will foster justice for power-less people and respect for the integrity of the natural world.

ANOTHER FACE OF TOURISM

Case

Rolando, a community organizer, was very disturbed by the growing prostitution among the women in his barrio. He believed the prostitution was related to both the fishing industry and tourism. He convened a meeting of the youth of the Philippine fishing community where he lived to discuss future action. The meeting was attended by forty young men in the twenty-five to thirty-five age group. Some of them were fishermen, some owned *sari sari* stores, and a few were unemployed. The majority were illiterate. Their agenda included different issues relating to fishing.

At first the discussion centered on the depletion of fish resources due to bad management of the fisheries and overtrawling. Many trawlers from Japan and a few from Taiwan invaded the coastal waters of Zamboanga. They seriously disturbed the seabed and fish resources. The local fishermen believed that it was because of the irresponsibility, carelessness, and greed of the trawling companies that some species of fish were no longer available. This matter had been discussed a few months earlier when the fishermen found two foreign trawlers in their coastal waters. The fishermen went out with their *barotos*, brought the two trawlers to the beach, and angrily smashed them to pieces. The police then arrested some of the fishermen. In spite of the fishermen's action, the trawlers continued to violate the marine rules, moving freely into the five kilometer range of the traditional fishermen. The fishermen were convinced that the large fishing companies had the support of the national and local authorities since no one stopped the companies' trawlers. The fishermen continued their struggle to stop the trawling in coastal waters. With Rolando's assistance, they submitted a memorandum to the officials of the Bureau of Fisheries. Two officers of the bureau began to help the fishermen in a number of ways. However, fishermen believed that because of this assistance the officers were suspended on charges of corruption. This kind of authoritarian action by the government led to discontent among the fishermen.

The fishermen also discussed the threat to their survival by tourism development. For two generations they had lived along the beach. Most of the land was owned by the government. A few hotels had been built on the beach. Now they heard that the government had earmarked the entire sea front for tourism. Twelve thousand people had already been evicted from the area. The government planned to construct motels, hotels, parks, and roads on the beaches. These would be hotels which only the rich could afford. Politicians, high officials, and businessmen were regular customers of these kinds of hotels.

The young men also spoke about Lamberto, a man who owned two trawlers and a freezing plant. Lamberto had been an exporter of prawns for fifteen years before becoming the owner of one of the new beach hotels. It appeared that he could provide anything for his guests. His trawlers brought Johnny Walker, Marlboro, Zippo lighters, Rolex watches, Ray Ban sunglasses, and foreign soaps. He could even get girls from his factory to entertain the guests. Through the newspapers Rolando had learned that Lamberto sat on the local board of the tourism department. Lamberto was advising the government to invest more money to beautify the beach. He had very specific plans to develop tourism. He advised the government to remove the fishermen from the beach and told the press, "They are the dirty people who spoil the serenity of the beach." When a girl from his factory was killed in Lamberto's hotel, Rolando organized the fishermen to agitate in front of the hotel. They later met with the Superintendent of Police. The postmortem reports said the girl's death was due to sickness. Lamberto proved his innocence. The police told Rolando and the group of fishermen that they were troublemakers and communists and that their movements were being watched.

The issue of prostitution was also discussed by the young men. Some members of the group whose mothers, sisters, and wives were selling their flesh kept silent. But later, as the discussion proceeded, everything came out in the open. Rolando and some village youth had heard Marina shouting at some men the previous night. The young men were shocked when they came to know that a respected housewife such as Marina was engaged in prostitution. Her actions hurt them. Juan, a young man who worked with the group, urged them to stop this kind of degrading activity by the women.

Rolando thought about Marina's family, her husband and her two children. The thirty-two-year-old woman was now a prostitute. Within four years her life had changed. Her husband, a fisherman, used to earn about forty pesos a day. Though he did not own a *baroto*, he had never had any difficulty supporting his family. It was a happy family. Marina took care of the children and helped her husband sort the fish. If any fish remained unsold, she would dry them and later sell them. She never went to work anywhere else.

As time passed, the trawlers continued to disturb the seabed and deplete the supply of fish. Marina's husband could not earn enough money to support the needs of his family. Sometimes there was nothing at the end of the day. He was also getting old and was no longer capable of facing the rough sea. Marina had to look for some alternative way to keep the family going. She had seen some of the women in her village working and found a job in a nearby lodge. Rolando now realized that it was then that she was pushed into becoming a prostitute. This realization made him angry and prompted him to gather the youth for action.

The young men's discussion turned to arguments, attacks, and counterattacks with each one fighting and blaming the other. Juan said, "We must save our women from prostitution." Another young man asked, "Why has prostitution increased in our village? We never faced this kind of problem before. Who is responsible for this?"

Ruben, another young man, asked aggressively, "Why are you fools wasting your energy here? If you have the courage, why don't you challenge Lamberto to close his business. He is playing dangerous games with the lives of the poor girls and with ours as well."

Juan again spoke out loudly, "We have nothing to do with anybody. We must look at ourselves. Poverty does not mean that we must sell our bodies for others' enjoyment." Someone in the group asked softly, "How are we going to survive? What alternative is there for us?"

The young men were at a loss and looked to Rolando for his opinion.

Teaching Note

With the economic collapse of the so-called socialist countries of Central and Eastern Europe and the Soviet Union, capitalism has been praised by many international leaders as the most viable economic option for humanity in our day and age. Capitalism calls for an open-door policy for trade, commerce, transport, and communication. But capitalism and open-door policies have not been the saviors for all.

Even before the collapse of the socialist countries, capitalistic approaches to progress have been tried in many countries. Modernization through capitalism is seen as a "wonder drug" for economic development. A nation's people are called upon to make adjustments and sacrifices for achieving the miracle of economic prosperity, but this economic approach does not bring the promised benefits to everyone. This case about a historically self-sustaining fishing community shattered by the effects of modern development challenges many generally accepted views about modernization and capitalism.

I. Goals

A. To understand better the effects of modernization on common people in an economically developing country.

B. To understand better the benefits to some groups of people from development approaches backed by modern technology, global networks, and large financial resources.

C. To discern patterns of collaboration between the local, regional, and international forces necessary for modern technology, finance, and global development approaches to thrive.

D. To explore different options to counter the destructive effects of some development approaches on the most vulnerable communities.

E. To energize discussion participants to investigate viable alternatives for just and sustainable development.

II. Useful Background Information

An overview of the colonial history of the Philippines which includes the groups that initiated the independence struggle against Spain and the United States will help discussion participants understand the context of this case. A useful approach for studying current Philippine history would be an analysis of groups that control the political and economic system today. Which groups are in opposition to the established parties?

III. Case Discussion

A. Persons

Identify which persons and groups have relevant roles in the case, and discuss their primary concerns. There may be contradictory perceptions about some persons in this case, so it is important to urge participants to try not to be judgmental but to put themselves in the position of each person in order to imagine his or her concerns. This approach will help participants make a more objective analysis and be more honest about sharing their own perspectives.

Rolando: a social activist, community organizer, and popular leader concerned about the increasing poverty and marginalization of the village.

Lamberto: a businessman and hotel owner who appears to work closely with local and state officials.

Marina: a respected middle-aged housewife and mother who seems to have turned to prostitution to feed her family.

Juan and Ruben: angry young people concerned about their community.

Fisherfolk: indigenous people working in a traditional vocation who are concerned about survival, loss of land, identity, and community values.

Owners of trawlers from other countries.

National and local **government officials.**

B. Issues

Some of the issues which may be raised are:

Depletion of fish resources.

The effects of tourism on indigenous communities.

Land rights of the indigenous people, the government, and the developers.

Collaboration between persons of power and marginalization of those who are powerless.

Prostitution among barrio women.

Poverty as a threat to family life.

Ask about the impact of these issues on selected people previously discussed. For example, what are the effects of the tourism industry on Marina and Lamberto, or the impact of the depletion of fish resources on the local people, and on the international fishing industry?

C. Alternatives

Distinguish between short-term and long-term resolutions for the community. This approach will help address immediate concerns about such issues as prostitution as well as just and sustainable development strategies for the community's future. To add depth and authenticity to the discussion, urge participants to share personal experiences with suggested alternatives.

A few alternatives could be:

Mass media publicity about the plight of the fishing community.

Support and solidarity from movements and organizations committed to social justice.

Alternative economic approaches and resources to balance the loss of income.

Challenging local political representatives to take up the cause of the fishing community.

D. Resources

Although "Another Face of Tourism" takes place in the Philippines, the case situation echoes throughout the developing world. Negative effects of many development approaches have led to the creation of international and regional forums to challenge many current approaches and to support development that is more supportive of common people. Getting information about these resources to local communities and directly supporting vulnerable communities are steps participants could explore.

Many examples of effective alternative development strategies have been designed and practiced by individuals, communities, organizations, and nation-states. Religions and faith communities have also reflected on alternatives and have often been positive motivating forces. Local examples of such alternatives could be evaluated and discussed depending on the preparedness of the group.

Commentary

"I came that they may have life, and have it abundantly" (John 10:10 RSV).

All major living religions including Christianity focus on the fullness of life for human beings. The abundant life of which Jesus spoke refers to a life of dignity lived in relationships; that is, in relationship with God, in relationship with one's neighbor, and in relationship with creation. In this case study the selfishness of a few makes it difficult for some of the people to live a life of dignity. Some people tend to think of abundance of life only in material terms. Presumably, the more material wealth one has, the more happy and content one will be. But life does not work that way; overanxiety for material wealth creates its own problems.

SITUATION OF THE CASE

The young people are caught in the dilemma of preserving the social values of their society, especially the dignity of women, and at the same time accepting the reality of lowered incomes. They are conscious of the damage done to fish resources by foreign trawlers. Their livelihoods, societal values, and the land they had been living on for generations are threatened by the loss of fish species and the destruction of spawning beds. Marine products, a rich source of protein for the fishing community, are increasingly being exported, depriving community members of nourishment. Fishermen in the community soon realized that their *barotos* were no match against the trawlers. Even the civilized and democratic method of submitting a memorandum to the officials and ministers concerned did not bring any results. All this caused deep discontent among the fisher folk.

The alternative of tourism that the government is proposing further humiliated the people by dislocating them from their traditional dwelling places to make room for the construction of motels, hotels, and parks which fisher folk cannot afford to utilize. On the contrary, rather than being able to use these facilities, the women of the community have become prostitutes—victims of the tourist hotel culture.

Similar situations can be found today in many countries around the globe as some economically developing countries are forced to accept tourism to earn the hard currency required for building their economy. The developing countries turn to companies and investment from the industrialized North or finance new hotels from their own wealthy elite, whose interests are more in profit making than developing the well-being of an economically weak community. But close scrutiny discloses that the development required for a tourist industry to thrive on a global scale is usually too costly.

The young people in the case are moving in the right direction by organizing a meeting to discuss the ill effects of trawler fishing and tourism in their region. Whether they will be successful will depend on how well they will be able to mobilize their own people and whether they will be able to secure cooperation from outside their community and in the power centers of their country. In the last several decades, both large-scale mechanized fishing and tourism as described have destroyed communities and enriched the pockets of a few. At the same time, in some cases, constant struggles averted such a disaster.

ISSUES THAT EMERGE

In this case we see tension between macro-vision and micro-impacts. Today, many of the discussions on development are centered around the economic uplifting of the entire nation, region, or community, but what is generally not explained is the human cost involved and the social disturbance created by the process. One can start by saying that in any drastic change of economic development, sacrifices will be involved and that such sacrifices have to be made while bearing in mind the long-term benefits to the entire affected population. Although such arguments are quite logical, several examples, such as the one in this case and other cases presented here, have indicated that the outcome has not always followed the convincing logic of development. Therefore, any society needs to assess carefully the possible effect of its developmental scheme on all sections of the population.

Tourism is an emerging concern in different parts of the world. There are predictions that in the coming decades tourism will surpass all other transnational industries. Progress of a community is judged on the criterion of possession of more sophisticated airports, aircraft, luxury liners, five-star hotels, duty free shops, intercontinental telecommunications, and computer networks rather than on the values that safeguard and promote the abundance of life promised by Christian faith. Some modern-day prophets swear that the "Kingdom of God" is established in a community once it has acquired these material means or is on its way to acquiring them. What about people who cannot afford them such as the fisherfolk in the case? Affluence and prosperity will trickle down! The problem is that the fisherfolk will have to be relocated to allow the prosperity of development to materialize, and they will have to be taught new vocations, maybe tending the park and the golf course and providing women for entertainment. But will the promised prosperity come to everyone?

One region which has become caught up in this false promise of the miracle of overnight prosperity is Central and Eastern Europe and the former Soviet Union. It has been five years since political changes took place in this region. In one sense changes were long overdue, but the anticipated economic miracle which was to bring consolation to all the inhabitants did not follow. Rather, what has happened is that a small section of the population became overwhelmingly rich, relegating the majority to a life of poverty. Suddenly many cities have become breeding grounds for various antisocial activities and crimes such as illegal trade in arms and military technology, drug trafficking, and sex industries, all under the protection of the local Mafia. These activities are due in large part to the breakdown in the social welfare system and the rise in the rate of unemployment. Even a region which has seen long-term industrial and technological development could not cope with the sudden introduction of a system of development alien to its ethos.

From the point of view of the wholeness of human lives, development is too costly to be left solely to the political and economic overlords of a country. People concerned with the ethical, moral, religious, cultural, and ecological values of a community should get involved. It is only natural that politicians, and in many cases economists, will be guided by the short-term goal of maximum profit. In this case the fishing community which had a self-sustaining economy for two generations was shattered in a few years because of the vested interest of the few. Concerned groups should be vigilant at every point when new legislation and development schemes are introduced and they should try to get a cross-section of the population involved in debate and decision making.

A life of dignity is lived in healthy and whole relationships. The unemployment situation created a division between those who depend on a steady income and those who depend on family members or borrowed money. Relationships between men and a few women broke down as some of the women were forced into prostitution because of economic hardship. Eventually there will be broken relationships between those who would like to give up the struggle and those who would like to pursue a just solution. There will be animosity between the economically well off and the economically deprived.

A broken relationship becomes a breeding ground for other negative feelings. Since its inception the church has been committed to creating an egalitarian community by trying to build bridges between the rich and the poor, the smart and the not so clever, the strong and the weak, women and men. But the church has not always been successful. Its institutional preservation sometimes preoccupies its attention and drains its energy. In such cases reverting to its core beliefs is a rejuvenating experience. One of the core beliefs of Christianity is reconciliation, which is accomplished by breaking down barriers erected by humans. That significant vision needs to be brought out in practice with all sincerity. This case is a good test for such a Christian involvement in the life of a community.

RESOURCES OF GRACE

Churches and Christian communities are called to be committed to the well-being of people according to their own understanding and needs. In mission outreach, attending to the physical needs of people has been very much a part of the Christian witness, but much of it has been at the level of charity and aid. In the past the church has made the assumption that the state would tackle those forces that are not conducive for the healthy growth of a society. Churches are beginning to realize that such expectations are not always fulfilled by the state, even though the rhetoric is endlessly repeated by the state bureaucracy. Churches have no option but to constantly evaluate and, when necessary, wrestle with the economic forces that operate at the local level and may also have global connections.

Traditionally, churches kept themselves from any open engagement with economics or politics, but in reality no community can avoid the sociopolitical and economic forces of its environment. If a community does not venture into critical analysis of the political and economic forces operative in its context and take an appropriate step of engagement, it ends up supporting the status quo as a silent partner. The temptation for churches to be passive partners in the oppressive structures of society will always be there. Churches are often caught up in the dilemma of knowing the truth but feeling unable to do anything about it. Churches and Christians have been criticized as being excellent good Samaritans; they console the victims but let the robbers go free to continue beating people and stealing their possessions (Parable of the Good Samaritan, Luke 10:29–37). But there are several instances from around the world where Christians and churches have moved further and have challenged the forces that victimize innocent people. Many prophetic churches through the ages have stood against slavery, race discrimination, colonization, genocide of indigenous people, and atrocities against minority communities. In many such cases individual Christians and the church as a whole have paid a heavy price.

The systematic study and analysis of sociopolitical and economic forces by the churches is one of the significant features of contemporary witness. A number of churches and church-related organizations are able to evaluate existing economic forces from Christian faith perspectives. What they have discovered is what they knew all along: all is not well with the present type of economic development. So economics has become a matter of faith; economics has become a concern of mission.[1]

As to tourism and its adverse effects on a community, several organizations and institutions have been formed to study and campaign against tourism's negative impact on people. One such organization, which is supported by churches and church institutions in Asia, is the Ecumenical Coalition on Third World Tourism (ECTWT, also known as Contours) based in Bangkok, Thailand. ECTWT, working closely with the churches in Asia, has brought awareness about some of the damage caused by the rush of Third World countries to promote tourism: displacement of people, destruction of traditional economic support systems, threat to local culture and trade, ecological destruction, increase in drug trafficking, and growth in prostitution—including child prostitution. ECTWT's ministry has inspired regional and local networking involving both churches and secular institutions. In North America the Center for Responsible Tourism educates travelers to the negative effects of tourism and advocates guidelines for responsible travel.[2] However, such new initiatives are not widely accepted by the churches and need constant nurturing.

For many Christians, giving heed to forces such as economics and politics as a matter of faith is still a difficult theological struggle. But for many people, especially in countries with severe economic deprivation resulting from unjust trade and tourism policies, economics has become a life and death question. The church has no choice but to respond to these injustices as a matter of faith. In several liberation and contextual theologies, which see critical analysis of a situation as an integral part of doing theology, economic forces that operate in any given context become a key issue. In the articulation of such contextual and indigenous theologies lies hope for an expression of faith that is not limited to metaphysical issues but addresses factors which affect the day-to-day lives of individuals and communities.

NOTES

1. See Aart van den Berg, *Churches Speak Out on Economics: A Survey of Several Statements*, Geneva: WCC, 1990; and *Christian Faith and the World Economy Today: A Study Document from the WCC*, 1992.

2. The Center for Responsible Tourism, P.O. Box 827, San Anselmo, CA 94979.

VISIT TO A SHRIMP FARM

Case

"I'm worried about the long-term effects on the local people and on the Gulf."

"If you're really thinking long-term, this is the best kind of program to support."

Tom Sellers, an economist and one of twelve members of a church denominational Task Force on Sustainable Development, was listening to his colleagues as they discussed their visit to the Granjas Marinas Shrimp Farm. The farm was one of the newest and most financially successful business ventures in Honduras. In ten years Honduran shrimp had become the country's third most important export after bananas and coffee. The shrimp industry was increasing in importance as world prices for bananas and coffee declined.

The task force visited the shrimp farm, located on the southern coast, on the fifth day of an intensive study tour of Honduras. With a primary goal of "looking, listening, and learning," the team had driven from San Pedro Sula in the northern mountains, through the dry plains surrounding the capital of Tegucigalpa, to the humid coast along the Gulf of Fonseca. Tom's advance reading for the trip indicated that before the introduction of the timber industry, Honduras had been heavily forested. During the two-day drive across the country he saw thousands of acres of barren hills devastated by erosion and drought. The group stopped along the way to meet with local communities and to visit a variety of development projects. Tom was particularly struck by the poverty of the *campesinos* and the faith, courage, and creativity with which they survived.

The task force had been at work for more than a year, reading extensively about issues of economics, Third World development, theology, and the environment. In an effort to better understand U.S. international economic policies, a focal point of their work, the task force agreed on the importance of seeing first-hand the impact of these policies. Honduras was chosen for many reasons. This small country of fewer than 5 million people is the poorest in Central America; seven of ten inhabitants live in poverty.[1] The United States is Honduras' primary trading partner, and for many years Honduras was the recipient of more U.S. aid than any other Central American country. Honduras has a variety of nongovernmental development models, and the task force denomination has long-standing relations with ecumenical grassroots organizations which extended a warm invitation to the task force.

As the task force members discussed the shrimp farm, Tom's thoughts returned to the images and conversations of the visit. After driving across miles of salty marshland and passing through two checkpoints monitored by armed guards, the van entered the seventh largest shrimp farm in the world. The van traveled between rows and rows of neatly constructed ponds on either side of a land bridge. Carlos, the Marinas guide, explained that on the twenty-square-mile site there were nearly five thousand acres of ponds in production and plans for three thousand more. Tom had learned earlier that the beaches now under production had previously been public lands, which were turned over to private companies for development.

Their first stop was near the oxygenation tanks. A worker explained that some of the shrimp larvae are bred in a laboratory and flown to Honduras from Miami. The majority of larvae, however, come from the nearby mangrove swamps. Local fishermen are contracted to fill fifty-liter containers with larvae, which they collect in very fine nets. The larvae are then poured into heavily aerated tanks and left there for twenty-four hours to "isolate and acclimatize" them. The group learned that, since there is no practical way to sort the millions of tiny organisms collected, the technicians put pesticides into the tanks to kill all forms of larvae except two types of shrimp. This procedure leaves between 300,000 to 400,000 shrimp larvae in each tank. When Tom asked what effect the destruction of all the other larvae species, including other types of shrimp, had on marine life in the Gulf, he was assured by the worker that "this is no problem. There are lots of fish in the Gulf." The shrimp are transferred to larger nursery tanks, then raised to maturity in the open ponds.

The task force members drove another mile to the main processing plant, a large concrete block building. After climbing a steel staircase, they entered the plant supervisor's glass-enclosed, air-conditioned observation room. Tom saw six men in the hall below shoveling ice and shrimp onto long conveyer belts and about fifty women de-heading and sorting the shrimp. Having learned from Carlos that the shrimp were bathed in a chlorine solution, Tom expressed his surprise that only a few women had protective gloves. The supervisor responded that when the women "begin to work here, some do have a problem with their hands. But it's minimal." Tom also noted that there were no chairs or benches in the large open-air processing area.

The supervisor explained that the shrimp farm provided work for more than eight hundred direct and indirect employees. Direct employees such as the technicians were hired and paid salaries by the farm; indirect workers were contracted and paid by the hour or by the job. The farm management had no direct relationship with contracted workers; management paid contractors, who were responsible for paying their workers. He referred to the fishermen who collected shrimp larvae as an example of contracted or indirect workers.

In response to questions from the task force, the supervisor said that the women worked six days a week in one of two twelve-hour shifts. They were allowed three breaks during the twelve hours. When the plant had large orders, particularly in the wintertime, the workers could process 50,000 pounds of shrimp a day. When there were small orders, the processing plant was open only part time. When asked how many of the 110 women—who each signed an annual contract—might quit, the supervisor replied, "Only about eight. There are very few sources of work here. People can't afford to leave." The supervisor also noted that all Marinas shrimp were shipped north for U.S. consumption. Growth of the industry had made cheaper shrimp available for their primary purchaser, a large U.S. restaurant chain. In addition shrimp sales brought more than $30 million in foreign exchange into Honduras in 1991.

Adjacent to the processing plant were an employee cafeteria and the office of the workers' *solidarista*. The task force members welcomed the offer of cold drinks to help them cope with the intense heat of the coast. Carlos, who had been an elementary school teacher, spoke with great enthusiasm about the workers' association. He emphasized that it was not a union or labor organization. Although the workers had no retirement benefit beyond the percentage of their salary paid directly to the Honduran government, and no medical coverage, their *solidarista* provided its members with loans, a food co-op, and the cafeteria. The *solidarista* membership, composed of the "direct" or salaried employees of the shrimp farm, elected its leaders democratically. The walls of the office were lined with pictures of numerous cultural, athletic, and social events. Tom had seen no pictures of women. He asked Carlos about the women members and was told that all the women who worked at the shrimp farm were indirect employees; they could not belong to the *solidarista*; they did not have a union of any kind. Carlos thought the women were paid daily minimum wage, about U.S.$5, by their contractors. Tom learned later that pay for most women was less than half of this amount. The women received no pay when the plant was closed because of small orders.

Since he was there to listen and learn, Tom did not question Carlos about the inclusion of women in the *solidarista*, but he was feeling increasingly uncomfortable about the situation of indirect workers. Tom had learned that the women privately complained that their hands were peeling from the chlorine and that they had backaches from standing all day, but they "wouldn't think of bringing these complaints" to the supervisor.[2] As Tom wondered what would drive women as young as fourteen and fifteen to accept these working conditions, he thought about the villages through which the vans had driven on the way to the coast. The local host traveling with the task force explained that in this area the primary income was from the export of beef and melons. All the rich farmland in the valleys was owned by twelve or fifteen families. The *campesinos* were pushed up into deforested hills with very poor soil and little rain. With no hope for employment, many men left their families to seek work in the North. Tom learned that many men sent money to their families for a year or two, but they stopped all support when they established another family in the North.

The *campesina* women, children, and old men left in the rural areas suffered from illiteracy, malnutrition, and a serious lack of adequate housing and health care. Many of the *campesinos* with whom the group met in the north were certain that recent policies of structural adjustment introduced by the Honduran government at the insistence of the World Bank and U.S. advisors were having drastic effects on their lives. The government decisions to devalue the currency, cut public services, remove foreign exchange controls, and no longer subsidize basic food products had long-term goals of stabilizing the economy, but the immediate impact was even higher unemployment and a sharp rise in the cost of food. Tom was knowledgeable about the complex economic theories which supported these measures, but he now felt he better understood why the women would be willing to take any job that could help support their families.

The last stop on the farm was to view six giant diesel turbines. Twice a day, for six hours during high tide, 180,000 gallons of fresh water per minute were pumped from an estuary of the Gulf into the shrimp ponds. The cleansing water flowed back into the estuary at an outtake area "near the sea." Tom noted the bright red, white, and blue USAID (United States Agency for International Development) stickers on the turbines, which indicated the equipment had come directly from the U.S. agency or had been bought with U.S. funds.

As Tom reflected on the day, he was struck by the magnitude of the impact of U.S. policies on Honduras. In the 1980s Honduras joined the U.S. effort to support the "contras" fighting against the Sandinista government of Nicaragua. Between 1980 and 1984, U.S. military aid to Honduras increased from $3.9 million to $77.4 million, significantly strengthening a once-modest Honduran military.[3] Tom learned that as U.S. funding decreased dramatically in the late 1980s, the

Honduran military sought to maintain its strength. As part of its pension program, the military now owned many Honduran businesses including a cement factory, a funeral parlor, and a coastal shrimp farm. Although the military businesses competed with private industry, the military paid no taxes to support the Honduran economy.

Tom had read that USAID had loaned some $11 million to build Honduran shrimp ponds.[4] He was impressed by the income generated by the new industry, but he was worried about long-term effects. He recalled an interview with Gulf fishermen who strongly opposed the new industry, stating that the land now dredged and fenced by the shrimp farms was once national territory open to the thousands of families who made their living fishing. One fisherman noted that not only were they now cut off from miles of once-rich fishing areas, but "these waters used to be full of fish. Now you fish the whole day and come home with only a pound, a half-pound of fish."[5] While the fishermen blamed the depletion of the fish on the netting of larvae, the shrimp farmers said the cause was the *campesinos* who had come from the hills searching for work.

Tom recalled that concern about both the human and environmental impact of the shrimp farms was expressed by Del McCloskey, an expert in shrimp development in the Honduran USAID office. In reference to the fishermen's claims, McCloskey acknowledged, "We have no idea what sort of impact we are having on those populations." Tom also remembered McCloskey stating, "We are very concerned that we may be promoting a new industry that is having a major environmental impact—adverse environmental impact."[6] Tom wondered to what extent these concerns were countered by the enthusiastic response of John Sanbrailo, the Director of USAID, who strongly supported U.S. government export policies: "What you see happening in Latin America is as historically significant as the fall of the Berlin Wall, the changes going on in Eastern Europe. You have a new model out there. We in the United States foreign aid program are attempting to implement that in Honduras and in other countries—help these countries make the transition to more market-based economies. What we see is a more buoyant world economy that's good for everybody."[7]

Tom agreed that on paper the shrimp industry was exactly the type of program he had advocated for years. Honduras had found a market in the global economy which it could uniquely and profitably supply. The foreign income would help Honduras repay its foreign debts and move the country away from dependence on foreign aid. The industry also employed thousands of workers in a poor rural area with high unemployment. But as he reflected on the day, Tom continued to ask himself, which people would most benefit from the policies his government was advocating? How should the church express concern for marginalized *campesinos,* fishermen, and women struggling to survive in a rapidly changing world? Was the depletion of Honduras' natural resources worth the push to compete in international free trade markets? Perhaps most important, who should have the power to make these decisions?

Tom suddenly realized the members of the task force were looking at him. The group had been in a debate about the shrimp farm. "You're the economist, Tom. Should the church affirm our government's support of this kind of development program?"

NOTES

1. Background information and economic data taken from U.S. State Department document, "Honduras Economic Trends Report, July 24, 1992"; U.S. State Department, "Background Notes: Honduras, May 1992."

2. National Public Radio, "All Things Considered," April 18, 1992. Transcript and audio tape.

3. "AID Congressional Presentation FY 1988," Washington, D.C.: Agency for International Development, 1988.

4. National Public Radio, "All Things Considered."

5. Ibid.

6. Ibid.

7. Ibid.

Teaching Note

I. Goals

A. To assist discussion of the strengths and weaknesses of a particular type of development which is promoted by Western government agencies and international banking organizations. The primary model for the Granjas Marinas Shrimp Farm is frequently referred to as "growth-centered development." Shrimp farming is considered by many people to be one of Central America's most successful businesses. It uses locally available resources and local labor to create a distinctive niche in the global market, and it produces significant cash income for further development and repayment of international debts. Thousands of development programs throughout the world have adopted this model with a goal of improving the living standards of local communities. However, individuals and nongovernmental organizations concerned with the environment and the quality of life of local communities are raising questions about the long-term effects of this type of development.

B. To encourage church members to become knowledgeable about the goals and effects of development policies in general.

C. To consider the theological implications of the ways governmental and nongovernmental agencies and church bodies attempt to alleviate poverty.

II. Questions for Discussion

A. Put yourself in the position of the owners, supervisor, and other "direct employees" of the shrimp farm. What are the long- and short-term advantages and disadvantages of the business for these people?

B. From the perspective of the "indirect workers"—primarily women and fishermen—what are the advantages and disadvantages of working for the business? Consider such issues as working conditions, international markets, foreign exchange, and the impact on local and national economies.

C. Discuss the environmental impact of the shrimp farm. Note that Granjas Marinas is only one of several shrimp farms along the Gulf of Fonseca.

D. Beyond those issues already discussed, are there other issues raised by the case which Tom should consider in his response to the task force? Participants might suggest, for example, the overall impact of U.S. policies, including military policies, on the economic development of Honduras, or the role of women in Honduran society.

E. If a primary goal of development is to reduce poverty, what theories inform growth-centered development? Consider theories of privatization, "trickle-down" economics, the role of industry, market focus, and the perspective of some people on limitless natural resources.

F. What advice would you give to Tom? What economic *and* theological principles inform your response?

G. If you were advising the task force from a Christian perspective, what guidelines would you suggest for faithful and responsible ways to address poverty in the developing world?

H. Write down a message that you would like your church to send to your own government about development policies. Share your message in small groups. What personal experiences or components of the case discussion influenced your message?

III. Additional Resources

This case was originally published in a churchwide study document titled, "Sustainable Development, Reformed Faith, and U.S. International Economic Policy," for the Presbyterian Church (USA). The full study document is written as a six-session discussion guide for local congregations. The study and leader's guide can be obtained from the Committee on Social Witness Policy, Presbyterian Church, 100 Witherspoon St., Louisville, KY 40202. The study contains additional case studies and discussion material for such topics as the meaning of sustainable development, approaches to development, and international trade. The goal of the study is to introduce the issues without recommending specific positions. The basic biblical texts for the study focus on a theology of accompaniment. The leader's guide contains discussion questions, suggestions for group worship, a wide variety of reprinted articles, and an extensive bibliography of many facets of sustainable development.

Commentary

THE CONTEXT

The Republic of Honduras is the second largest and the poorest country in Central America. Its population in 1990 was estimated at 4,679,000.[1] Seventy percent of the population lives in poverty. "More than three-fourths of Honduras is mountainous. The lowlands are confined to the coastal plains and river valleys. The southern lowland area is formed by the valley of the Choluteca River, which drains southward, across a small coastal plain, into the Gulf of Fonseca."[2] The Gulf of Fonseca, shared by Honduras, El Salvador, and Nicaragua, empties into the Pacific Ocean. Honduras is heavily dependent on the production and export of bananas, coffee, sugar, shrimp, and timber.[3]

Agriculture, which employs almost three-fifths of the labor force, accounts for about one-fifth of the gross domestic product. Bananas are the main cash crop and are exported by U.S. companies. Both coffee and sugar are produced primarily for export, and shrimp, the most important part of the fishing industry, is primarily exported to the United States.[4] The main trading partners besides the U.S. are Japan and Germany. Honduras has generally had a trade deficit, partly because of the higher cost of imported petroleum. The Gross National Product (GNP) is not growing as rapidly as the population.

The Constitution adopted in 1957 included programs of moderate social reform. However, land reform has benefited relatively few peasants. Military leaders ruled, with one exception, until 1982 when a civilian government was elected to office.[5] Although the military has remained in the background, it continues to be influential and has openly opposed the activity of leftist guerrillas.

FREE MARKET ECONOMY

In most parts of the world "economic power is closely linked with inherited wealth, political power, scientific and technological knowledge, and military power."[6] In a world driven by a global market economy, poor countries have to compete with rich, powerful countries. These poor countries are disadvantaged for several reasons: lack of capital for investment, lack of a qualified and educated labor force, lack of infrastructure, and lack of technical expertise. Many poor countries are also controlled by small power elites which are usually dominated by the military and supported by some business elites.

National development programs need capital investments, which have to be borrowed from the industrially developed countries in the North, or from the international consortia of banks through the World Bank and the International Monetary Fund (IMF), or other international loan agencies. Loans are usually given with strings attached. Most countries receiving loans from the World Bank or IMF are required to make structural adjustments, which generally involve a currency devaluation and reduction or abolition of government support for basic food, commodities, health services, and other social welfare programs. Such structural adjustment adversely affects the majority of the people who are poor and marginalized.

The free-market economy, which promises economic boom and prosperity for all, has not alleviated the misery of the poor and marginalized people of the world. Instead, it has brought tremendous wealth only to a few nations, mostly in the North. The gap between the rich and the poor nations continues to widen, between the industrially developed countries in the North and the developing countries of the South. The free-market system has created small pockets of newly rich elites in the midst of the large majority of poor people in most of the countries in the South. Although a move into the global economy has brought some new jobs to such areas as the poor villages near Honduran shrimp farms, the global free-market economy has not opened up jobs for the millions of young people joining the labor market every year. Instead there is a trend among large companies and industries to "downsize" in order to be more competitive and to realize higher profit margins. Downsizing results in a substantial decrease in employment in many parts of the world. The loss of jobs by millions of people in the past few years has brought frustration, anxiety, and suffering to millions of families. People are willing to take even minimum wage jobs just to survive. Some accept "slave wages" to feed their families.[7]

"Desperate to reduce its dependence on bananas, coffee, and other unstable export commodities, Honduras has turned to shrimp farming for badly needed foreign exchange."[8] This policy, which is supported by the USAID (United States Agency for International Development), has made the shrimp industry a very important development project. Shrimp has become "the third most important export after bananas and coffee" and the newest and most financially successful business venture in Honduras.

ENVIRONMENTAL CONCERNS

The apparent success story of shrimp farming is not without drawbacks. First, the shrimp farms, according to a USAID-sponsored report prepared by Florida-based Tropical Research and Development Inc., "destroyed mangroves and contaminated water supplies around the ecologically sensitive Gulf of Fonseca on Honduras' Pacific coast."[9] According to this report, "Declining water quality in the shrimp zones is a serious concern. The cause of poor water quality . . . is organic loading from shrimp-pond effluent, particularly in San Bernardo area."[10] Furthermore, "all ten water samples analyzed in the study contained detectable levels of pesticides, some of which were at concentrations approaching dosages lethal for selected test organisms."[11]

This report was countered by ANDAH (Honduran National Aquaculture Association) which has twenty-four members representing the industry's largest exporters. According to ANDAH, "The shrimp industry knows that if they don't safeguard the natural ecosystems, their industry will fall apart. So they are the most interested in conservation." Further, according to the Technical Director of ANDAH, "Twice a year, on World Environment Day and World Food Day, ANDAH releases 10,000 reproductive shrimp into the Gulf of Fonseca as a symbolic gesture."[12] One might ask if this gesture is adequate when compared with the 300,000 to 400,000 shrimp larvae collected every day from the mangrove swamps for only one of the shrimp farms. Many species of shrimp larvae are killed by pesticides in the heavily aerated tanks along with millions of tiny organisms. The church task force members must consider the validity of these studies and ask if the shrimp industry, which is backed by powerful figures in the Honduran military, is really concerned with long-term protection of the natural ecosystem.

"Poor people suffer disproportionately from environmental degradation. Often they live close to polluted areas, in inadequate housing conditions with poor sanitation; as peasants they often possess poor, degraded, and arid land; as landless agricultural workers they are often exposed to toxic insecticides, pesticides, and herbicides; often they see their drinking and fishing waters polluted and their health directly endangered."[13] This is the fate of the poor people of Honduras. Honduran peasant women working in the shrimp industry have extra burdens, as they have to work long hours, in environmentally unhealthy working conditions, without fringe benefits, and are paid very low wages.

ECONOMIC JUSTICE

What lesson can be learned from the timber industry which left thousands of acres of barren hills devastated by erosion and drought? Before the timber industry Honduras had been heavily forested. The same is true in Haiti and many other countries that did not nurture their natural resources.

These two development projects, timber and shrimp, which use a growth-centered approach, aim for rapid economic growth to provide job opportunities and to yield capital income for further investments. The goal is to lift the standard of living of the people.

Experience in many growth-centered development projects does not support this thinking. While there may be short-term benefits for some people, there can be serious consequences for future generations.

The USAID-sponsored report also made critical comments about the industry's impact on Honduran society. Although the shrimp farms have provided employment opportunities for a large number of women, their incomes "have not led to substantially better housing or more material goods."[14] The women's working hours are long (twelve hours a day, six days a week), and their working conditions are unhealthy. They are not provided with protective gloves for handling the chlorine-treated shrimp, and no chairs or benches are available in the large working area. Many women have complained that their hands peel from the chlorine and that they have backaches from standing all day. But they do not dare bring these complaints to their supervisor. Since there is an excess supply of labor, they are afraid of being laid off.

These women do not receive any payment when the plant is closed because of a decrease in orders. While the men are hired as direct employees, receiving regular salaries and freedom to organize as *solidaritas*, with privileges such as food co-op, cafeteria, and office, the women are hired through a contractor as indirect employees and are paid only for the time they work.[15]

It is not surprising that Tom was particularly struck by the poverty of the *campesinos*. Tom learned that the closed and guarded beaches had previously been public lands that were turned over to private shrimp companies for development. Thousands of families have lost their access to the beaches and have found the supply of fish radically diminished, as the shrimp industry has taken control of the rich marshes which are the breeding ground for the once-vibrant marine life in the Gulf. The *campesino* families have lost both land and sustenance.

PASTORAL STRATEGY

As an economist Tom had advocated programs such as this shrimp industry, confident that this type of enterprise would enable Honduras to repay its foreign debts, move the country away from dependence on foreign aid, and provide employment to workers in poor rural areas with high unemployment. The experience of this field visit and observation has presented him with a different reality.

Who has benefited most from this project? Definitely not the marginalized *campesinos* and *campesinas*, nor the fisherfolk, nor especially the women workers who still struggle to survive. Powerful Honduran military figures and wealthy businessmen able to influence government policies, such as turning public land into private enterprises, control many of the shrimp operations. Workers are not allowed to organize unions for their own protection because of the strongly anti-union attitudes of the shrimp industry.[16]

Tom has also heard evidence that the shrimp industry has contributed to environmental degradation by endangering the survival of the mangroves and contaminating the water supplies around the ecologically sensitive Gulf of Fonseca.

Now, what should Tom recommend to his church concerning his government's support of this kind of development program? What should his church do to help rectify the adverse impact that the people of Honduras have experienced?

Tom's experiences in Honduras should first make the reader conscious of the difference between theory and practice. The fact that shrimp industries have not been fully successful in raising the standard of living for more people, as was expected by Tom, should be analyzed carefully. A short-term gain has to be weighed against the long-term loss. The positive financial success of the project should be weighed against the marginalization and impoverishment of the *campesinos*, fisherfolk, and women workers and the environmental pollution the industry brings.

As a basis for pastoral strategy, Christians should "Remember the Future":

1. The future is more than just a continuum of time. It is also the *eschaton*. The future also means the fulfillment of the Kingdom of God, the fulfillment of God's promise. It is the full manifestation of the Kingdom of God which has already begun in the New Testament.

2. Remembering the future means recalling to memory the life of Jesus, his teaching and ministry, his "opting for the poor," his suffering unto death on the cross, his resurrection from the dead, which gives hope for the life to come. The future is an event when God will fulfill God's promise as written in Isaiah 65:17–23,

> For I am about to create new heavens and a new earth; the former things shall not be remembered or come to mind. But be glad and rejoice forever in what I am creating; for I am about to create Jerusalem as a joy and its people as a delight. I will rejoice in Jerusalem and delight in my people; no more shall the sound of weeping be heard in it, or the cry of distress. No more shall there be in it an infant that lives but a few days, or an old person who does not live out

a lifetime; for one who dies at a hundred years will be considered a youth and one who falls short of a hundred will be considered accursed. They shall build houses and inhabit them; they shall not plant and another eat; for like the days of a tree shall the days of my people be, and my chosen shall long enjoy the work of their hands. They shall not labor in vain or bear children for calamity; for they shall be offspring blessed by the Lord—and their descendants as well.

3. Remembering the future also means understanding that the future is a part of the present and that the present is a part of the past. What is happening now (the thousands of acres of dry, barren hills) is, in many ways, the result of past policy. What will happen in the future will be the result of or influenced by what is being done through policy and action in the present. The present society is the product of the past, and the future society has already begun. What we do or not do with regard to the shrimp farm will have significant bearing for the future.

4. Remembering the future, therefore, means being thoughtful and considerate of the future of our society. We must be attentive to the needs of future generations and mindful of their welfare. We must acknowledge, respect, and honor the rights of future generations to the natural resources that the earth has to offer. We should neither squander nor destroy the limited natural resources. We did not inherit this earth from our parents; we borrow it from our children and grandchildren. We are accountable to future generations. In the concrete terms of this case, we need to be more concerned with the deterioration of the water supplies and the Gulf of Fonseca.

5. Remembering the future is also a process of reflection and action that must be taken today. We must critically observe and analyze what is happening in our daily lives, in our local communities, and in the global society, and how our private lives and public communities are interrelated. In the case study, the Honduran shrimp industry's financial success is influenced by the USAID's support and this financial success has contributed to the impoverishment of the fisherfolk who were once sustained by the Gulf. Would a change in U.S. policy with regard to this industry have an impact on it, such that the workers' situation would be improved and the environment preserved? How can the church, which has good relations with the grassroots ecumenical movements, empower the fisherfolk and the shrimp farm workers to improve their condition? How can the task force encourage the church to lobby the U.S. government to look more seriously into the environmental issue?

The church can help support the grassroots ecumenical organizations to empower the people through organized effort and cooperation and to challenge the industries to be more open to organized labor, increased wages, and improved working conditions. These actions can promote more just and equitable economic development. Empowering the powerless in the community is one of the most important goals in a pastoral situation.

NOTES

1. *The New Encyclopedia Britannica,* Micropedia, 15th Edition, 1993, Vol. 6, p. 33.

2. Ibid.

3. *Latinamerica Press,* November 4, 1993, p. 6.

4. *The New Encyclopedia Britannica,* ibid.

5. Ibid.

6. *Christian Faith and the World Economy Today: A Study Document from the World Council of Churches,* Geneva, 1992, p. 19.

7. *Latinamerica Press,* p. 6.

8. Ibid.

9. Ibid.

10. Ibid.

11. Ibid.

12. *Christian Faith and the World Economy Today,* p. 23.

13. *Latinamerica Press.*

14. Ibid.

15. Ibid.

16. Ibid.

THE FATE OF TÉ BOUKÉ

Case

Tom and Marion Dalton slowly climbed the steep, barren hill behind their cabin. They had lived in Haiti in the rural village of Té Bouké (tired land) for nearly three years. The Daltons were volunteers with a European church development organization. They understood their mission as witnessing to their Christian faith while they lived in the village and worked with community leaders and organizers to help improve the quality of the meager crops.

After months of struggle, with many challenges and some real successes, neither Tom nor Marion could remember being more frustrated than they were by the issues now before them. Several of the village farmers had asked the Daltons to import strong fertilizers from North America. The couple agreed that the chemicals could immediately improve the current crop of maize, but this step challenged some of the basic principles of long-term development they hoped the village would adopt.

In addition, Tom and Marion had received a notice that Dérius, the "Chief of Section" (county sheriff) and his *attachés* (aides) wanted to talk to them about their work with the villagers. Tom and Marion knew of other development organizations and projects that had been harassed by autonomous and often corrupt local officials; they assumed they had been left alone up to this point because they were foreigners. They were aware that some Haitian *animators* or development workers had been jailed and some murdered by local officials who felt their authority and control were threatened by community organizing.

During three hundred years of colonization and political struggle, the once lush hills and mountains of Haiti had been almost totally denuded of large stands of timber. The mountain range in which Té Bouké was situated was a heartland of coffee production only fifty years ago. European colonists, international corporations, and powerful Haitian landowners cut and sold thousands of acres of timber. More recently, during the twenty-nine-year Duvalier reign from 1957 to 1986, large

This case was first published in a church-wide study document, "Sustainable Development, Reformed Faith, and U.S. International Economic Policy," Louisville, KY: Presbyterian Church (USA), 1994. Used by permission.

timber concessions were given to regime supporters who ruthlessly cut down the remaining rain forest. The growing population of poor people searching for fire-wood further denuded the hillsides. The result has been massive erosion of topsoil leaving deep gullies of rock and clay and miles of low scrub brush. Erosion also made the hills steeper. People occasionally came into the local clinics to be treated for injuries sustained when they fell out of their gardens.

Today less than one-third of Haiti's land is able to produce crops. The largest tracts of farmland are used to produce coffee, sugar cane, cocoa, and sisal for export. Most of the remaining plots of land, used to produce sweet potatoes, bananas, beans, rice, and maize for local consumption, are being rapidly depleted by overuse. There are fewer than six hundred miles of paved roads in the entire country; the trip into the remote mountain village of Té Bouké is long and diffi-cult. Although the journey from the capital city of Port-au-Prince is less than ninety miles, it takes nearly six hours for a four-wheel-drive vehicle to travel over rutted dirt roads and across unbridged mountain streams. Travel by car or truck is virtually impossible when it rains.

Before they arrived in Té Bouké, Tom and Marion spent several months studying the history and culture of Haiti and learning Creole, the language spoken by the Haitian people. Tom's college degree was in agronomy, the scientific study of agriculture. Marion was a business major. The couple were invited to be staff members on a team of Haitian community organizers working to improve the quality of life in impoverished rural mountain villages. A primary goal of the plan was to help the villagers become self-sufficient. One of the basic organizing prin-ciples was to involve the villagers as much as possible in the planning and deci-sion-making processes. The Daltons, as well as the community organizers, were particularly concerned about development projects which lead poor people to become dependent on expensive products which demand scarce cash resources.

Tom and Marion, the first foreigners to live in Té Bouké, received a warm welcome from the six hundred villagers. In a few weeks they were settled in a small cabin constructed near the outskirts of the village. At first they spent time getting acquainted with the village residents and elders, with the Reverend Eugene, the feisty Baptist pastor; Pé Ivon, a quiet Haitian Catholic priest who lived in the next village and served a chapel in Té Bouké; and Andrémon, the local Voodoo priest. Not long after their arrival, the Daltons witnessed the fervent prayers and proces-sions of the villagers, most of whom are Catholic, in a celebration in honor of St. Peter. That afternoon they were baffled to see the same people on their way to Andrémon's *Hounfor* (Voodoo temple) carrying hens to be sacrificed. The Daltons reminded themselves that they were not there to judge the Haitians' complex spirituality. Their mandate was to witness to their own faith by offering support through their technical advice and their presence.

The couple immediately began their support work for the four Haitian *animators* who came into the village monthly. Ironically, Siplé and Dieuleme, two of the *animators*, had once lived in Té Bouké, but were forced to leave because of threats on their lives by Dérius and his *attachés*. The *animators* had organized the village farmers into small discussion groups. The farmers would decide what they wanted to do and what was needed to accomplish their goals. The groups would share with Tom and Marion their plans, and the couple would assist with implementation.

The villagers' first project was to acquire better farming equipment. Their present tools were worn out from years of use in difficult conditions. The cost of trips to the market in Port-au-Prince had increased tremendously, and farm tools purchased from small merchant stores on the main road in the valley were quite expensive and of uneven quality. The villagers wanted their own supply store in Té Bouké. Working with Tom, Marion, and the community organizers, a number of the farmers formed a cooperative and pooled their funds to construct a building. Tom and Marion helped the co-op apply to the church for a loan to assist in the initial wholesale purchase of quality seeds and tools. Marion helped the farmers develop a system to record inventory and sales. Within two years the advance from the church was repaid, and the farmers who had invested in the co-op had received a small share of the profits.

The Daltons assisted the villagers by gathering a variety of trees to provide food and to curb soil erosion. The church agency advanced the funds to purchase bread-fruit and nut trees as well as coffee bushes. Tom used his truck to bring in the young trees. Several villagers attended a regional workshop to learn how to care for them. Next, responding to the emerging awareness of the village women about the need for better nutrition for their children, the Daltons helped the women acquire several hundred baby chicks so that fresh eggs would be available in the village. Tom trained the villagers in the care of the birds and sold a rooster and two or three hens at below market cost to each participating family.

Marion and Tom were clear that they were not the only ones teaching. They continued to be impressed by the creativity and energy of the villagers and the incredibly long hours they toiled to build a future for their children. The couple had recently shared with the community organizers their appreciation for the growing self-confidence of the villagers as they identified and designed community projects. Marion was particularly impressed by the vitality of the village women who seemed to be the driving force in the community.

The challenges now facing Tom and Marion were ones they had seen coming for several months. Since their arrival in the village, they had been a sort of buffer between the area authorities and village project participants. Now word had come to the Daltons that the Chief of Section had received complaints from merchants on the main road who had lost Té Bouké's business since the opening of the village store. The small successes of the village projects were also disturbing some powerful people from whom the farmers had previously received loans at very high interest. Dérius sent word that he wanted to talk to Jean Pierre, leader of the farm cooperative, in addition to Tom and Marion.

At the same time, there were important decisions to be made regarding the next agricultural season. When they arrived in Té Bouké, the Daltons found the soil in the garden behind their cabin almost completely devoid of nutrients. Tom suppressed his inclination to plant nitrogen-rich native plants and let the land lie fallow and replenish itself. He knew he could never convince the farmers, whose lives depended on the maize crop, not to plant every square foot of their small parcels of land. However, during their first year, Tom and Marion did not follow the village practice of planting maize over a large area after burning off the grass and last season's stubble. Rather, they tilled a smaller garden very deeply, turning the grass into the soil. They also added to the soil plant and grass clippings from their yard and all the vegetable peelings from the kitchen. Their second year in the village they had an extremely good maize crop in the kitchen garden. Several village farmers said that the Daltons' crop was so good because they were educated. Marion and Tom disagreed. "You can have a crop just like this if you are willing to try to farm in a different way." Many of the farmers, however, were afraid to try new methods. Maize was their most important food crop. If a farmer had a poor harvest, his family could starve.

The next growing season a few farmers were willing to try the new method on a small portion of their land. The work was tedious and involved manually plowing the grass into the land, rather than burning it off, and letting the land lie fallow for one season. The hope of one good crop in the following season implied having less corn in the current year. A few weeks later a group of farmers from Té Bouké left the village to attend a meeting in the lowlands with the community organizers. The farmers returned with exciting reports of a farm they had seen where the maize crop was much finer than anything in their village. They had talked with one of the workers who told them that the church development agency they worked with had imported tons of fertilizer from North America. The crop would be so large this year that their village could sell the surplus maize and have enough money to build a school.

On their return to Té Bouké the farmers talked about having enough maize to be able to sell some and have money for a school. Jean Pierre, the spokesman for their group, went to the Daltons' home that same evening with the request for a large quantity of chemical fertilizer. Tom and Marion knew they would wait to speak with the Haitian *animators* before making any final decisions. But as they stood looking over the village and the surrounding hillside fields, they shared their concerns with one another. Tom and Marion agreed that dependence on expensive fertilizers could threaten the growing independence of the village. However, they disagreed on other issues concerning imported fertilizers.

Tom thought that the soil was so poor on the hillsides that it needed much more than expensive imported chemicals. He was convinced that the farmers needed to plant more trees, such as the leucena, and crops that could supply nitrogen naturally. They needed to plant grasses in contour ditches to conserve the remaining topsoil and avoid the fast runoff of rain water. But these changes took years of hard, slow manual labor. Tom saw some advantages in a combination of building up the soil naturally and adding a limited amount of chemical nutrients, but the fertilizers would have to be carefully controlled. The soil in Té Bouké was very sandy, and nitrogen and potassium were 100 percent water soluble. If the farmers misused the chemicals, they could seriously contaminate the village water supply. Tom recalled a situation involving leaching of chemicals used by farmers in Iowa and Illinois. The level of nitrate in the ground water became so high that babies fed infant formula made with the contaminated water turned blue from lack of oxygen. And those were farmers who could read the warning labels on the chemical containers.

Tom strongly stated his conviction: " If the farmers turn to chemicals now, they could be fooled into thinking they no longer need to build up the soil. They might have a few years of good crops, but in subsequent years heavy dependence on chemical fertilizers could turn the earth salty and ultimately kill the few healthy and critical bacteria remaining in the soil. Their fields could be as barren as these rocky, scrub-covered hills. In addition, the margin of profit on this land is so small that only one crop failure would mean that the farmers would be unable to make payments on their loans for the fertilizer." Tom was sure that a number of the Haitian *animators* agreed with him.

Marion looked out over the village before responding. "Part of me agrees with you completely, but another part is very uneasy with this approach. We have never experienced the hunger and insecurity these families have lived with for generations. Who are we to suggest that the farmers of Té Bouké shouldn't have the materials to give them the best possible crop as soon as possible? As a business person, part of me says there's absolutely nothing wrong with a good short-term profit. An excellent crop of maize would energize the entire village and could provide a small financial cushion for those who live day by day. If there is a crop failure, the church would be able to extend the loan. There are also significant technological advances in farming every year. Why not look for new approaches to counteract the harmful effects of chemical fertilizers? A number of the community organizers are also wrestling with these questions."

Marion and Tom believed that the farmers were beginning to trust them to help with the vital crops. But if the Chief of Section and his thugs decided to persecute the cooperative in Té Bouké, not only would many years of hard work be jeopardized, but the very lives of some villagers. The Daltons had heard by short-wave radio that two villages in the northern part of the country had been burned the week before, their projects destroyed, and their leaders arrested or in hiding. Marion and Tom agreed that before they came to Haiti they had no idea of the enormous costs of challenging the status quo. In all likelihood they would be able to leave Té Bouké safely, but the villagers had no place to go. The Daltons were also aware from comments by the parish priest that the villagers had come to depend on them for protection. They could try to postpone a meeting, but they would need to decide before too long how to respond to the Chief of Section.

Even in the face of the political uncertainties and anxiety about the villagers' safety, the Daltons' desire to support the farmers' dreams for improving the quality of life in their village was unshakable. Healthy crops were a vital link in reaching that goal. While Tom and Marion agreed that they would place the options before the organizers, they wanted first to clarify for themselves the moral and faith implications of responding to the farmers' request for chemical fertilizers.

Teaching Note

This case situation takes place just prior to the 1991 military coup which overthrew the government of President Aristide. While the political and economic climates in Haiti have changed since that time, the central issues raised by the case remain the same for rural villages and development agencies throughout the world.

I. Goals

Several goals could be reached through a discussion of this case. Among them are:

A. To explore multiple implications of long-term and short-term development strategies.

B. To appreciate the ingenuity and to better understand the perspectives and needs of poor rural communities.

C. To consider both the benefits and the potentially negative effects of the disruption of the status quo in developing countries by mission agencies and non-governmental organizations.

D. To encourage participants to learn about the development strategies of their own governments and denominational bodies.

II. Questions

The following questions are not designed to lead participants to conclusions but to encourage them to ask more questions and explore the assumptions underlying their responses. As many of these questions will stimulate in-depth discussions, the facilitator will need to be selective. One major decision may be to choose between focusing on the question of imported fertilizer or on the question of how the Daltons should respond to Dérius and his *attachés*.

A. Focus on the local residents of Té Bouké. Describe what their daily life is like. How are their lives directly and indirectly affected by the history of Haiti? How are they affected by the current political situation? Why did most farmers initially resist Tom's approach to farming? In reaching for their goal of self-sufficiency, how have the residents changed the status quo, particularly in relation to Dérius, the Chief of Section, and his *attachés*?

B. Describe the Daltons. What are the goals of their mission in Haiti? What faith assumptions inform these goals? The case closes with the Daltons facing several dilemmas. Focus first on the question of fertilizer. With the assurance of time to share the reasoning behind their votes, ask participants to take a straw poll.

Record the number of people who support Tom's position and those who support Marion's position. Discuss the factors which influenced those who support Tom's belief that the community should not import large quantities of chemicals. What factors influenced support of Marion's position to import the fertilizer? Encourage participants to go beyond the reasoning set forth by Marion and Tom, reminding them that the *animators* are also divided about this issue. After the discussion, ask if anyone changed her or his mind after hearing the rationale for other positions.

C. Who should make the decision about the fertilizer? Why? If the villagers or *animators* make a decision with which Tom and Marion do not agree, how should they respond? Why?

D. Are there ways to balance long-term and short-term development needs? What guiding principles can the farmers, *animators,* Marion, and Tom follow in meeting immediate basic human needs while nurturing the environment for the next generation? Balancing these two goals is a critical issue for the church and for most nations of the world. What biblical insights would address the tension between these two goals?

E. Ask participants if they are aware of the guidelines which shape the social services and development policies of their congregation or denomination. Advance preparation by the facilitator and the presentation of resource material will be very important for this discussion. Ask which biblical and theological principles inform these policies and guidelines. What principles inform their national development policies? Should the church be involved in shaping national and international development strategies? Why or why not?

F. What issues should Tom and Marion consider in making their decision about responding to the "invitation" to meet with the Chief of Section? In dealing with this question it may be helpful to return to the initial discussion of the village residents and how they changed the status quo in relation to Dérius and his *attachés*. Participants should keep in mind the relative safety of the Daltons as foreigners and the danger to the villagers in light of recent persecution of other villages and local leaders.

Whom should the Daltons consult? What resources can they draw on to help them make a responsible, wise, and loving decision? What approaches can the Daltons or other international agencies take to protect communities from persecution by local authorities who are threatened by community development and increased independence of their constituents? What preventive strategies can agencies develop?

G. Should the Daltons have come to Té Bouké in the first place? Why or why not?

Commentary

Té Bouké or "tired land" describes the entire island nation of Haiti as well as the village in the case. Haiti is a desperately poor country devastated by an oppressive colonial history, decades of dictatorial internal rule, violent and corrupt local governance, and agricultural patterns that have denuded the forests and depleted the land. Further suffering has come to Haiti through the military takeover which deposed a popularly elected president and the economic sanctions and other forms of intervention by the United States and the world community to restore the democratically elected government. Haiti is not unlike many other nations in the developing world facing similar dilemmas of economic justice and ecology. The strong parallels make the name Té Bouké "Legion."

Tired land and tired people are struggling for survival in the remote village of Té Bouké with the help of Haitian *animators* and overseas partners. The development workers are seeking to implement a locally designed plan to give the rural people a measure of self-sufficiency and some independence from local and international economic and political forces. The problems in Té Bouké illustrate the need to develop pastoral strategies that are influenced by concerns for economic justice and ecology from a global perspective.

The case is seen through the eyes of Tom and Marion who are European lay mission volunteers. Like every actor in the slice of life that is a case study, they bring their own history, biases, commitments, and limitations. They understand their task to be not only improving the quality of crops and life in Té Bouké but also "witnessing to their Christian faith." The tone they project is one of shared ministry with the Baptist pastor and regional Catholic priest and cultural respect for the religious traditions of Haiti. Although Tom and Marion imply that they will defer final decisions to the *animators* and the village leaders, they have already begun to analyze some of the questions raised by the farmers' request and the growing independence of the village:

• How does one deal with the tension between meeting basic human needs and being responsible for the ecological needs of the village? Added chemical fertilizer could help the land produce more maize to feed the village now, but it could also further deplete the soil and make Haiti more dependent on a nonrenewable petrochemical resource.

• How does one balance short-term and long-term development needs? The villagers and their supporters appear to be facing a choice between an immediate food surplus versus crop diversification, soil improvement, and fewer burdens for future generations.

• How does one address corrupt and often violent political pressures? Resistance to the demands of the Chief of Section and *attachés* for the sake of independence may cost lives.

• Who makes the decisions and implements strategies when there are participants with different levels of power and vulnerability? Do the village leaders decide about the fertilizer acquisition by community vote and a consensus process, or do Tom and Marion make the decision and use their position of power to simply "not succeed" in making the church connection to purchase large quantities of chemical fertilizer?

• How do the problems facing Té Bouké relate to the problems of other poor communities in the world?

Faithful and caring response to these questions calls for pastoral agents who have a broad theological understanding of the underlying issues, sensitivity to the cultural and social lives of their hosts, and awareness of the systemic and global implications of the issues.

A THEOLOGICAL CONTEXT

The crisis in agricultural life in Té Bouké may be grounded in theological questions. Whose land is it? Does the land belong to the people of Té Bouké? To their ancestors? To the Chief of Section? The Psalmist declares, "The earth is the Lord's and all that is in it, the world and all those who live in it"(Ps. 24:1 NRSV). In the language of the earliest Christian creeds, "God is the maker of heaven and earth," the ultimate purpose, provider, and proprietor of the world.

Speaking biblically, the residents of Té Bouké "lease" the land they are caring for on behalf of God. When God decrees that humankind should have "dominion" over "all the earth," God also indicates that humans are made "in the image of God" (Gen. 1:26). Just as God's creation is an expression of God's loving kindness, God's dominion of the universe is tempered by love and caring. The decisions that humans who are created "in God's image" make about the use of the earth should be shaped by the values of the creator/owner. Dominion is not a vocation of domination but one of stewardship. Human beings are charged with protecting God's good creation for the sake of the common good of all.

God's grant to humankind of a special place in the created order brings with it honor as well as responsibility. The concept of the image of God is the foundation for the understanding of the intrinsic dignity of all God's children. Every human being from the Haitian farmer to the Chief of Section has God-given worth and identity that are violated at the cost of denying God's love and the goodness of the created order. Human responsibilities are both ecological and societal. In other words, stewards of God's good creation are expected to implement God's justice and to guard the dignity of other humans as well as the integrity of creation.

JUST AND SUSTAINABLE HUMAN DEVELOPMENT

With visions of crop surplus, extra income, and a new school, the farmers of Té Bouké ask Tom and Marion to obtain a large quantity of chemical fertilizer. The desire on the part of the farmers of Té Bouké to be like the villagers in the lowlands is understandable. Aided by another development agency, the lowland farmers used tons of imported fertilizer to yield a larger maize crop and to gain extra income to build a school. How should Tom and Marion respond to the request of the people in this hill area where the soil is probably already more depleted and farming more vulnerable than in the valley? Whether the answer is ultimately "yes" or "no" after dialogue with the organizers, a responsible process of decision making will be helped by the community members thinking through some issues of development.

Basic assumptions stand behind the agricultural innovations in Té Bouké's farm co-op store, the tree planting project, and the chicken and egg nutritional initiative. These assumptions also inform an understanding of just and sustainable development that challenges the dominant notion of growth-centered development.

The aim of a growth-centered approach is rapid economic growth in order to provide jobs and capital income, and consequently raise the standard of living in poor countries. Growth in developing nations is seen to come primarily through private businesses financed by domestic savings, foreign investment, and income from exported products, usually raw materials or crops. This approach directly benefits and strengthens those already in power who have large amounts of land or access to national and international loans and foreign aid. In many poor areas of the world this approach to development has also led to large debts, depletion of natural resources, decrease in locally available food crops, and dependence on such external resources as chemical fertilizer. This growth-dominated approach has been modified in some areas to include notions of "equity" to address poverty and "adjustment" to world economic conditions. Even the promoters of the growth concentration, such as the World Bank, now acknowledge, however, that growth-centered development has done little to address extreme poverty.

Advocates for just and sustainable human development see the reduction and ultimate eradication of poverty and its consequent suffering as the primary goal of economic development. The Haitian development advisors in Té Bouké and other church partners may be helped as were the authors by the report of a Presbyterian Church (USA) task force which developed a working definition of just and sustainable human development as "the comprehensive enhancement of the quality of life for all, present and future, involving the integration of the economic, political, cultural, ecological and spiritual dimension."[1] A justice-based approach to development seeks the common good of God's creation within the limits of a fragile environment. An effective pastoral strategy for the church requires informed advocates of holistic development, not merely prophetic statements against poverty. Two of the many extremely complex issues raised by the Té Bouké farmers' request are care of the earth and dependence on technology.

Care of the Earth

Sustainable human development entails care of the earth over many generations. In Té Bouké the demands of meeting immediate basic human needs make it difficult to reject using chemical fertilizer simply because it could further deplete the soil. An immediate increase in food production is balanced against the long-term rebuilding of the earth through the tedious process of turning the grass into the soil, planting nitrogen-rich trees, and letting some land lie fallow in rotating cycles. This process is made more difficult because the survival of many families depends on use of all the land each year. It is easy to understand why the farmers see large quantities of chemical fertilizer as a solution to their poverty.

Tom fears, however, that a false sense of food security promised by the fertilizer option will further distract farmers from the long-term agenda of agricultural practices that restore the soil. Improper use of chemical fertilizers could even poison the ground-water supply. The peasant farmers and their children could eventually pay dearly for a short-term solution, just as the people of Haiti have been the victims of shortsighted policies when dictatorial leaders sacrificed the trees and soil to benefit a limited number of people. Just and sustainable development requires the protection of all the resources of the earth for the sake of equitable development for all the people. One of Tom's greatest challenges may be sharing his concerns with the farmers in a way that respects their views and widens their perspective to the past and future of the land and their nation.

Overdependence on Technology

Overdependence on technology threatens the independence and perhaps even the survival of the people of Té Bouké and thus also threatens sustainable development. Marion raises the possibility of new technological advances which could counter the negative effects of chemical fertilizers and help build the soil more rapidly and efficiently than the labor-intensive process Tom has introduced. However, if the community becomes dependent on the chemicals, and there is a crop failure due to natural causes or human failure, the farmers would neither be able to repay the loan nor purchase additional fertilizer for the next year's crops. They would begin a cycle of debt to pay for the fertilizer out of future crop sales or of greater dependence on the good will of foreign donors. This type of dependency continues the demeaning subordinate-dominant relationship of colonialism which endangers "the equal dignity and solidarity of peoples."[2]

Dependence on costly, advanced technology seldom benefits the poorest communities. The "green revolution" in India, which held great promise for solving problems of hunger, offers an example of this point. The revolution in hybrid seeds and new, more powerful fertilizers increased agricultural output, which tended to force prices down. In order to cover their costs and make a profit, growers using the new methods needed to find higher prices for their crops. They shifted from local markets to export markets. India became an exporter of grain and even began making contributions to international food relief programs. There were still hundreds of thousands of desperately poor, hungry people in India. The benefits of technology's promising advances were limited to those growers who could afford hybrid seeds and nitrogen fertilizer. The vast majority of the rural poor with small land holdings could not afford the advanced technology, and the landless poor could not afford to buy the grain for food. The failure was not in the technology itself but in overdependence on it to solve the problem of hunger.

Recall that it is a church development agency providing imported chemical fertilizer in the lowland village in Haiti. A moderate amount of carefully used chemicals can provide enormous benefits for farmers. However, the long-term costs of importing and using the fertilizer, including potential health hazards of misuse and sustained dependence on an external agency, must be carefully weighed. The commentators hope that the leaders of the church working with the lowland village have seriously considered these costs. Whether the role of the international church is in direct aid or in supporting development policies at local or international levels, church leaders must be clear about the implications of their involvement and must train pastoral agents in the complex issues of just and sustainable human development.

The Haitian *animators,* with the assistance of Tom and Marion, are seeking to implement development policies that will lead to self-sufficiency and dignity for rural farm families. They offer a potentially powerful and effective model for the international community to follow.

STRUCTURAL TRANSFORMATION

For Té Bouké to escape the cycle of poverty there needs to be transformation in the basic social and economic structure of the nation. The decision about the fertilizer is important, but other matters of justice must be addressed simultaneously if Té Bouké and similar villages of the world are to have the opportunity for self-sufficiency and independence. One of these justice issues deals with debt.

International Debt

The commentary noted some of the potential dangers to the villagers if they were unable to repay debts from imported fertilizer. On a much larger scale the debt of poor communities and nations has become a global problem encompassing the North as well as the South. One of the most devastating effects of international debt is that those who suffer most are the very poor, who have reaped little or no benefit from the loans, but who usually bear the heaviest burdens of repayment. Many nations of the South or developing world were led into patterns of debt by political and military leaders who borrowed heavily to acquire technology and to build infrastructure such as roads and dams. The borrowing agents for some nations were nonelected leaders whose corruption led to personal gain and serious mismanagement of the funds. In other poor nations, loans were made in good faith with strong encouragement from international banks and loan agencies. For many nations, regardless of the motives of the borrower, the loans brought spiraling debt rather than economic renewal. Borrowers in the 1980s were caught by falling prices in the global market for their exported products, rising interest rates, and rising costs for oil and imported and manufactured goods.

In order to earn capital to repay loans, many borrowing nations turned to massive sales of their natural resources, and they converted land once used to produce locally consumed food to produce export products. These policies directly affected the poor who were evicted from the land. Debtor nations also borrowed more money to meet interest payments. In order to continue borrowing, many poor nations were forced by the World Bank and International Monetary Fund to make structural adjustments.[3] These adjustments called for devaluing currency, modifying trade policies, and removing government price support for basic goods. Those programs "have been particularly hard on the poorest people in the poorest countries by cutting government subsidies for food and health care."[4]

Although the two largest international lending agencies have begun to revise payment policies to focus on poverty reduction, "developing countries owe more than they earn from exports in a year and carry a burden that stifles attempts to fight poverty."[5] The Third World owes an amount equal to about half its yearly income. This is true even though "some [countries] . . . have repaid significantly more than the amount they borrowed in interest and principal, but the principal remains large."[6]

Both the Old and the New Testaments admonish the faithful to "lift up the poor" and "restrain the rich." Pastoral theology must seriously search for and advocate means to reduce and finally eliminate the burden of international debt that cripples human development programs worldwide. This challenge implies that in order to minister effectively to the poor, pastoral agents must expand their knowledge of structural global economic problems and be willing to confront prophetically the "principalities and powers" which impoverish people. Of equal concern is the degree to which concerned church workers can count on the solidarity of the national and international Christian community as they seek justice.

Oppressive Local Power Structures

While small countries like Haiti are often crippled by global realities, there are local and national realities which can be equally oppressive. Powerful area authorities pose an immediate and possibly violent threat to Té Bouké's community leaders. Dérius, the Chief of Section, his *attachés,* and area business owners have been challenged by changes in the status quo that reduced their power and control. As the farmers of Té Bouké became more independent through their own farm store and loan programs, profits were reduced for local business owners and powerful people who make loans to the rural farmers. In retaliation for earlier attempts at change, two previous *animators* were forced by threats on their lives to leave the area.

Marion and Tom have become buffers between the people and the area representatives of political power and profit. If the people of Té Bouké are willing, Marion and Tom may need to be prepared to make the need for structural changes in Haiti an issue of national and international solidarity with other people of poor villages, by exposing the political and economic oppression from which the people suffer. Will the church Tom and Marion serve be as willing to be in solidarity with the village on issues of justice as they have been in providing mission funds for trees and farm supplies? Pastoral theology must include an understanding of why and how to address structural injustice which robs poor people of their dignity and denies God's love of creation.

Bishop Dom Helder Camera in his struggle for economic justice for the poor in Northeast Brazil used to quip, "When I feed the poor, they call me a saint. When I ask why the poor are hungry, they call me a communist." The same accusation was made against Father Jean-Bertrand Aristide when he was elected President of Haiti. He was deposed by the military when he began to focus his energy and postelection policies on the plight of the poor. Forces which oppress the poor and cause their suffering violate not only humanity but God's will. In searching for ways to honor God for God's compassion and gift of life, Micah asks if God will be pleased with "burnt offerings" or "thousands of rams" or even the sacrifice of his first-born child. The response is startling in its simplicity: "What does the Lord require of you but to do justice, and to love kindness, and to walk humbly with your God" (Mic. 6:6–8, selected phrases). Justice for and kindness to all of God's children is as basic as Christ's commandment to "Love your neighbor as yourself" (Matt. 22:39 NRSV).

While the scriptures offer guidelines that call the church to stand against oppressive structures and individuals, how pastoral agents should respond to the call is not at all clear. Tom and Marion, as those least likely to be seriously affected by the area's political and economic leaders, could seek to expose the oppression through articles in free and independent media outside of Haiti. They could begin a campaign to challenge European and American corporations that deal with oppressive businesses and governments. And they could seek to bring in other faith communities to stand alongside the people of Té Bouké. However, any decisions made by Tom and Marion must be agreed upon by the village people. Tom and Marion can always leave; the *animators* and villagers must stay and will suffer the consequences of any decisions to challenge directly the power and control of the Chief of Section and his supporters.

PARTICIPATION AND DECISION MAKING

Economic independence will bring increased political independence. However, just as with the use of chemical fertilizer, one must be clear about the cost. The Haitian *animators* and the people of Té Bouké who will pay the price must make the decisions.

Participation and decision making are critical areas of holistic human development. From the beginning of their development program, the *animators* operated on principles of working not only for but with the people. Small discussion groups decided on needs, goals, and plans. Love and respect for the six hundred villagers made consultation with them integral. Respect also calls for Tom and Marion to share with the residents their concerns not only about the chemical fertilizer but about long-term sustainable development.

Independence and empowerment of the community rest not only in how much the people trust the organizers, but also in how much the organizers trust the people. Marion and Tom must work within the limitations of communication and time. The test of their accompaniment of the people on the journey toward sustainable self-sufficiency may be how they continue to work with the people, even if at this juncture the decision of the people and the *animators* is not what Tom and Marion hope. The process by which the community addresses this particular question of development may be much more important than any specific decision about chemical fertilizer.

Economic justice is a right of all humankind and encompasses the material necessities required to live with dignity and the freedom to participate in the quest for the common good. All human beings also have a right to an environment adequate for their health and well-being.[7] The villagers in the tired land of Té Bouké still have hope of participating in the new heaven and new earth. Pastoral agents, whether lay or clergy, must be equipped by the seminary and the church to address the fundamental issues of holistic human development from Té Bouké to Tokyo as they follow the ethical standard to love their neighbors as themselves, which is not far from the reign of God (Mark 12:22f.).

NOTES

1. "Christian Vision and the Global Challenge: Toward Just and Sustainable Human Development," Draft Report of the Task Force on Sustainable Development, Reformed Faith, and U.S. International Economic Policy, Louisville, KY: The Presbyterian Church (USA), April, 1995, p. 115.

2. Ibid., p. 18.

3. Hilary French, "Rebuilding the World Bank," in *State of the World 1994*, Lester Brown, ed., New York: W. W. Norton, 1994, p. 172.

4. Hal Kane, "Third World Debt Still Rising," in *Vital Signs 1994: The Trends that Are Shaping Our Future*, Linda Starke, ed., New York: W. W. Norton & Company, 1994, p. 74.

5. Ibid.

6. "Christian Vision and the Global Challenge," p. 17.

7. The World Commission on Environmental Development, *Our Common Future*, New York: Oxford University Press, 1982, p. 348.

PART IV

RECONCILIATION AND PEACEMAKING

From now on, therefore, we regard no one from a human point of view; even though we once regarded Christ from a human point of view, we regard him thus no longer. Therefore, if any one is in Christ, he is a new creation; the old has passed away, behold, the new has come. All this is from God, who through Christ reconciled us to himself and gave us the ministry of reconciliation; that is, God was in Christ reconciling the world to himself, not counting their trespasses against them, and entrusting to us the message of reconciliation. So we are ambassadors for Christ, God making his appeal through us. (II Cor. 5:16–20a RSV)

A mandate for every baptized Christian is to be an agent of reconciliation. To be "in Christ" and a "new creation" calls every believer to be an ambassador for Christ. But everyone falls short of Paul's vision of reconciliation. Christians fight. Congregations fight. Sometimes Christian churches fight one another. Frequently, individuals and churches are not agents of reconciliation but agents of division, not ambassadors of Christ but of the evil one—the devil—who, in promoting sin, is the ultimate symbol of alienation from both God and neighbor.

Conflict in itself is not portrayed as evil in human history or in the biblical tradition. Like life, the Bible is full of conflict. Conflict is inevitable, necessary, and ultimately a sign of health. There is no *metanoia*, no meaningful conversion, no transformation of self or society without conflict. Seldom does "everything old" pass away and everything "become new" without holding on to the old and resisting the new. The question in the Christian community is not *whether* people disagree, but *how* they disagree. The challenge is not even how to avoid conflict, but rather how to manage it so that the energy focused on conflict can be channeled into just and healthy change.

A Chinese symbol sometimes translated as "crisis" or "conflict" is made by two characters which together mean "danger overlaid with opportunity." Admittedly, conflict can be dangerous, even life threatening, but it need not be destructive. Conflict can also bring opportunities for new life, new awareness, personal growth, and perhaps most important, justice. Without conflict the deeply entrenched economic and social institution of slavery might not have ended; without conflict women in many parts of the world would still not be able to vote. The struggle for justice is the struggle for change, and real change seldom comes without conflict. "If Christians are committed not only to peace but also to justice, we must be prepared to enter into conflict."[1]

Jesus, prophesied as "the Prince of Peace," is clear in the Beatitudes that peace-makers will be called the children of God (Matt. 5:9). Peacemaking is a calling, a vocation: empowering reconciliation with justice is a gift of God's grace. "Circumstances compel us to face the reality of conflict and find ways to make it non-combative, constructive, and where possible, reconciling."[2]

Several of the world's major religious traditions, including Judaism, Christianity, and Islam, affirm that God seeks peace and reconciliation. In Ibillin, Galilee, on the grounds of Prophet Elias College is a moving memorial composed of two curved walls facing each other; between them is a small courtyard with two benches. Inside one wall an inscription in Hebrew reads, "In remembrance of Palestinian martyrs." Inside the facing wall the inscription in Arabic reads, "In remembrance of Jewish martyrs." On top of each of the stone benches between the walls is inscribed the single word, "Listen." It seems that the only memorial in Israel that recognizes the suffering of both Jews and Palestinians is called *The Listening Post*. At its core, empowering reconciliation which leads to shalom-making is about pro-active listening. One committed to reconciliation seeks to hear what the other person says, not only with ears, but with one's heart, and body, and life.

A Ugandan pastor ("Who Are the Victims?") struggles with how to listen with his heart as well as his head to a woman who has robbed his parishioners and the German medical sisters whose hospital serves the whole community. Can the pastor hear the woman's desperation to feed her children even as he hears the fear of the sisters and their threat to leave the community? This pastor faces a test of pro-active listening and of his commitment to seek justice for all the victims of systemic violence.

In the midst of conflict, reconcilers are not asked to search scripture and tradition to find support for their own positions. Rather, "Christ invites us to seek His will through a shared exploration of the whole Gospel, though a discovery of where we have not been listening."[3] The Reverend Monica ("Should a Woman Lead the Church?") faces great resistance to her ministry of word and sacrament in her assigned parish in India, as do many women in ministry around the world. Her challenge is to discover God's will for the unity of her congregation in light of the rejection by some members of her role as teacher, preacher, and administrator of the sacraments. To become an agent of reconciliation she must listen to those who oppose her; she must feel their pain and anger as well as her own.

The church and those within it are asked by God to nurture genuine candor and Christian charity in their conflicts and dialogues. Christians are called to "speak the truth in love" but not to be so presumptive as to assume that any Christian, congregation, or church has a monopoly on holiness, grace, and truth. True *koinonia* or fellowship in God's family is rooted in the Spirit. God's gift of true *koinonia* is built by agents of reconciliation who can love and accept others as they love themselves and who are willing to assume responsibility for one another. Empowering reconciliation seeks a "mutuality in the Spirit that transcends differences."[4]

Koinonia is seriously threatened when differences between cultural and religious values clash. In the midst of grief over a young woman's death in childbirth ("Lobola for a Dead Woman") a confrontation between members of a family and a congregation in Zimbabwe threatens to destroy the unity of the church and community. Finding mutuality in the Spirit will call for careful listening, honesty, and openness to God's voice in unexpected places.

Prayer can unite the head and heart if the one who is praying truly listens for God's presence. Dependence on prayer can be more life-giving than dependence on the church's doctrines, traditions, or even on its community. Prayer seeks a "way through which believers respond to the working of God's love."[5] The following prayer was written by a group of pastors and lay leaders who were developing guidelines for constructive conflict resolution in the context of the church. It offers a fitting entry to three cases which reveal not only the dangers of conflict but opportunities for reconciliation and renewal.

PRAYER FOR CONFLICT RESOLUTION

God, you have called your people to a ministry of reconciliation.
When we find ourselves in places of conflict, may we discern your will
in a world for which Christ gave his life.

In our deliberations with those with whom we differ,
keep our hearts, minds and spirits open to your speaking
through each person and in each circumstance.

May we honor and respect each other,
remembering that you dwell among us and within us,
as you are a listener to every conversation.

May your Spirit reign in all that we do to overcome alienation
as we prepare ourselves to gather around that table
of justice and peace in the life yet to be our joy.
As your Son made us one in baptism,
may we strive to cherish diversity
as we are prodded to become one fold.
This we pray through
Jesus Christ, our Reconciler. AMEN.[6]

NOTES

1. Ron Kraybill, *Peaceskills: A Manual for Community Mediators*, Cape Town: Centre for Conflict Resolution, 1994, p. 2.

2. Working Group of the Massachusetts Council of Churches, *Constructive Conflict in Ecumenical Contexts*, Boston, MA: Massachusetts Council of Churches, 1996, p. 3.

3. Ibid., p. 9.

4. Ibid., p. 7.

5. Ibid.

6. Ibid., p. 14.

WHO ARE THE VICTIMS?

Case

The Reverend Yelasa, rector of Nima parish, left the police station at Miti where he had just visited Bigara. In the course of their conversation, Yelasa had learned that Bigara was a mother of three children.

It had been three weeks since five thugs, including Bigara, had robbed the homes of three of Yelasa's parishioners. Yelasa's parish was in a college community of faculty families and two hundred students. Nima was twenty kilometers from Miti, the nearest town.

As Yelasa traveled back to the college community, he thought about the tremendous changes that had taken place in Uganda in recent years. For more than twenty-five years the country had endured a series of military governments which brought political upheaval and economic destruction to his beautiful homeland. Some 70,000 Asians, the backbone of the merchant community, were expelled. More than 300,000 Ugandans died; the people of entire villages were massacred. Warring factions of undisciplined soldiers fought for power and terrorized local communities. Reconstruction did not begin until 1986 after Yoweri Museveni came to power. He ruled with a tight hand and began to put a stop to the bribery, to encourage cultural diversity, to rebuild the markets and roads, and to bring security back to the villages. However, the years of war had left deep scars. Recovery was slow, and some areas were still threatened by heavily armed bandits.

Although Nima is not far from Miti, it is quite isolated. There is electricity at the college and the neighboring areas because of the tea estates. The main road had recently been repaired. However, the telephone wires, which were broken down fourteen years ago during the war, had still not been repaired.

Yelasa's thoughts returned to Bigara. The memories of the night they first met were still fresh in his mind. Yelasa had become a victim himself when he was on a pastoral visit at the home of the principal of the college. Five young people, including a woman, had surrounded him and the family of the principal. The thugs held guns which had been hidden in a leather bag.

At first the thugs made a pretense of being sick and said they needed to see the German medical sisters who would be able to help them. They insisted that Yelasa take them to the house where the sisters lived. One of the thugs suddenly zipped open the leather bag, and all at once each of the thugs held a gun. They surrounded the group, their guns cocked. Yelasa realized he would risk his life if he did not yield to their demand. One of the principal's family said, "We shall take you to the German sisters."

Yelasa and the others walked with their hands raised. Yelasa was ordered to call the sisters out once they reached the house. This order caused Yelasa a lot of anxiety. On reaching the house he knocked hard at the window pane but did not speak. After the third knock a sister inside switched on the lights. She was ordered by the thugs to open the door, which she did promptly. The two thugs who entered the house demanded dollars and Deutsche marks. The other thugs kept an eye on the hostages who were made to lie prostrate on the floor. The thugs kept saying, "Reverend, pray for us." Several times they asked, "Reverend, are you praying for us?" As Yelasa lay there, he recalled, he had interceded for the thugs as well as for the hostages. Since the thugs were not organized, one would say one thing and another something different. This situation saved Yelasa from saying a public prayer.

As they left, the thugs locked the hostages and the sisters in one room. Kalla, a member of the college community, was kidnapped and forced to show the robbers the way to the capital, Kampala. They drove away in a Suzuki car stolen from Mr. Galiwo, a nearby neighbor. Yelasa later learned that some kilometers from Kampala the thugs had stopped the car and ordered Kalla out. He was picked up by members of a local defense unit who took him to the nearest police station to make a statement. An hour later it was reported to the same police station that the car had been found abandoned near Malago. The following day the robbery was reported to the area police in Miti who went to the college community to see for themselves where the robberies had occurred.

After their traumatic experience, the German sisters said that unless they could be sure of security they would withdraw their services. Yelasa, who was also the vice-chairman of the dispensary board, and the dispensary administrator decided to convene an emergency meeting of church and community leaders to discuss the security situation and find a solution to the problem. The resistance council (RC) chairmen in neighboring communities were also invited to the meeting. The gravity of the situation called for the involvement of the local administrative authorities as well. The withdrawal of the German sisters would have grave implications for the health services offered at the dispensary which had served the surrounding area for ten years.

Three weeks later, before the leaders could gather, and just as the community was beginning to recover from the robberies, the thugs returned. This time money and other valuable property were taken from two other houses within the college community, and the dispensary ambulance was stolen.

An hour after the thugs had driven off, the incident was reported to the area police station, and immediate action was taken by the patrol unit. Later that same night the thugs were intercepted on Gayaza Road, and the ambulance was recovered. One of the group was shot dead, and two narrowly escaped during the encounter with the police. Bigara was captured and jailed in Miti.

The two robbery incidents and his visit to Bigara left Yelasa perplexed and uncertain how to respond. The principal of the college, who was also a member of the dispensary board, and his family still lived in fear after the ordeal. The German sisters were likely to withdraw their services. Mr. Galiwo and his wife Lena whose car was stolen no longer lived in their house for security reasons. In fact, the whole college community was living in fear. People from the communities that benefited from the services of the dispensary were angry with the robbers for disrupting community life. The continuing presence of the dispensary, which had brought essential services to the area, was seriously threatened.

While Yelasa was trying to give pastoral care to those who were affected by the events of the past few weeks, he was also concerned about Bigara and the economic conditions in his country, which may have contributed to her life of crime. Although there had been great improvement, the country was still struggling with poverty. The government had agreed to a program of structural adjustment in order to secure international loans, but this program led to retrenchment for people from all sectors, including the army.

As a result of the years of war, there were also too many guns in the country. Although it was now legal only for the security forces and local defense staff to carry guns, there were not enough police to stop illegal gun ownership.

Amidst such a predicament the recurrent question in the Reverend Yelasa's mind is, "How can a pastor minister in such a situation?"

Teaching Note

I. Goals

This case lends itself well to teaching about reconciliation in a violent situation, where many people are victims and many may be called to serve as agents of healing. This teaching note focuses on reaching the following goals:

A. To better understand the impact of war on social order.

B. To explore the role of the church in the aftermath of war.

C. To discern practical and theological implications of reconciliation within a disintegrated society.

II. Case Context

It is important for discussion participants to familiarize themselves with the situation in an African country that has just been at war and with the resulting dislocation of society. In Uganda during the time of the case, unemployment has increased and its consequences have affected more than the working people. Survival has become the preoccupation of most people in the country. The societal infrastructure has broken down, telephone and postal services are interrupted, public transportation has ground to a halt.

The breakdown of the social order and the paralysis that follows also affect the institutions of civil society. Norms and value systems crumble, leaving the concern for survival to create its own systems of values and norms that are not shared communally and for which there are no enforcing institutions. Crime becomes endemic. Even mothers resort to crime to survive. Since this phenomenon is not particularly African, it is incumbent on the facilitator to help participants see this situation as common to many countries of the world. The participants will derive more value from the case if they can internationalize the sense of desperation and chaos. The discussion leader may be able to draw on insights of participants who have experienced war or been in a community after a major disaster. Spend enough time on this analysis of the situation to facilitate a good understanding of it.

III. Actors in the Case

In teaching the case the facilitator should lead participants to characterize the main actor and distinguish him from the many secondary actors in the case. The dilemma in this case revolves around Yelasa and his ministry. However, to understand Yelasa's dilemma, it may be important to discuss some of the other characters first.

A. The international community is present with the missionary group of German sisters and their medical contribution. The sisters represent both an institution and also concerned people in their home country. What are the implications of their presence for people recovering from war? Why are the sisters considering returning home? What is the effect on the people in Nima and the surrounding communities of the sisters' debate about leaving? Yelasa serves on the dispensary board; how might the sisters' reactions affect Yelasa's response to Bigara?

B. Discuss briefly the community of Nima in which Yelasa ministers. Ask participants if they lived in Nima or were a part of the college community, what they would be most concerned about. Responses may include the isolation and lack of phone lines to contact police when there are problems, the threatened loss of the dispensary, fear of additional robberies, and anger at the thieves who terrorized them.

C. What does Yelasa know about Bigara? What are Bigara's primary concerns?

D. Identify who Yelasa is and ask participants to try to imagine themselves in his role as pastor to the college community. Trace his feelings through the case chronologically. His emotional reactions during the robbery, for example, probably ranged from fear and humiliation to possibly guilt and anger. What were his feelings when the German sisters said they were considering leaving? When he went to visit Bigara? On his drive back to the community?

Ask what Yelasa is most concerned about at the end of the case. Be alert to conflicts in interests.

IV. Options for Response

A teaching approach to help participants become more involved in the discussion is a "group role play." The case facilitator or a preselected participant assumes the role of Yelasa and sits with the participants in a circle. Tell participants to be themselves and respond from their own perspectives. Yelasa has come to a group of pastors to ask for their advice. What should he do to begin the healing in his community? What are some concrete steps he can take? How can he help Bigara? Yelasa should press participants for reasons to support their suggestions. If participants disagree with one another in suggested approaches, he should encourage them to be in dialogue with one another about their differences.

In his role Yelasa should feel free to draw on the concerns the group suggested earlier. He may want to remind his advisors that he sees the postwar situation to have created conditions in which a person such as Bigara may have no option but to engage in criminal activities for the survival of her children. On the other hand, the German sisters have come from a distance to help people such as Bigara and her countrymen and -women. The pastor's role on the dispensary board may make it difficult for him to choose openly to support a criminal like Bigara who has terrorized the sisters.

Yelasa should also ask which theological resources are available to him, both to inform him and motivate his decisions. What community resources are available to help heal the community and bring reconciliation between people who are anxious and in pain?

Commentary

CASE CONTEXT

The setting for this case is a village, far from the capital and deep inside Uganda, where communication infrastructure is not as good as that near or inside cities. The African country of Uganda has just been through a long war with the resulting dislocation of society. Uganda has had two recent periods of war and suffering. First was war during the Idi Amin period. Suffering and death engulfed Uganda when the army that was directly under the control of Amin indiscriminately slaughtered innocent Ugandans in every part of the country. Lawlessness prevailed, and guns were available everywhere as citizens started arming themselves, first for self-defense and later for offense. Whoever had a gun had the law in his or her hands and did not have to respect legal institutions, since the ruler himself, Idi Amin, did not respect the rule of law. Neither did his army. Police stations were still scattered around the country, but they were ineffective because they did not have vehicles, telephone service, or personnel who could deal effectively with the high tide of crime and lawlessness. Those policemen who were still at their posts were demoralized by the lawlessness of the head of state and his army.

The second phase in the history of the case setting is that of the struggle against Idi Amin, his overthrow, and the series of civilian governments that succeeded him and then each other in rapid succession. These governments inherited a country with an economy shattered by the war and by the expulsion of thousands of people of Asian descent, primarily Indian, who had controlled a large share of the economy. There was a grave shortage of basic necessities everywhere in Uganda. Unemployment was rife, and almost everybody, including decent and law-abiding citizens, struggled for survival through various means, some of which were criminal. Government leaders had to retrain and reorganize government institutions and law enforcement agencies. Many recruits came from hardened elements of the society, who had learned to survive by any means. Above all, the leaders had to work hard to restore respect for the law among the Ugandan people.

In that country at that time, unemployment increased dramatically, and the consequences affected more than the working people. Survival became the preoccupation of every able-bodied person. The societal infrastructure that includes roads, telephones, and postal services had broken down, and public transport ground to a halt. The breakdown of the social order, and the paralysis that always follows, affects the institutions of civil society. Norms and value systems crumble, leaving concern for survival to create its own systems of values and norms that are not shared communally and therefore have no institutions to enforce them. Crime becomes the order of the day. In that situation, even mothers, such as Bigara, resort to crime as a means of survival.

In this dark and gloomy situation, a small number of people still cared for human life and respected the imperatives of the gospel. Among them were the churches, church personnel, and lay Christians. They represented a ray of hope in that hopeless situation. It is always through the agency of such people that people of good will in other parts of the world rally to the assistance of suffering people. Uganda was no exception.

The general and widespread breakdown of law and the collapse of traditional systems of values and norms are neither Ugandan nor African phenomena. They are common to many countries throughout the world. In many major cities, large-scale unemployment and poverty have led to the disintegration of the social fabric. Families fall apart, and children end up in the streets where they learn the art of survival through hard criminal ways. They resort to theft and sometimes end up selling drugs in the streets. The parents lose their homes because they cannot pay the rent. They have to sleep in the parks and subways. Young people form gangs and engage in violent conflicts with other gangs and with the police, who have their hands full attempting to combat crime. More often than not, the police are engaged in a losing battle against crime and drug abuse. The politicians talk, but their measures are often ineffective.

It is also common in many African countries to have teams of nongovernmental organizations from different parts of the world offering various forms of assistance. Such assistants operate in, among other fields, education, agriculture, and health as is the case in Uganda. Generally, such foreigners are visible; they are the nonpoor who live in groups and constitute easy and unprotected targets for thieves and violent elements. The missionary group of German sisters in this case study is such a group.

CONCERNS

"Who Are the Victims?" introduces a conflict between groups of people who ought not to be opposed to one another. The pastor, the missionary group of sisters, and other victims of the armed robbery are on one side, and Bigara and her children are on the other. These people are not natural opponents. They are all responding urgently to the predicament of a country in turmoil and its desperate people. They are responding to structural problems that society faces.

The German sisters are driven by Christian faith and compassion to go to Uganda and assist in preserving life by dispensing medicines. They are efficient, and their work is appreciated by the people of the area. Bigara, especially, is driven by love of her hungry children to a state of desperation, because she cannot find a job and money to buy food for them. The state and its agencies are not able to help her and her children. There is no compassionate neighbor for her. The state organizations come down on the side of the German sisters and not on the side of desperate people such as Bigara. Arresting and imprisoning her is a choice, made by the state and implemented by the police, on the side of those who are not desperate against the desperate ones. The official position will, of course, be that the police maintain law and order. But what is the value of law and order for a person such as Bigara if the law cannot ensure that her children have food on the table?

The second pertinent issue is the threatened withdrawal of the German sisters and the problems that threat raises. If the sisters were to withdraw, they would leave a very desperate situation in which more lives would be at risk, including those of Bigara and her children. Bigara does not realize this fact; if she did, it would be a secondary issue, the first being the feeding of her children. On the other hand, the question of security for compassionate German sisters cannot be overlooked. The humiliation and ill treatment of the sisters, as well as of the Reverend Yelasa and the other residents, were traumatizing. The sisters' departure would also affect the credibility of the Christian faith. People would ask questions about the strength of a faith that does not want to take risks and instead only operates under conditions of peace and comfort. What kind of discipleship is this in which the follower wants to be safer than the master? A situation such as that in Uganda calls for a suffering discipleship and a preparedness to suffer for other human beings. This is the situation the German sisters and the Reverend Yelasa face.

A third issue concerns personal responsibility and the necessity of repentance on the part of Bigara. It cannot be enough to regard her as a victim of circumstances, because she is not alone in this predicament. There are other mothers who may be in equally desperate situations, but who do not engage in criminal activities. She made a choice to engage in such activities and has to accept personal responsibility. Her repentance before she is forgiven is a legitimate expectation. Reconciliation, which seems to be what Yelasa will have to aim for, cannot be cheap; it has to be in response to genuine repentance and a promise to lead a positive life in which the lives of other human beings are also valued. There cannot be forgiveness without justice. Only by including justice will peaceful coexistence for all parties involved in this tragedy be ensured.

THEOLOGICAL ISSUES

There is no doubt that the German missionary community is moved to a concrete medical mission as a form of discipleship aimed at affirming common humanity. In other words, their acts of love for their neighbors in need have to be made concrete, and that is what they are doing (Matt. 25:31–46). The problem is the limits and conditionality of that love. The extent of their commitment when their own lives are in danger will say a lot about their understanding of their following of the suffering Christ. The behavior and response of these German sisters reflect their Christology. A true discipleship that chooses the side of those who are suffering without anyone, especially the powerful, on their side will inevitably lead to the cross. The depth of such discipleship or its climax lies in its preparedness to suffer and give away one's life for the sake of the suffering neighbor. It should not be a preparedness to suffer conditionally, that is, suffering only for those who appreciate the help they receive while not including deviants such as Bigara.

If reconciliation is the fundamental goal of discipleship in situations where society and community have been destroyed, it should not demand repentance as a condition. Through Jesus, God offers reconciliation with those who are not worthy of it. Such reconciliation can lead to conversion of the recipient when the culprit is brought into the community of love and experiences the warmth of the love of the members of that community. That life of love will call up a new life in the one who is being loved. Such acceptance and forgiveness should not be made conditional upon conversion and confession of transgressions. It should be borne in mind that humanity's sins were atoned for, unconditionally, when humanity did not deserve such atonement.

The relation between Yelasa and Bigara also raises theological questions. In dealing with her, Yelasa has to choose the side of the oppressed as God did in divine condescension (Kenosis-Phil. 2:6, 7). Yelasa has to choose the side that God chose and see as well as understand the world from that perspective to help Bigara. God did not wait for human beings to improve or for their situation to be better before hurrying to redeem them and the world. God came at the worst of times, at the worst state of the world, and descended to the lowest among us: to those who have no one on their side. That is the depth of God's solidarity, and that should be the basis of Yelasa's choice, even if it may be misunderstood and may alienate many people who are not guided by the same theology. His actions may also be politically risky and may be seen by the police as encouraging repetition of such crimes as the one committed by Bigara.

STRATEGIES AND TACTICS FOR RECONCILIATION

Yelasa is in a difficult situation in this case due first to his own emotional involvement in the matter. He was humiliated and harassed by the robbery and ended up in emotional turmoil. But those problems should not delay or stop him from carrying out his pastoral responsibilities. He should not forget that the desperate situation in Uganda has made everyone a victim. It has divided people and turned them against one another when they ought to be clinging to one another more firmly because they need one another even more. Yelasa will need to engage in the search for reconciliation between the parties and hope for his own healing in the process. He will need to show compassion for all the parties concerned without being lenient toward the wrong that has been done. To do so, he has to create conditions that will facilitate mutual acceptance and the participation of all parties in this situation.

The first and most difficult task is dealing with the imprisonment of Bigara and the condition of her children. Should Yelasa strive to secure her release to enable her to look after her children and to get her to participate in a process of reconciliation? He should. He will also need to secure the participation of the victimized and traumatized community in the effort to rehabilitate Bigara. In a situation where there is a breakdown of law and order, it might be that such a release from prison will convey the wrong impression to those who are inclined toward lawlessness. It is possible that they will interpret Bigara's release as an indication that crime pays. However, it may also be that when they see Bigara changing and leading a positive life, they will think differently. If so, Yelasa has to convince the missionary sisters that helping Bigara will make a contribution to their security in the long run. Should Yelasa not strive to promote the rule of law by refraining from interceding for her? That will be the question from the police and other hard-liners in the community. He has to convince them that his faith advocates winning the sinners over by love, not punishment.

If an opportunity is created for Bigara and the German sisters to meet again, Yelasa has to deal with whether it is advisable to bring them together without preparing both parties for such a meeting. He has to consider the psychological impact of bringing the victims in contact with their captor and find a way to reduce the negative impact by discussing the matter with each party beforehand. He should bring fellow pastors and lay leaders into that effort and keep them as part of the solution.

SHOULD A WOMAN
LEAD THE CHURCH?

Case

As the Reverend Monica was preparing for next Sunday's Holy Communion service, an incident from the previous Sunday came into her mind. She reflected on her leadership role on Women's Sunday and began to think about the agony she had experienced during her brief period of ordained ministry.

After her graduation from theological college in Southern India, Monica was appointed to work as warden in a home for physically handicapped children. She was also asked to assist the Reverend Francis, pastor of a local urban church of four hundred families. At that time Monica was not ordained. Not being ordained had never hindered her from participation in church activities. She took an active part in Sunday school and vacation Bible school, and she was president of the women's fellowship.

Even though she was convinced of women's right to ordination and felt called by God to ministry, she had not fought for ordination. She knew that because ordination of women was a controversial issue in the church, some of the local churches did not readily accept it. But then the church council passed a resolution to ordain women, and Monica was one of the eight women chosen to be ordained.

Women's Sunday, a regular feature of the year, drew closer. Mrs. Savithramma, secretary of the women's fellowship of Wesley Church, requested that Monica conduct a special Sunday service on Women's Sunday. It was a privilege for the Reverend Monica to conduct a service on this day especially because she was now ordained as deacon. She carefully prepared the order of worship involving office holders and other active members of the women's fellowship.

On Women's Sunday, the Reverend Monica arrived at the church at the correct time and entered into the altar with the Reverend Francis. Hymns, lyrics, lessons, prayers, and sermon were fitting to the occasion. As the service was going on, Mr. Anand rose from his seat to show his resentment to the Reverend Monica. He disturbed the congregation by taking four members with him out of the church. But the Reverend Monica managed to continue with her order of service.

An anonymous pamphlet agitating against the Reverend Monica and with several demands was distributed to the homes of all church members. The demands were that the Reverend Monica was not to conduct the service from the altar, preach from the pulpit, nor celebrate and assist in sacraments.

A short time afterwards, it came to the notice of the parish committee that Mr. Sundar had formed a group to support the Reverend Monica. The formation of the two groups destroyed the previous unity and peace of the church.

Mr. Anand's group and Mr. Sundar's group were very angry with each other. Mr. Anand was saying, "Wesley Church is one hundred years old with a Methodist background. No women ever preached from the pulpit nor entered into the altar. The Reverend Monica is the only person to break the tradition." He based his position on I Corinthians 11:2ff. "I commend you because you remember me in everything and maintain the traditions even as I have delivered them to you. But I want you to understand that the head of every man is Christ, the head of a woman is her husband, and the head of Christ is God." Some members of this group said, "If she comes to the altar again, we will pull her out."

Mr. Sundar's group was in support of the Reverend Monica, saying that she is a trained theological graduate. In the early church there were deacons ministering. Members of this group quoted from Romans 16:1. "I commend to you our sister Phoebe, a deaconess of the church at Cenchreae, that you may receive her in the Lord as befits the saints, and help her in whatever she may require from you, for she has been a helper of many and of myself as well." They also noted that Lutheran and Methodist churches in the state, which until recently had only men pastors, now had ordained women posted for pastoral work. Even some of the ex-Anglican congregations of the Church of South India had also accepted women as their presbyters. "Both men and women are partners in the mission of the Lord, and women cannot be discriminated against." Almost all the members of the women's fellowship supported Mr. Sundar's views.

The Reverend Francis was carefully watching the developments. He tried to arrange a meeting, inviting both groups to enlighten one another about women's ordination. Mr. Anand's group and his supporters refused to attend the meeting.

The Reverend Monica felt the bitterness of the situation in the church and began to think about whether she should take part in the life and activities of the church or request the Bishop to relieve her of pastoral work. The Reverend Monica also recalled the Reverend Francis' assurance that he would support her in whatever she decided to do.

Teaching Note

Empowerment of people through the various programs of the church will result in these people seeking their rightful place to make their own contributions. Empowerment leads to changes in the existing order and patterns of the church. Changes are not always welcomed with open arms, especially by those who are affected by the change. Changes are difficult and seldom take place without some resistance. This case provides an opportunity to discuss a situation calling for change and to consider responsible ways to manage resistance.

I. Goals

Some of the goals which can be pursued through discussion of this case are listed below.

A. To bring awareness about the discrimination against women in the church. While many Christian communities are willing to accept the leadership of women in the secular realm, they have difficulty accepting women in church leadership, especially as ordained ministers. This resistance to women in leadership is sometimes based on cultural understandings of the spiritual office and sometimes on interpretations of the Bible. The outcome of such a response is discrimination against women, which the authors believe cannot be supported by the gospel.

B. To explore the historical background of certain practices and traditions in the Protestant Church. The knowledge of the interaction between gospel and culture in the early formation of the Christian community is a great asset for discerning the way forward for Christians living in the sociocultural realities of today.

C. To discern the role of the church vis-à-vis the social and cultural ethos of the society in which believers live. Christian community is not only a spiritual and religious community, it is also a social community. As a social community it is subject to social and cultural conditions. Christians are continually challenged to discern whether the church is a captive community or an agent of change. Because it is extremely difficult to be objective about the culture in which one is immersed, discussing the elements of captivity and liberation in each social and cultural community is a significant challenge.

D. To evaluate theological views on ordination and leadership in the church. Protestant Church order is understood as a human creation. It is created so that the life of the community is organized for better utilization of its resources and for smoothly carrying out its vision. As a human creation, all the church orders including ordination are subject to review from time to time, so that the community is able to discern the best order for its witness and service in the world.

II. Background Information

The Indian Constitution enshrines equal rights for all its citizens—male and female. In the organized sectors women are paid the same salaries and enjoy the same job privileges and have access to trade unions and cultural societies. But in large sections of India women are relegated to secondary positions and as such are subject to various forms of oppression. They are also discriminated against in the organized religions.

Women's ordination is now carried out in mainline Protestant denominations such as the Church of South India, Church of North India, and the Lutheran and Methodist Churches. But the number of women who are ordained and in ministry is small. There are congregations and Christians who are still not comfortable accepting women as their ministers.

III. Case Discussion

A. Issues

The issues suggested below are not exhaustive. The discussion leader should be attentive to other issues that may surface. Concentration on one or two issues, depending on the primary energy and interest of the group, will facilitate in-depth probing into the matter.

> Insecurity resulting from changes
> Ordination—preparation and qualification
> Interpretation of the Bible
> Holistic Christian education programs
> Conflict resolution and management
> Authority in the Church—teachings and disciplines
> Role of culture and the liberating message of the gospel
> Meaning of sacraments in the Protestant tradition.

B. Persons

Identification of and with the persons in this case may help move the discussion from an objective to a subjective analysis. This step is important because the response of many people to the issue of women's ordination may be emotional and based on unexamined cultural assumptions. Their response may also be based on thoughtful reflection about the issue. Some people will be very sympathetic to Monica, while others will be supportive of Anand. It is important to give space for participants to express their honest reactions to the positions of various case characters. Openness on the part of the discussion leader will offer participants a safe place to ask their real questions, to examine their assumptions, and to be able to hear different understandings.

After identifying the primary people in the case, consider what feelings they may have.

Monica: theologically trained, ordained, experienced, bitter, and anxious

Francis: supportive of Monica, committed to the ministry of women, cautious in his actions

Anand: resistant to Monica's new role, resentful about women's ordination, capable of convincing people

Sundar: open to women's ordination, prepared to counter the resistance of Anand and his supporters

Congregation members: divided and uncertain. Although several women have been vocal in their support of Monica, it is possible that many other members of the congregation are undecided about her role and would be open to being convinced by either side of the debate.

IV. Alternatives and Resources

Suggest that participants put themselves into the role of a colleague to whom both Monica and Francis have come for advice. What are the most important factors to consider in determining responsible alternatives? Consider, for example, their need to minister to persons who have taken opposing positions while maintaining integrity about their own positions. Discuss the strengths and weaknesses of alternative responses. On what biblical and theological understandings are alternatives based?

Thoughtful and supportive colleagues are an important resource when one is faced with a serious problem. What other resources would be helpful to Monica and Francis?

V. Conclusion

Close by asking participants to name one important insight or learning from the discussion that may influence their ministry.

Commentary

In the Protestant tradition ordination is a church rite held in high esteem by churches and communities. Traditionally men with physical disabilities were not accepted for the ordained ministry of the church. The assumption was that this office required a "perfect" and "mature" person. Not very long ago several Western Christian missionaries and mission board officials were hesitant to ordain converts from Asia and Africa and others in the mission fields. The converts were considered deficient in one way or another.

Some of these assumptions, though untested, have become part of church tradition and practice. Some have even crept into church rules, regulations, and constitutions. Therefore, some Christians still hold to the belief that only men can be ordained for ministry. They feel that men are physically, intellectually, spiritually, and morally superior to women. Women are not considered for ordination because of the presumed deficiency. In some instances where Christians live in a religiously pluralistic situation, this church practice has been reinforced by the culture and other religions. The secular mass media gave a lot of attention to the issue of women's ordination when the Church of England decided to ordain women for the priesthood in 1994. This action was preceded by decades of debates and several setbacks. Today, even though women are being ordained in increasing numbers in Protestant churches, women's ordination is still an issue in many cases. This case study highlights one such struggle.

SITUATION OF THE CASE

The relatively united and peaceful Wesley congregation faces division within its fold as two opposing groups are formed. One group is under the leadership of Mr. Anand who wishes to defend the age-old tradition of the church and the teachings in the Bible as he and his supporters understand them. The other group, led by Mr. Sundar, is committed to implementing needed changes that they see as upheld in the Bible. It is not clear how long Francis and Monica have been ministering in the Wesley congregation. Apparently, earlier clergy did not raise the matter of women's ordination, nor did they discuss scriptural support for it. That could be the reason a part of the congregation seems to be unprepared for Monica's role and disturbed by it.

The Reverend Francis faces a dilemma. On the one hand, like any pastor, he does not wish to see division in his congregation. On the other hand, as a pastor and leader, he feels the need to support Monica as she struggles for a just cause.

In India, the setting of the case, the larger community still practices discrimination against women, but the system is not so closed that women cannot exercise any rights. Women are in leadership roles in politics and other public spheres. Indira Gandhi was a powerful prime minister, and several other women have had significant political roles in India. Indian women serve in the government bureaucracy, help in maintaining law and order as police personnel, are pilots, and are portrayed as heroines in the mass media because of their achievements in sports. In the dominant Hindu religious tradition, goddesses are common. In fact, the Hindu patrons of both knowledge and wealth are goddesses. In modern day Hinduism the women gurus (teachers) are as popular as male gurus, depending on their capacity to win followers and control a religious network. Even though Indian Christians live in such an environment, where Christianity is concerned, they keep women away from leadership in the church. This exclusion is partly because of the type of Christianity they have been taught, partly because of the attitudes they developed in regard to the teachings in the scriptures, and also partly because of the threat of losing male domination as already witnessed in the secular realm.

Further, there are still strong cultural and social factors in Indian society that promote the status quo insofar as male/female relationships are concerned and that have a firm grip on the social thinking of the masses. For example, the traditional dramas and plays performed in India are primarily based on Indian mythology and often depict women in subservient roles. In popular religiosity, worship of goddesses is common, but such honor and respect is normally not expressed in daily practice. In general, the movies, a prime entertainment medium in India, project the age-old role of women as obedient and faithful beings. The practice of dowry paid to a groom's family by the bride's family, the stigma attached to widows, and the economic dependence of women are great hindrances to the liberation of women. These cultural factors have a strong impact on Christians in India as in any other community, and the use of specific scriptures that portray women as subservient are why, in spite of the active role of women in every other aspect of church life, men still dominate church leadership. But changes in society, especially in urban areas, and changes in Christian education about the equality of women are contributing to the changes in the role of women in churches. This case is a good example of such change.

ISSUES

Tradition

Tradition is valuable to any community. No human being is an undiscovered and isolated island. All members of the human race are connected to each other and, in any given time or place, to the whole of nature. Certain basic beliefs and values which have been transmitted to them from previous generations keep humans together in a community.

Among the many parts of any tradition are the place and role of the genders and of persons from different generations. Each society's attachment to tradition depends upon historical circumstances and the society's capacity to absorb changes, to start new traditions, and to let go of some aspects inherited from the past. No tradition remains static, but custodians of any society will have a large say regarding changes. They can initiate or resist change depending on the power they possess and their ability to exercise it.

The issue in the Wesley congregation deals with who has the final say regarding tradition. Both disputing groups feel they are right. In a way, the case exposes the problem with teaching authority in the Protestant tradition. Protestants are not very good at accepting doctrinal formulations simply because a board, committee, council, assembly, or synod votes on it. During periods of conflict, the final criterion usually upheld is the Protestant principle of *sola scriptura*. Teaching authority on the interpretation of the scripture in the Protestant tradition is not so rigid as in some other Christian traditions. An issue in this case is the differing interpretations of the scriptures.

Interpretation of the Scriptures

The Protestant tradition has universally accepted the canons of the Old Testament (Hebrew Bible) and the New Testament, sixty-six and twenty-two books, as the prime standard of faith. But an undisciplined and unguided freedom to interpret these books is not always very healthy. Differing interpretations have resulted in the emergence of numerous denominations, groups, and sects. Anand bases his position on I Corinthians 11:2ff., in which Paul suggests that his followers keep the tradition he delivered to the Christians in Corinth, which speaks of women being subservient to men. Sundar, on the other hand, quotes Romans 16:1 to prove that there were women deacons in the Apostolic Church; Paul wrote,

"I commend to you our sister Phoebe, a deaconess of the church at Cenchreae, that you may welcome her in the Lord as befits the saints."

In such circumstances, who decides which is the correct interpretation? Protestant tradition has ways of dealing with this issue. Normally, the theological commission of a church arrives at a consensus after going through a process of study and after consulting biblical experts. In the practices of some churches, even what is agreed upon by the theological commission has to be voted upon democratically by the larger body as one major step in doctrinal and other faith matters. But in this case the denomination of which Anand and Sundar are a part has already made an appropriate decision on the ordination of women for ministry and implemented that decision by ordaining eight women. The issue here is convincing the group that supports Anand's interpretation about the appropriateness of the church's stand on women's ordination. Much of this convincing is left to Christian education and nurturing in which churches are not always successful. Those Christians who fail to be convinced sometimes break away to preserve what they feel is important. Both Francis and Monica are concerned about this possibility. Francis contemplates solving the problem by calling for a meeting of both groups. Monica considers whether she should totally withdraw, and she struggles with making a decision.

Decision-making Process

Protestant denominations in general have followed a democratic way of arriving at a decision. Of course, there is a scriptural basis for such a procedure: the Jerusalem council in the Apostolic period (Acts 15:1–21) and the great ecumenical councils of the undivided church such as the Councils of Nicaea in 325, Constantinople in 381, Ephesus in 431, and Chalcedon in 451. But the democratic way of dealing through councils can also mean the imposition of the majority opinion on the minority. One can argue that the democratic way may not be the way to settle the matter of faith.

Christian life is not primarily organized as a democratic model of making decisions for the whole community. As an institution the church is governed by state regulations for religious and voluntary organizations, but the Christian community is centered around loving concern, a spirit of reconciliation, and mutual empowerment. Because of these emphases, concern for the belief and faith of fellow Christians is highlighted by Paul in his letter to the Corinthians. He advises that those who are strong in faith should care for the feelings and faith of those who are not strong in their convictions. The issue in the church at Corinth is the

Christian attitude toward eating meat offered as sacrifice. Paul sees no spiritual damage in eating such meat. "All things are lawful, but not all things build up" (I Cor. 10:23). For him "the earth is the Lord's, and everything in it" (I Cor. 10:26). But Paul pleads that if such behavior might be offensive, one should be sensitive to the feelings and the needs of others. "Let no one seek his own good, but the good of his neighbor" (I Cor. 10:24). Believers have to exercise their freedom with caution. Paul is not urging that one should compromise the truth, but that one should explore the possibility of achieving the goal without too many disturbances to one's neighbor. Francis and Monica are facing this dilemma. As ministers they do not wish to upset the congregation, while at the same time they wish to uphold the truth.

The overall uplifting of women and their liberation is another issue in the case. The Christian community in India, although part of the larger human community, is about three percent of the total population and is bound to be shaped by the forces operating in the larger society. Because of the strong grip of certain traditional practices, cultural and social constraints, and economic disparities, the status of women has not changed very much even in the late twentieth century. Women are still in bondage. The traditional belief is that a female is under the protection of her father until she gets married, under the protection of her husband once she is married, and under the protection of her son when she becomes a widow. Some Christians take shelter under such traditions and practices on the grounds that they wish to be faithful to their culture. But those arguments cannot be sustained if the cultural traditions contradict the spirit of the gospel. Christians in every community are called to expose and challenge those forces that are dehumanizing. Their call is to be pioneers in liberation as the salt and the light of the earth (Matt. 5:13–16).

The call to be salt and light on earth demands that while Christians have to be particularly concerned about the health of community life in the church, they should be equally committed to fighting against those evils in the larger society that are bound to have an effect on Christians.

One of the challenges that this case poses is the issue of reconciliation and peacemaking in the church. Even though Anand and his followers are resentful and are fighting against Monica's role in the church, they are surely aware of the trend in society to move toward more gender-inclusiveness. Whether they are willing to accept defeat or not, they are at the losing end of this disagreement. The challenge to Francis, Monica, Sundar, and their supporters is how to work out an agreeable solution so that peace and harmony is maintained and the community spirit upheld. In India and other Asian societies, people who take a public stand do not wish to lose face under any circumstances. So in situations of conflict, losing or saving face can become more of a major issue than the original cause of the community conflict. Therefore, the issue is how Anand and his sympathizers can be won over to the cause of peace and led into the path of reconciliation without being made to feel defeated or brushed aside as trouble makers. If the church is true to its calling to be a community of reconciliation and an agent of change, it is important that the church be equally responsible toward those who dissent and those who are ready to collaborate.

ALTERNATIVES AND RESOURCES

There are at least four viable approaches for facing the challenge posed in the case: transferring the Reverend Monica to a new congregation; intervention by the leadership of the denomination; systematic studying of the Bible and Christian education; working toward reconciliation and/or taking disciplinary action against Anand and his followers.

One of the easiest options for the denomination or church leadership in a crisis such as this is to solve the problem by transferring the Reverend Monica to a new congregation or engaging her in some other church activities while waiting for an appropriate time to place her in another congregation. While such an act can bring the conflict to an end, it could hurt Monica, Francis, and the members of their congregation who are expressing solidarity with Monica. Furthermore, transferring Monica will project the view that she is weak and does not have the leadership ability to manage conflictual situations. Occasionally such drastic steps are taken by the church leadership, but they should be a last resort and done with much care and attention to the feelings of all the parties involved. Resources available in the secular world on conflict management in an institutional setting will be of help here. Lay persons in the congregation who are well informed and gifted in conflict management could be approached for guidance.

Second, if the congregation comes to understand that the church hierarchy supports Monica, it will certainly help at least that section of the people in the congregation who normally trust the judgment of the leadership. The social status and moral authority of the church hierarchy may make the congregation more receptive. Someone from the church hierarchy, such as the bishop, moderator, or president, who is experienced in the ministry of the church in a variety of situations and has risen to the leadership level, may be able to explain and give assurance to congregation members that, from the larger perspective of the church, they have to cope with this new situation of women ordained to the ministry. This person will be in a position to give information about the global view among Christians on the matter of women's ordination and how this vision has been implemented in various churches around the world. As early as 1853 the Congregational Church at South Butler, New York had ordained Antoinette L. Brown for ministry.[1] Today, some churches have also consecrated women to the office of bishop. Such information properly presented by the church leadership could help the situation.

Third, systematic Bible study and Christian education involving a cross-section of the congregation is necessary for dealing with the issue at hand and other theological issues that may arise in the future. Both conflicting parties have cited single references from the Bible. Such an approach is not healthy. The Bible should be approached holistically. The congregation needs help from the ministers and the Christian education committee or the education department of the denomination to do so.

Most churches have women's fellowships and women's departments and will be able to supply materials dealing with the issue of the role and place of women in the church and society today. Monica, as president of the women's fellowship, would be knowledgeable about the resource materials that are available. Many countries have national councils of churches that organize discussions from ecumenical perspectives, sharing one another's experiences with mutual challenges they face in the contemporary world. Materials from such studies by the National Council of Churches, the All Africa Conference of Churches, the Christian Conference of Asia, and the World Council of Churches are of immense help in Christian nurturing. One such study which involved discussion many churches found helpful is the World Council of Churches document on *Baptism, Eucharist and Ministry (BEM)*, 1982. Since the other church in the neighborhood, the Anglican Church, ordains women, a joint program of study might also be explored to expose members of the Wesley Church to women in ordained ministry.

At Wesley Church, leadership for the opposing groups comes from men. It is important that women and youth as well as men are involved in the Bible study and Christian education program. If, in the process of study, men find that the women and youth think differently from them, they may be more convinced to heed the changing views and opinions of the time. Of course, there is the danger that some men may become more adamant if they are challenged not only by other men but also by women and youth.

Fourth, a concrete effort should be made to arrive at a peaceful solution through reconciliation. Every community is bound to experience crisis, but the test of the community's health is its ability to handle the crisis and utilize it as a source for evaluating its community life and strengthening its fellowship without forcing anyone to lose integrity. The resources of the gospel can be of immense help: the plea for humility; loving one's neighbor as oneself; and sacrifice for the sake of others. One of the gifts the Indian community, as well as several others, can offer is the role of elders (in age and wisdom) in reconciliation and peacemaking. Traditionally elders enjoy a special place in Indian society. They are seen as those without serious personal vested interests. Their long life experience gives them certain authority, and if the situation demands, they can stand as moral guarantors or guardians when someone else is hesitant to take an action which is not part of the tradition. The Reverend Francis could explore the possibility of elders intervening to create a situation of confidence among the parties in conflict.

The elders could also remind the Wesley congregation that without a certain level of harmony and cooperation among the members of the church, their ministry and mission will be severely affected and that the image of the church as an agent of reconciliation will be tarnished if Christians are not able to put into practice what they constantly preach. Professional help in conflict management can also be explored as another source for achieving an amicable solution.

Disciplinary action is an alternative which could be utilized. Although disciplinary action may not carry much weight in the late twentieth century, that option sometimes helps the situation, especially if theological argument is used only as camouflage. Sometimes in theological disputes in the church it is the nontheological factors which have a prominent role. In Anand's case, careful study should be made about whether issues of class, caste, linguistics, and regional feelings are at play. If so, while reconciliatory methods should be explored first, the use of disciplinary action should not be ruled out. Besides being a faith community, the church is also a human institution and needs to be governed by certain rules, regulations, and commonly agreed-upon goals. If some members deliberately disrupt those rules, regulations, and goals, they should be disciplined for the sake of the larger community.

NOTE

1. Jane Dempsey Douglass, "Glimpses of Reformed Women Leaders from Our History," *Walk My Sister: The Ordination of Women, Reformed Perspectives*, Ursel Rosenhäger and Sarah Stephens, eds., Geneva: WARC, 1993, p. 107.

LOBOLA FOR A DEAD WOMAN

Case

A fortnight was almost over. Chipo's body still lay in the mortuary while the wrangle for payment of lobola for her continued.[1] The Reverend Manatsa was concerned that Itai might be even more distraught now than when his wife had died.

The Reverend Manatsa, pastor of Rugare Methodist Church, explained the situation to the church elders whom he had called to a meeting. He wanted them to help him identify the best approach to resolving the dispute between Chipo's and Itai's families. Both families were members of his congregation. Mr. Roorayi, Chipo's father, demanded that lobola be paid for his deceased daughter before he could join Itai's father, Mr. Tabaiwa, and his family in performing the burial ritual. The amount he wanted, Z$16,000 (approximately U.S. $2,000) plus a heifer for Chipo's mother, was considered a very high lobola.

Chipo had become pregnant while doing A-levels at Goromonzi High School. At eighteen Chipo had grown into a well-respected girl in the school and had been appointed head girl in charge of the girls' hostels. News of her pregnancy was a shock to the whole school. According to school regulations she had to leave immediately. She went to Itai, her boyfriend and father of the expected baby. Itai was well known to Chipo's aunt, Mrs. Marara, who advised Itai to have his family prepare lobola and to marry Chipo as soon as possible. Meanwhile Chipo would stay with her aunt. Itai agreed with his family on the importance of lobola.

When Itai's family came to discuss lobola, Mr. Roorayi refused to consider the marriage proposal. His refusal was based on his belief that since the families were of the same clan (held the same totem or extended family names), they were related. Marriage into the same clan is regarded as incest. Chipo and Itai were not happy with this argument. They felt that the relationship was quite distant and would not constitute incest at all. They decided to marry anyway. Since both Chipo and Itai were over eighteen years old, according to Zimbabwe's Age of Maturity Act they could enter into legal contracts without their parents' consent. Bolstered by this legal provision, they had their marriage solemnized by a court magistrate.

The new couple lived together very happily for six months in an apartment in the city. Many of Itai's friends admired the couple's good life. Itai, a chief accountant with United Bottlers, was well paid and had a beautiful company car. Although Itai was from a poor family and had not worked long enough to have saved much money, at the age of twenty-five he was making a good salary of Z$32,000 (U.S. $4,000) per year.

Itai and Chipo knew they were not welcome in Chipo's family home, but on weekends they occasionally traveled the twenty kilometers outside the city to visit Itai's family. However, every visit was filled with nearly visible tension, because Itai's parents regarded the couple as rebels and feared that there would be serious repercussions if the marriage dispute was not resolved. Mr. Tabaiwa was also worried that the child would arrive before the ritual of *masungiro*.[2] Although he and his wife no longer followed this practice, Tabaiwa knew that it was important to the Roorayi family.

Shortly before Chipo's baby was due, an examination at the prenatal clinic indicated a sharp rise in her blood pressure. The doctor recommended a Caesarean section. Chipo was admitted immediately because her condition was critical. The following day Itai and his mother sat apprehensively waiting for the operation's results. Finally, they were summoned into the doctor's office where they were told of Chipo's death. The doctor confessed that he was not able to control her blood pressure, but he was able to save their baby boy.

When his wife gave him the news, Mr. Tabaiwa said that his fears had been realized. Chipo had died before the customary procedures for marriage had been settled. Despite his anxiety, Mr. Tabaiwa sent one of his brothers to inform Mr. Roorayi of his daughter's death.

Upon receiving the news, Roorayi seemed to lose his senses for a while. He paced back and forth in the house talking to himself. "Chipo was the most brilliant of my seven children. We expected her to study medicine at the university after her A-levels. Then she got pregnant. We tried to use customary beliefs to stop the marriage, but she went ahead and married this Tabaiwa boy without my consent. Now she is dead. My ancestral spirits have punished her. How shall I bear all this? I am broken. . . ."

Turning to Mr. Tabaiwa's brother, Mr. Roorayi said, "No one from my family will come to perform burial rituals until lobola for my daughter is paid in full." With these words he left the room. The messenger understood the importance of the reference to ancestors and reported Mr. Roorayi's words to Mr. Tabaiwa. Mr. Roorayi believed that one's family includes both the living and the dead. Neither incest nor ignoring traditional practices was acceptable to either his living family or his ancestors. In addition, because Chipo and Itai had not followed traditional practices, she had never actually become part of the Tabaiwa family. Chipo's spirit could not rest without a proper burial which must include members of her whole family.

Meanwhile, friends and relatives had already begun to gather at Mr. Tabaiwa's small home for Chipo's funeral. Many of Mr. Tabaiwa's extended family members traveled from great distances for the funeral. Members of Rugare Methodist Church joined the mourners and brought food. They also helped with cooking and serving food to all the people gathered there. The proper time for the funeral was as soon as the family had gathered, usually in three or four days. But the first week turned into a second. The Reverend Manatsa came to the Tabaiwa home every evening to conduct services. During the day he visited the Roorayi home to try to persuade them to join the funeral and to consider settling the lobola issue after the burial. He felt his efforts were fruitless, as Mr. Roorayi remained adamant about his demands.

The Reverend Manatsa told the elders how worried he was about Itai, who had hoped to give his wife a decent burial. Now he was faced with this dilemma. Itai did not understand why Chipo's parents should demand lobola now that she was dead, yet had refused it when she was alive. He also did not understand why the church did not go ahead and bury Chipo if her parents continued to be stubborn. The Reverend Manatsa was also worried about the funeral expenses which increased each day and seemed to weigh heavily on the Tabaiwa family. This expense was in addition to the high lobola demand and the implications of a large debt for Itai should he decide to marry again.

After sharing his concerns with the church elders, the Reverend Manatsa waited for their suggestions.

NOTES

1. Although colloquially called "bride price," lobola is not considered payment for a bride but a symbol of the groom's family's recognition of the bride's worth. At the time of marriage the family of the bride brings gifts (*roora*) to the groom's family. These practices help establish strong ties between the two families. The custom of lobola is deeply ingrained in southern African culture. Traditionally, lobola was given in cattle, goats, or sheep with each animal having symbolic significance. However, as families have become less agrarian and rural and increasingly urban, various animals given as lobola have taken on monetary value.

2. Also known as *ukudliswa amasi*. The slaughter of a cow (a goat in some communities) unifies the ancestors of the husband and wife before the birth of their child, which comes from the union of the two families.

Teaching Note

I. Goals

There are a number of avenues to approach this case. Its inclusion in the section on Reconciliation and Peacemaking, however, prompts using the case to focus on conflict resolution. Consequently, the goals of this teaching note are to help participants recognize some basic skills which are effective in resolving family and community conflicts.

   A. To analyze the situation;

   B. To identify primary parties and stakeholders in a dispute;

   C. To distinguish between a party's position and his or her needs or interests;

   D. To consider distinctive factors in the mediator's role;

   E. To raise the importance of process in reaching mutually agreeable, sustainable resolutions.

   This basic approach to conflict-handling skills can be applied to any of the cases in this section. A facilitator who wishes to address the goals stated above would be best served by having participants read the commentary after case discussion rather than before.

II. Case Context

The case offers background information for international readers regarding southern African concepts of clan, lobola, and traditional burial practices. Ascertain from participants if there is sufficient understanding of lobola and concepts of African family relationships to grasp distinctive cultural implications of the case. It may be helpful for the facilitator to supply additional descriptive material on these topics or glean fuller descriptions from any African participants.

   Further Questions: What additional factors seem relevant for understanding the setting of the case? Consider the signs that Itai has moved away from traditional values as well as the rural lifestyle of his family: his and Chipo's life in the city and the distance from their families; their choice of Western law and the court system over traditional family laws; their friends' understanding of good life; Itai's insistence that the church proceed with the funeral without Chipo's family.

   Ask participants to identify factors in the case which are similar to family and church conflicts in their own setting and not tied to the cultural context of southern Africa. Participants may raise issues of generational differences, problems of communication, the fact that the pastor seems caught between disputing parties in his congregation, and the apparent inability of disputing parties to comprehend the other's viewpoints.

III. Parties and Stakeholders, Positions and Interests

A. Identify the obvious parties in the dispute (Itai and Chipo's father Mr. Roorayi) and identify their apparent positions in the conflict. (Mr. Roorayi: "Pay lobola or my family will not go to the burial"; Itai: "The church must bury my wife even if the stubborn Roorayi family refuses to attend.")

B. A basic mediation principle is, "Ignore position and focus on needs and interests." Consider the interests which underlie these positions. What are Mr. Roorayi's feelings and deeper concerns? Some might be a sense of betrayal and rejection by his daughter; grief about her death; concern that traditional values are acknowledged and honored and that his ancestors' spirits and the spirit of his daughter are reconciled with one another and with the living. In what ways might the demand for high lobola be an instrument of justice or restitution? The high lobola being demanded may also indicate that he feels vindictive, but there is no clear evidence in the case to either support or discount this possibility.

What are Itai's feelings and deeper concerns? Some might be grief over the loss of his wife and mother of his child; anxiety and possibly guilt about the escalating cost of the funeral for his family; fear of his and his family's inability to pay the high lobola; confusion about traditional values; perhaps anxiety about extended absence from work which may jeopardize his job.

Mr. Tabaiwa may be considered a party to the conflict, but he has not expressed a clear position. He and his family, especially his brother or brothers who would negotiate any lobola, will probably play a role in resolution of the conflict. What might be his feelings and deeper concerns?

C. Identify the stakeholders in the conflict—those who may not be directly involved but who have strong interest in the outcome. These would include the church elders, members of the congregation, and extended family members. What might be their primary concerns? What are the implications of the conflict for the church? for the wider community in which the Roorayi and Tabaiwa families live?

IV. Role of the Peacemaker

The Reverend Manatsa has assumed the role of a mediator and shuttle diplomat moving between the Roorayi and Tabaiwa homes. To help parties reach their own mutually agreed-upon resolution, a mediator must remain fair and impartial. What evidence is there that the pastor is responding to Mr. Roorayi's concerns? Is there evidence that the Reverend Manatsa may be partial to Itai's position? What are the pastor's primary interests? Are there ways in which he may have become a party to the conflict?

Is the Reverend Manatsa the best person to help mediate the conflict? Why or why not?

V. Process and Outcome

If parties in conflict do not trust the process of resolution, they will not usually trust the results of that process. The Reverend Manatsa does not seem to have been successful with his role as a shuttle diplomat. What are the advantages and disadvantages of his decision to turn to his elders for advice?

Ask participants to assume the role of a church elder and offer advice to the pastor. Which approaches could best respond to the real needs and interests of the parties and stakeholders in the dispute? What process might be most acceptable? Ask discussion participants to be concrete and give their rationale for suggestions.

VI. Resources of Grace

What biblical and theological images might be resources to peacemakers in confession, forgiveness, justice, reconciliation, and restitution for the individuals, families, and communities in this dispute? What might help heal the past and repair relationships for the future?

Prayer can be a powerful resource of God's grace. In this situation what should the pastor, elders, and others pray for?

Ask participants to relate this conflict in Zimbabwe to pastoral issues in their own communities.

What kind of training do pastors and lay leaders need to handle conflict more effectively?

Commentary

"Blessed are the peacemakers, for they will be called children of God" (Matt. 5:9 NRSV).

The Reverend Manatsa finds himself in a difficult situation, caught between a grieving husband and a distraught father. He is also caught in a painful generational conflict which has the potential of dividing his congregation and perhaps the community. He faces critical decisions about how best to respond as a pastor and a peacemaker.

Components of his response must be culture-specific as he addresses issues of lobola and family relationships as traditionally understood in southern Africa. However, there are also general and perhaps universal principles and basic skills of conflict resolution which may be useful as the Reverend Manatsa seeks peace between the two families and in the community.

THE ROLE OF CULTURE IN PEACEMAKING

In many cultures peace, often viewed as absence of conflict, is produced by decisions made by persons or structures having strong authority. This decision-making process is often the one followed by courts and judges or by kings and chiefs who may listen to various sides of a conflict and declare their decision. In some parts of the world, religious leaders have this kind of authority. In other communities peace is built through consensus. This commentary will take the position that both lay persons and clergy in Christian ministry, although they may have been granted strong authoritarian power by their communities, are able to facilitate effective, sustained reconciliation between individuals, families, and communities through a process of face-to-face dialogue in which parties to the conflict can reach mutually beneficial agreements. This process seeks to honor individual needs and self-worth as people in conflict are called to assume mutual responsibility for decisions. For many Christians this type of peacemaking is based on an understanding that Christ's model of authority is not built on power, but on wisdom, compassion, and sacrificial love which bridges all cultures.

The importance of cultural similarities and differences is relevant to this case in another way. The case presents issues of cultural misunderstanding even on the part of people with the same linguistic and geographical background. Statements in the case imply that Itai has little or no understanding of Mr. Roorayi's perspective. Everyone views the world from his or her own unique perspective, which usually develops from a long history of personal experiences. Mr. Roorayi's understanding of the connections between the living and the dead, for example, and his strong commitment to traditional values have shaped his world view and consequently his strong stance on lobola. Itai's perceptions of reality have been shaped by urban values of success and by trust in a European court system and in a market economy as represented by United Bottlers.

Anyone entering the situation as a peacemaker does not need to agree with Mr. Roorayi, Itai, or any other parties in the conflict, but he or she must communicate sensitivity and understanding of their perspectives. For peace to be sustained between the parties, there may also need to be some acknowledgment and mutual understanding of the perspectives that have led to the conflict.

ATTITUDES ABOUT CONFLICT

Christ's powerful model of a ministry of healing and forgiveness and His commandment to love one's neighbor as oneself repeatedly call disciples to a ministry of reconciliation between persons and with God. The biblical mandate calling Christians to a "ministry of reconciliation" is also strong and clear in Paul's Second Letter to the Corinthians (5:18) and to the Ephesians (4:1–3). Clergy and lay leaders, however, often assume they have failed when conflicts arise. Consequently, they may respond to conflict situations with avoidance or denial. The pastor and other members of the Rugare congregation were surely aware of the dispute between the Roorayi and Tabaiwa families as soon as Chipo dropped out of school and left with Itai for the city with no traditional marriage. There is no indication that the pastor or other church leaders came to either party before Chipo's death and before positions hardened.

The strong biblical call for reconciliation implies that conflict is natural and to be expected within the human community. The promise of redemption opens the way for viewing conflict as a path to growth and new possibilities. If conflict can be viewed in this way, persons of faith may be freed to envision the creative possibilities of conflict resolution. When Itai's family's offer of lobola was initially refused, Itai and Chipo rebelled and turned to the court system, rejecting traditional values with a tremendous affront to her family. An African scholar has suggested that if Itai's uncles had returned to Mr. Roorayi after his first refusal and offered "damages" for Chipo's pregnancy before discussing lobola, they may have been successful, and the bitter dispute between the families might have been avoided.

PRINCIPLES OF CONFLICT RESOLUTION

While persons of faith have a clear calling to be involved in reconciliation and often have excellent intuitive gifts to guide their path, they may be assisted by some basic principles of third-party mediation and conflict resolution.

1. Shift Attention from Positions to Needs and Interests

Both Mr. Roorayi and Itai have taken strong positions. Mr. Roorayi insists that no family members will attend the funeral unless lobola is paid in full. Itai insists that the church must bury Chipo without her parents if they are too stubborn to attend. As long as these positions are maintained, there is little chance of a peaceful resolution between the families.

Hard positions such as these are often the result of pressure and defensiveness. They are also the result of what Ron Kraybill, Director of Research for the Centre for Conflict Resolution in Cape Town, refers to as "unmet identity needs."

> "Identity needs" might be described as a deep drive to be recognized and acknowledged as beings of dignity and worth. Regardless of station or circumstances, all people experience powerful needs to be included, respected, recognized, and involved by the people who are important to them and in the decisions integral to their lives. These are not merely wishes or desires. They are needs in the sense that people cannot function constructively in society unless they are met.[1]

An effective way for a peacemaker to proceed when parties are locked into hard positions can be to shift attention away from the positions they have taken and focus on discovering critical underlying issues. Mr. Roorayi may be convinced not only that his daughter died as punishment for abandoning traditional values, but that her spirit will never rest until proper restitution is made. He may feel responsibility for her death because he did not accept lobola when it was offered. He may also be in grief and denial about his daughter's death. Mr. Roorayi's sense of self-worth as a father was seriously threatened by Chipo and Itai's rejection of traditional values. His sense of identity may be threatened by the encroachment of Western values from the nearby urban area. Whether Mr. Roorayi's motives for demanding a high lobola for his daughter stem from grief, a sense of appeasing his ancestors, or punishment of Itai and his family for "stealing" his daughter, understanding his motives may be a key to reaching a peaceful resolution.

The Reverend Manatsa conveys to his elders concern for Itai's grief over Chipo's death and the financial burden of the prolonged funeral process on the Tabaiwa family, but he does not seem to have probed further into other possible interests. Although Itai's father expressed deep concerns about the couple not following accepted cultural marriage patterns, Itai gives no indication of any feeling of responsibility for the situation. To what extent is Itai's pressure on the church to bury his wife motivated by a desire for the church to justify to himself and perhaps to the community his decision to marry Chipo without her family's consent? Once Chipo is buried, there will also be much less pressure on the Tabaiwa family to give lobola for Chipo. Is Itai deeply worried about his job or his family's ability to make arrangements for lobola? Greater understanding of the pressures on Itai may lead to discovering creative options for resolution.

Agreements which are not mutually beneficial and do not recognize the needs of the parties will not be maintained by the party or parties that feel slighted. One of the most important roles a mediator or peacemaker may play is to help discover and clarify the often unstated, deeply rooted interests and needs of parties to a conflict. This process is greatly assisted by the peacemaker's taking time to listen with genuine interest and asking open-ended, thoughtful questions.

The peacemaker must also be fair in his or her treatment of the parties. In relating the situation to his elders, the pastor expresses more than once his deep concern for Itai's state of mind, but he does not seem to express the same concern for Mr. Roorayi, who may be expressing his grief in different ways. Peacemakers also need to examine their own interests and motives, particularly if these might block the process of resolution.

2. Identify the Stakeholders

Stakeholders are those persons who may not be so visible or vocal as the parties in a conflict but who are deeply interested in the outcome and often have an impact on the resolution process. Evidence in the case suggests that many members of the church are supporting the Tabaiwa family by bringing food and helping to cook for the gathered relatives. Yet there also appears to be pressure to honor the traditional burial practices and wait for the Roorayi family to come to the burial. Otherwise the church and the Reverend Manatsa would have proceeded with the funeral as soon as Mr. Tabaiwa's relatives had gathered. There are also uncles in both families who are very influential in southern African family decision making who may not belong to the church but who may well be taking sides in the conflict. It may be crucial to involve them in the resolution process.

3. Clarify the Role of the Peacemaker

As noted above, the Reverend Manatsa has assumed the role of mediator, and he is clear that he has not been successful. However, he does not appear to have looked at his own motives as a mediator in this situation. Historically there has been pressure on many Christian mission churches to interpret respect for one's ancestors as idol worship and supernatural witchcraft. In many cultures the church has also emphasized the importance of modernization and moving away from traditional patterns, which not only hold people back from joining contemporary society but are viewed as violations of human worth and dignity and as contrary to the scriptures. For example, many church bodies have taken stands against female circumcision and for the ordination of women clergy. Both stances are often counter to traditional societies. Although the reader does not have clear evidence in this situation, the Reverend Manatsa may need to examine his own theological position in regard to Mr. Roorayi's beliefs. While a good mediator may not agree with a party's beliefs, he or she must be able to listen fairly and communicate genuine understanding of the views of all parties. Unexamined presuppositions held by a mediator may block this process.

Equally as important as the skills and objectivity a mediator brings to reaching a sustainable, mutually beneficial resolution to a conflict is the fact that a mediator or peacemaker must not ultimately assume responsibility for the decision. As the Reverend Manatsa describes the situation, he has assumed responsibility for resolving the conflict and seems to have accepted Itai's demand that the church should solve the problem. In some ways the pastor has become a party as well as a stakeholder in the dispute. An effective, long-term solution can be reached only when the parties and not the mediator assume ownership for the resolution.

An effective peacemaker must assess whether he or she is the best person to mediate in a given situation. The Reverend Manatsa's role as peacemaker should lead him to be open to many alternatives and to seek the best person or persons to mediate the dispute. It may well be that one of the elders, an older brother, or respected traditional leaders of the community who are not part of the church can best play the role of healer. Manatsa's decision to consult his elders is an important step toward finding the right person or persons and the best process for resolution.

4. Recognize That Process May Be More Important Than Outcome

If the parties involved do not trust the process of reconciliation and resolution, they will not trust the results of that process. If Mr. Roorayi is pressured by the pastor or the church elders, who may use their authority to force a resolution, his bitterness could bring about a deep division in the congregation or even in the wider community. He may draw on the support of others in the church or community who feel that traditional values and the worth and dignity of those who hold them are being rejected by the church. In the same way, if Itai feels slighted or ignored and does not feel that he and his family are part of the decision-making process, not only his family but other young people who are moving to the urban areas may feel rejected by the church.

In giving their wise counsel, the elders need to be open to creative suggestions such as consulting with both families to discover which mediator or mediators would be most acceptable. They need to consider how the parties could best be involved so they can listen to and understand one another and become full participants in the decisions that are reached. In many African settings it would be appropriate to call on the uncles or family spokespersons who were first engaged in the offer of lobola. It may also be critical for the elders to consider issues of justice, whether traditional or contemporary, for the persons involved.

In discerning the most responsible and effective process for reaching reconciliation and resolution, the church elders must remind the pastor and themselves of the powerful resources of God's grace. In the biblical tradition, one of the principles of reconciliation is that it is God who is the Reconciler and not humankind. "(Christ) is our Peace . . . (He) has broken down the dividing wall . . . of hostility between us" (Eph. 2:14 NRSV). The resources of God's grace are those resources of prayer, the gifts of confession and forgiveness, and faith in the promise that God acts between and among God's children to bring healing and wholeness. The elders may need to discuss what they should pray for and to ask which process will allow the families not only to listen to one another but to hear each other's pain. Faith in God's promise of redemption opens parties and peacemakers to unexpected possibilities of God's presence in the midst of human community. Faith in God's forgiveness and acceptance also frees peacemakers from the unbearable weight of responsibility in those times when their careful and prayerful role does not bear fruit.

NOTE

1. Ron Kraybill, *Conflict and the RDP: A Primer on Process-Centered Development*, Cape Town: Centre for Conflict Resolution, 1995.

PART V

CARING FOR HUMAN NEEDS

Christian life is life in community, and the search for better community is central to the work of Christian ministry. Community life requires the members of the community to respect each other's opinions and views, but also demands acceptance of each other's being and life. Genuine community is more than just mutual acceptance and respect. Its members share their lives with each other, give attention to each other, and care for each other, especially in time of need.

Caring for human needs is central to pastoral ministry. Concern for human life involves more than sympathy and empathy. It requires compassion. In his ministry Jesus frequently showed this very attitude and feeling. "When he saw the crowds, he had compassion on them, because they were harassed and helpless, like sheep without a shepherd" (Matt. 9:36 NIV). One day when Jesus was going out of Jericho, two blind men were sitting by the roadside. When they heard that Jesus was passing by, they shouted for mercy and asked Jesus to give them their sight. "Jesus had compassion on them and touched their eyes. Immediately they received their sight and followed him" (Matt. 20:34 NIV). Indeed, God is full of compassion. James wrote, "As you know, we consider blessed those who have persevered. You have heard of Job's perseverance and have seen what the Lord finally brought about. The Lord is full of compassion and mercy" (James 5:11 NIV).

"Tony, we need you to help us build a sense of community. There are some good people here, but everyone just stays to himself or herself," said Jason Boyd, the Director of the Waverly Residence. Here is the challenge that confronts Tony Herrera in the case "They Still Call Me 'Stinky,'" the first of the three cases in this section that addresses the issue of caring for human needs.

Tony Herrera, a second-year theology student, was to work at the residence as an intern for the academic term. "And let them get to know you . . . as a minister of the gospel of Jesus Christ," said Jason. This second charge from Jason may be even more difficult for Tony to accomplish than building community. Waverly Residence provides housing for the working poor, mostly unskilled laborers; many are recovering from alcohol or drug addictions, a few have criminal records, and some have AIDS. How does Tony bring the presence of the church into the residence? How would he manage to let people know him as "a minister of the gospel of Jesus Christ"? The first Waverly resident Tony meets is Alicia Jones, who has full-blown AIDS. How can he help Alicia? The dilemma Tony faces is not only how can he help Alicia, but also how can he help the residents of Waverly to grow as a community.

The commentary on this case sheds light on how to deal with persons who have AIDS or who are HIV-positive, their families, and their churches or communities. "In order to minister effectively pastoral agents need to be equipped not only with wisdom and compassion, but with accurate information." A caring person must be able to distinguish between rumors and facts about AIDS. There is a tendency among persons infected with HIV to hide or deny their illness as long as possible because of shame or fear of being persecuted. Society often blames persons who are HIV-positive for their illness. Many are ostracized or rejected by their communities, their churches, and even their own families. These rejections are generally due to fear based on incorrect information or misunderstanding of the nature of AIDS and how the virus is transmitted.

Caring for human needs does not always involve people with physical illness. People who suffer psychological or mental disturbances also need love and caring, understanding and compassion. It is not uncommon for chronic physical sickness to degenerate into psychological or mental illness as well. On the other hand, psychological or emotional impairment may cause people to suffer psychosomatically. In both of these situations, human or interpersonal relations are directly affected. Spiritual malaise, although it may also affect human or interpersonal relations, does so only indirectly and subtly, and may not be so obvious or transparent. A need for spiritual healing is at the heart of the second of the three cases in this section, "We Want to Be Baptized."

It is understandable that Slamet and Suharti, siblings who have been living as husband and wife with their four children, feel morally and socially guilty. They know that they were sinful, but they were helpless to change the situation. Therefore, they have suffered spiritually for a long time. They yearn for spiritual comfort. As Muslims, although they did not practice their religion devoutly, they did not see any possibility of spiritual comfort or well-being. They attended Sunday worship services in a local church for about a year. They learned that joining the Christian church through baptism would enable them to receive forgiveness of their sins; they believed this act was the answer to their longing. However, as the case describes, the issue for the church leaders was not that simple.

Churches have different views with regard to their rites and rituals. Different churches have different traditions. Some churches hold traditions very strictly. Others are more flexible. Churches also have different theological teachings or doctrines. Most of the churches, however, at least believe that baptism is one of the sacraments of the church, commanded by the head of the Church, Jesus Christ himself. This sacrament is one of the signs of salvation given by God through Jesus Christ, the Lord of the Church. Therefore these churches take baptism very seriously. Whether baptism is by sprinkling or by immersion, and whether baptism is given only to adults able to confess their faith or also to babies or children of Christian parents, these issues have historically caused schisms in the church. Some believe that the actual act of baptism cleanses persons from their sins, others believe that the act of baptism is only a sign or a symbol of the cleansing of sins.

A central issue which emerges from the case is whether persons who are not and cannot be married legally (because they are siblings), but who have been living together as a married couple may, with their children, be allowed to receive baptism in the church. The commentary suggests that in dealing with such a difficult theological issue, "It is better to have a clear biblical and ecclesial understanding of the sacraments, especially baptism." In this case the church leaders face a possible conflict between "law and grace" both of which involve caring for human needs. The church leaders as well as the readers are challenged to reflect theologically on what is the best pastoral ministry in such a situation, with real concern for the human needs of everyone involved.

The third case in this section deals with the power of tradition. A community is usually united by commonalities in language, customs, and traditions which are handed down from generation to generation. Some of the traditions are loosely held by the members of the community; others are strongly held. Strongly held traditions that most members of the community consider of high value are usually based on an understanding of divine inspiration or intervention and, thus, have a religious aspect or form a part of religious practice. A strongly held tradition is the central issue in this case. Both the conflicting parties, Mr. Eze and his son-in-law Mr. Nja, are determined to hold on to apparently conflicting convictions. For Mr.

Eze, the tradition of initiation must be maintained for his grandsons; for Mr. Nja, baptism in the church has replaced his sons' need for initiation.

The Reverend John, who has taught his congregation to refuse initiation, now must deal with a conflict that affects the unity of his church. Mr. Nja is a respected elder of his church who wants the Reverend John "to save his dignity and the unity of the church." Mr. Eze is a leader of the village council of elders, which has threatened to expel the Reverend John if he intervenes in this case.

The commentary suggests that the real issue the Reverend John confronts is about gospel and culture. "What is the role of a missionary as a carrier and representative of foreign culture and as a messenger of a universal gospel in another culture?" Therefore, this case "offers an opportunity for a review and rethinking of the appropriate approach of a missionary in his or her mission work in a foreign culture." The commentary also suggests that the case does not merely involve family level conflicts but also conflicts between "two powerful institutions," the church and the village council to which every member of the church owes allegiance.

Although the presenting issues of the case involve questions of the power of tradition, there are equally important underlying issues of social and family power held by the conflicting individuals. It is important that in such a case care and concern be given to the feelings of all parties involved. Not only Mr. Eze and Mr. Nja but also Ada, daughter of Mr. Eze and wife of Mr. Nja, are caught in the middle of the conflict as is Eke, the child who is the subject of the controversy. Ada and Eke may not be in the front line of the conflict, but they are indeed at the center of the human and interpersonal relations in this conflict. Any pastoral ministry agent must be sensitive to the needs of these persons and seek the possibility of solutions which care for the needs of all those concerned.

These three cases deal with specific situations in three countries on three different continents. However, the issues are definitely not specific to the countries nor to the continents. Similar cases can and do happen in almost all parts of the world. Our concern is to see how such issues are dealt with in their own contexts, but also to see the possibilities of wider application in other contexts.

THEY STILL CALL ME "STINKY"

Case

Tony Herrera, a second-year theology student, had gone to the Waverly Residence in January to satisfy a course requirement. He was to work at the residence eight hours a week for the academic term.

As he reported for work on his first day, Tony walked quickly along the narrow streets, trying to stay near the curb and away from dark alleys. When he finally located the building, he was surprised at how nice the residence looked. Aside from the city jail, it was the newest building in the area. Jason Boyd, director of Waverly Residence, met Tony in the lobby.

"Tony, I'm really happy you're here," Jason said. "Come on back to my office." They passed the reception desk and a small laundry. Jason's office was on the right.

Jason explained that three years of funding had been secured for the residence from government and nonprofit organizations. However, what he hoped Tony could help provide could not be purchased for any amount of funding. "Tony, we need you to help us build a sense of community. There are some good people here, but everyone just stays to himself or herself. You know what I mean? I think Waverly would be a nice place to live if the people got to know each other and learned how to treat each other like neighbors. I want you to help me start some activities which might draw our residents together."

"Okay," Tony said quietly.

"Waverly Residence," Jason continued, "addresses some of the problems of homelessness and substance abuse. Our dormitory-style housing is for the working poor—generally unskilled laborers who don't earn enough money to buy a house or rent an apartment. We have about 125 residents. Many of them are in recovery from drug and alcohol addictions. We have a few artists, a few students, a few with criminal records trying to make a fresh start."

"We also have people here with AIDS. I, myself, am HIV-positive, so I have a special relationship with these people." Tony heard little else that Jason said. Pangs of doubt and fear began in Tony's stomach. Had he ever known a person with AIDS? Could he handle such close contact with Jason, knowing that he was infected with the disease? And the only ex-convict Tony knew was his cousin Ricky, with whom he had never exchanged more than a gruff "hello." Could he even communicate with these people?

During the next few weeks, Tony's fears subsided. Jason had seemed to sense Tony's anxiety and allowed him some time to get to know the residents before asking anything else of him. "And let them get to know you," Jason said, "as a minister of the gospel of Jesus Christ."

Alicia Jones was the first Waverly resident Tony met. She had full-blown AIDS. They met in the television room. Alicia saw Tony enter and introduced herself. She had been sitting in the room alone wearing a long, quilted, pale blue robe. Her hair was braided and gathered in the back with a red rubber band. Several days later she confided to Tony that she wore the robe to help conceal the smelly, cancerous lesions which covered her dark, blotchy skin.

Alicia also told Tony that after she learned she had AIDS she had asked her sister, who lived nearby, if she could move in with her, "maybe occupy the basement, or something." She could tell that her sister felt bad about telling her "no." After all, her sister did have to consider the welfare of her two small children. Alicia said she might answer the same way if the shoe were on the other foot.

When Alicia learned that Waverly was opening, she applied immediately. She said that when she was notified that her application was approved, she could have jumped for joy if she had just a little more energy. She liked the idea of living in a communal setting. That was sixteen months ago.

Gradually Tony and Jason began to implement some of Jason's ideas for building community. They bought board games, several decks of cards, and even a ping pong table. They started "movie night" with rental videos and later expanded it to "movie weekend."

Tony was particularly concerned with activities which he thought would help the residents be more sensitive to those with AIDS. He told Alicia he had some ideas which might help others be more accepting of her. Alicia smiled.

Over the next two months, with Jason's permission, Tony put together a number of AIDS awareness programs replete with food and music and speakers. Flyers were put under the door of each Waverly resident. Local AIDS professionals were also invited. Jason helped Tony arrange for volunteer AIDS counselors to be present one night a week for discussion sessions.

The day after the last scheduled awareness program, Tony was about to leave the residence for home when he realized he had not seen Alicia. He knocked on her door several times before she answered. It was a particularly bad day for her. She had to lay her emaciated body down before she could speak.

"I wanted to find out your opinion of the last awareness program," Tony said. "But if you don't want to talk, that's okay."

Alicia shook her head, indicating that Tony should not leave. After a long pause, she finally said, "They liked the food and the music. But they still call me 'Stinky.'"

Tony felt helpless as he walked away from the Waverly Residence that night. Over and over again he heard Alicia's words, "They still call me 'Stinky.'" How could he help her?

Teaching Note

The goal of this teaching note is to help clergy, lay leaders, and congregations better understand some of the issues inherent in a growing pastoral ministry to which the church throughout the world is being called. It is also hoped that those who study and discuss the case will join Tony Herrera in his journey toward greater understanding of the needs of people living with AIDS. The most effective case discussion will call for discussion leaders to do advance study on the number of HIV/AIDS cases in their areas and to gather concrete information on local and national church, community, and government resources that offer education and direct services. The commentary following this note offers global statistics and basic information on AIDS. Discussion leaders should be knowledgeable and feel comfortable about sharing facts about AIDS transmission.

I. Context

Begin the case discussion by asking those participants who know someone who is HIV-positive or someone with AIDS to raise their hands. The discussion leader may want to state that five years earlier, many would not have raised their hands; five years in the future many more will probably know someone with AIDS. At this point the leader could share updated international figures: in 1995 there were fourteen to eighteen million people infected with the HIV virus. Unless there are dramatic shifts in human behavior, scientists at the World Health Organization predict there will be from forty to one hundred million persons infected by the year 2000.

Next, ask participants if they have any ideas about what part of the world this case study comes from. Some may suggest that the case is situated in the North because they are convinced that AIDS is a gay disease only found in North America or in Europe. In fact, the case could be located in almost any urban center in the world. The discussion leader could then ask participants to share statistics on persons directly affected by HIV in their communities and be prepared to supply additional local and national information. This information could include the fact that although AIDS is spread through homosexual and intravenous drug contact, the disease is now primarily transmitted heterosexually. Heterosexual women comprise the group with the sharpest increase in the HIV-positive population. It may be extremely important to remind participants that the virus *cannot* be transmitted through casual contact such as hugging or holding. It cannot be transmitted by eating with or sharing a toilet seat or a glass with a person who is infected.

II. Persons

Because many people will be able to identify with him, it may be easiest for those discussing this case to begin by examining the role and feelings of Tony Herrera, the young theological student attempting to minister to Alicia Jones and other residents at Waverly. What are Tony's feelings as he begins his new ministry? Ask participants what they would feel if they were in Tony's place. What are his primary concerns as he begins his ministry? What are his primary concerns at the end of the case? What accounts for the changes in Tony's perspective?

A discussion of Alicia Jones could also begin by asking what she is feeling. Ask participants to get "into her feet." What are her primary concerns? Discussion leaders are urged to help participants be aware of stereotypes and assumptions they may have about people with AIDS. The case does not state how Alicia acquired AIDS. If participants assume she is to "blame" for her illness, discuss the vulnerability of women in most societies and the variety of ways people acquire the virus that causes AIDS.

What do readers know about Jason Boyd? What may have motivated him to manage Waverly Residence? What do readers know about residents other than Alicia? What may account for their reactions to Alicia?

III. Issues

What are the primary issues raised by this case? Consider the power of assumptions and stereotypes, rejection of people with AIDS, the loneliness and fear of people who are terminally ill, and the role of the church in caring for those who are outcasts from society.

If participants were in Tony's place, what kinds of information would they need to minister to Alicia?

IV. Alternatives

What are the goals of Tony's ministry at Waverly? He has begun a program of recreation and information sharing. What goals did this program meet? How effective has it been? What other approaches might Tony adopt? Why? In what ways do Tony's goals differ from the goals that Jason Boyd has for Tony's role?

At the close of the case Tony is worried that he has not really helped Alicia. Review her feelings and concerns as identified earlier in the discussion. Does she have needs that Tony has not recognized? Are there ways that Tony could help Alicia love herself and accept her illness? What resources of God's grace could Tony and Alicia call on?

V. Role of the Church

Who helps care for people living with AIDS in the participants' communities? How are the needs of people infected with HIV different from those of people with other illnesses? Should the church help care for persons who are HIV-positive or who have AIDS? Why or why not? In what ways could churches help that are different from care provided by secular organizations?

Commentary

"As you did it not to one of the least of these, you did it not for me." (Matt. 25:45 RSV)

In two recent case teaching seminars for church workers, one in Australia and another in South Africa, the discussion leader asked how many participants knew persons who were HIV-positive (infected with the Human Immunodeficiency Virus) or who had AIDS (Acquired Immune Deficiency Syndrome). Almost three-quarters of the twenty-five persons in each group raised their hands. The case leader noted that if they had been asked that same question five years earlier, only a few people would have raised their hands. If she were to ask them in five years, almost all will know someone with AIDS.

The number of people living with AIDS has reached epidemic proportions in much of the world. A mid-1994 publication reported that another person contracts HIV, the virus that causes AIDS, every fifteen seconds.[1] According to the World Health Organization, by the year 2,000 "over 40 million men, women, and children will be HIV-positive and over 10 million adults and 5 million children will have developed full-blown AIDS."[2] Although AIDS is an affliction with global implications, ministry to persons with the virus or with AIDS is highly personal, calling for deep compassion and often sacrificial love and caring.

In order to discover how Tony Herrera or any pastoral agent can minister effectively to Alicia Jones, it may be helpful to consider some of the factors which affect the way people with AIDS are seen by those around them.

FEARS ABOUT AIDS

Fear and disdain of people who have been infected with HIV have led to their being evicted from apartment buildings, fired from employment, and banished from home and community. Much of the fear surrounding people living with AIDS is because AIDS appears to be fatal. While some people who are infected with the virus have lived for many years, there is no known cure. This factor is surely reflected in Tony's anxiety when he meets Jason Boyd, in the refusal of Alicia's sister to allow the sick woman to live in her basement, and in the avoidance of Alicia by other Waverly residents. Many diseases are much more contagious than the virus which causes AIDS, but because these illnesses are not always fatal, they are not so feared.

The fear and anxiety about AIDS are heightened because the disease was first associated with homosexual people who are shunned in many cultures. Fear and disdain were accentuated when it was learned that intravenous drug users, who are also seen as "enemies of society," transmit HIV by sharing needles.[3] Although much more is now known about how the virus spreads, early stereotypes persist. The inhibitions and taboos of many Christian communities about sexuality also inhibit open discussion and education about how AIDS is transmitted.

RUMORS AND FACTS

Ignorance of AIDS can have devastating effects. In some countries, where little is known or understood about AIDS, rumors that AIDS can be cured by having sex with children has led to thousands of young girls being raped. Another study, one conducted in Latin America, showed that "men do not consider themselves gay if they have sex with both women and men, and so they don't take precautions."[4] In other areas AIDS prevention programs have been thwarted, as some cultural and racial groups have interpreted programs which advocate abstinence or the use of condoms as a means by which a dominant culture is seeking to curb population growth in the less powerful community. In many ways equally devastating is the hysterical rejection and banishment of persons who have been identified as being HIV-positive or as having AIDS.

To minister effectively, pastoral agents need to be equipped not only with wisdom and compassion, but also with accurate information. While there is not yet a known cure for AIDS, significant research has been done on how HIV is transmitted.

Perhaps the most important fact about AIDS is that the virus *cannot* be transmitted through casual contact such as hugging or holding or eating with a person who is HIV-positive. It is not possible to become infected by sharing a telephone, a toilet seat, or a glass of water with a person who is infected. With proper precautions medical personnel, families, and friends who care for people with AIDS on a daily basis are at no risk of becoming infected with the virus.

The virus which causes AIDS has been found in human tears, breast milk, vaginal secretions, saliva, blood, and semen. The two body fluids that contain the highest concentrations and are the most likely to transmit the virus are semen and blood. Intravenous drug users who share infected syringes and inject contaminated blood directly into their systems have a high rate of infection. A sexual partner can be infected by contaminated semen ejaculated into the mouth, anus, or vagina and is particularly vulnerable when she or he has a sore or tear in the skin that allows the virus to pass into the bloodstream. The virus itself is not fatal. Rather, the virus destroys T-cells, which are part of the body's immune system that fights infection. Persons infected with HIV are considered to have AIDS when they have so few T-cells that their bodies are no longer able to ward off fatal infections.

Abstinence from sexual contact is the only sure way to avoid sexually transmitted AIDS. Latex condoms, especially those treated with a spermicide, can greatly reduce the risk of contracting the virus, although condoms may fail from 10 to 30 percent of the time in the United States and up to 60 percent of the time in developing nations, due to poor manufacturing standards, transport, and storage.[5]

For several years following the discovery of HIV, there was noticeable contamination of blood supplies in Europe and North America. More recently, added precautions and technological advances in many Western countries have contributed to significant reduction of the possibility of acquiring AIDS through blood transfusion. However, contamination of the blood supply continues to be a problem in poor countries, where adequate screening for the virus is often not possible. This is a serious problem because "more than 90 percent of recipients transfused with infected blood and or blood products have become infected."[6] In countries where the poor sell blood to commercial distributors, there is increased risk of infection through transfusion. Both sellers and buyers resist attempts to curb this practice. Some countries have been able to move away from selling blood for profit only after massive public educational programs.

BLAME THE VICTIM

Most communities do not withhold compassion for people with life-threatening diseases and do not base their response on whether or not the patient is somehow responsible for his or her illness. Lung cancer, liver disease, cholera, hepatitis, and many other human illnesses can often be traced to human behavior, but patients with these diseases are not banished from their communities. People with AIDS or who are HIV-positive are often judged responsible for their illness, regardless of how they acquired the virus; for this reason they are often excluded from love and acceptance by their families, church, and wider community.

Tragic results of the church's condemnation and rejection extend not only to people with AIDS but to their families. At a time of great pain and suffering, when the church community could offer love and support, many families feel forced to hide their grief for fear of being judged and excluded themselves. The shame and fear of persecution associated with AIDS also leads those infected to hide or deny their illness as long as possible, increasing the possibility of infecting others.

In some Christian communities, blame is based on the belief that the disease is God's punishment for one's sins or for the "sins of the fathers." This interpretation of scripture can be traced in part to Old Testament references to those with leprosy. According to Mosaic law, a person with leprosy was to be banished from the community and must not only follow a stringent regimen of bathing but must also sacrifice lambs as "sin" or "guilt offerings" "to make atonement [and] be cleansed from his uncleanness"(Lev. 14:19 RSV).

In Jesus' time lepers were feared and reviled outcasts. Jesus' response to them was in defiance of both Mosaic law and social customs. As a sign of God's love to all, Jesus reached out, touched, and healed lepers, just as he healed those with other diseases. He modeled loving those most in need, calling his followers to do the same. Christ's example does not mean that followers should not use precautions in caring for those with communicable diseases. Christ's model calls followers not to blame but to love, accept, and care for those who are feared and cast out.

Jesus' words also challenge his disciples to move from judgment to compassion. His followers are reminded to "Judge not, that you be not judged. . . . Why do you see the speck that is in your brother's eye, but do not notice the log that is in your own eye?" (Matt. 7:1, 3). Jesus calls his followers to look at themselves before judging Alicia or Jason or any other person with AIDS.

There are other implications of society's tendency to blame those who contract AIDS rather than minister to them. In North America some people see AIDS as a homosexual disease. In Europe it is seen by some as a drug addict's or immigrant's disease. In parts of Asia and Africa AIDS is seen as a white man's disease. Some Christian communities declare that AIDS is a sinner's disease. People who blame particular groups for acquiring or transmitting AIDS feel safe from contracting the disease because they do not fall into those groups. They assume that because they are not homosexual, or white, or do not use drugs, they will not become infected. AIDS can be contracted from unprotected sexual contact with either men or women infected by the virus or from contaminated blood. Globally, AIDS is primarily spread through heterosexual sex and childbirth. People who deny these realities and hide behind stereotypes are not likely to learn how AIDS is actually spread or to assume responsibility for educating the next generation.

WOMEN AND AIDS

Knowledge of particular issues faced by women with AIDS may give Tony greater sensitivity to Alicia's situation. In many parts of the world infection rates for women are climbing. In a ten-year period AIDS increased in the female population of New York City by 40 percent and is now the leading cause of death among women age fifteen to forty-four.[7] Brazil has the highest rate of HIV infection in Latin America. In 1984 Brazilian women accounted for one in fifteen cases of HIV. Ten years later the ratio was one in four.[8] In Africa, home to 60 percent of the ten million people worldwide infected with the AIDS virus, infection rates are already higher for women than for men.[9] As noted above, in most of the world AIDS is primarily transmitted through heterosexual contact, and studies consistently show that the receptive partner in sexual intercourse has a greater likelihood of acquiring the infection than the insertive partner.[10]

Most women who contract AIDS are in their most productive years, between twenty-seven and forty. The social and economic effects on society are already catastrophic. In countries of the South women not only care for households and raise the children, they raise the majority of food crops. The tragedy is also carried into the next generation by the high incidence of mothers transmitting the disease to their babies. By the end of the 1990s sub-Saharan Africa "can expect to have from 200,000 to 300,000 HIV-infected infants annually."[11]

Many societies do not hold men and women to the same standard of fidelity. An increasing number of married women who are faithful to their husbands are contracting AIDS from their husbands. The "Itapecerica da Serra Statement of Brazilian Black Women" attributes the rapid increase of AIDS among black women to the lack of control women have over their own sexuality, to the fact that many women must depend economically on men to survive, and to the exclusion of women from those at risk in early information about AIDS.[12] Other women's groups point to deeply rooted cultural inequalities that prevent women from resisting sex or protecting themselves by insisting that men use condoms.

We do not know if Alicia has a husband who has abandoned her, if she has children who may be HIV-positive, if she used intravenous drugs, or if she was a victim of rape. We do know that she represents a growing number of women who are vulnerable and at risk, and that sensitivity to her situation may help Tony minister more effectively. Alicia may be especially helped by other women with AIDS who share her pain and loneliness.

SPECIAL ROLE AND RESOURCES OF THE CHURCH

Many governments, especially in the majority world where nations are struggling with debt, stabilizing the economy, or attempting to attract tourists, have not only given little or no attention to AIDS, they have denied its presence. Of notable exception is the government of Uganda, which works closely with the Church of

Uganda to support AIDS education programs. In most nations independent nonprofit organizations have taken up the challenge of addressing education and care of people with AIDS. Too often the church is noticeably absent.

The church is present with the residents of Waverly through Tony Herrera. He has taken an important step by introducing AIDS information sessions into the residence program. Tony could make an even greater impact if he takes AIDS awareness programs into his home congregation, beginning with education of his senior pastor and church leaders. The World Health Organization reports that "effective prevention programs could reduce the number of infections by as much as half in the developing world."[13] Knowledge about AIDS also lessens fear about people living with AIDS and can help reduce the level of social rejection. Greater knowledge and deeper understanding can only add to the number of Christians able to care for their brothers and sisters with AIDS. The games and movies at Waverly provide informal personal contact with Alicia, which also helps reduce other residents' anxiety about being around her. With Jason's assistance, Tony is wisely drawing on the skills and knowledge of local AIDS professionals and volunteer counselors. Collaboration between public and nongovernmental organizations gives mutual support and strengthens the positions of agencies working on educational and prevention projects. But the programs, information, and recreation have not eased Alicia's pain. "They liked the food and music. But they still call me 'Stinky.'"

In his efforts to provide programs, Tony seems to have forgotten Jason's initial request that the residents get to know him "as a minister of the gospel of Jesus Christ." Tony's personal care and concern for Alicia have led her to trust him and share parts of her personal story. Her greatest need may now be to talk about her spiritual health, about death, and about salvation, but Tony probably needs to initiate the conversation. He may even need to help Alicia ask the questions that are most troubling her. Tony is modeling in a small way God's overwhelming acceptance and love. As Alicia experiences Tony's love and concern, she may come to understand that God loves her. Tony needs to find ways to help Alicia realize that "neither death, nor life, nor angels, nor rulers, nor things present, nor things to come, nor powers, nor height, nor depth, nor anything else in all creation will be able to separate [her] from the love of God in Christ Jesus our Lord" (Rom. 8:38–39 NRSV).

Tony and Alicia may also be helped by Jesus' response to his disciples who asked about the man born blind: "Rabbi, who sinned, this man or his parents that he was born blind?" Jesus answered, "Neither this man nor his parents sinned; he was born blind so that God's works might be revealed in him" (John 9:1–3 NRSV).

Jason Boyd is not afraid to tell of his infection; he uses his gifts of organization and management to help people who survive on the fringes of society. God's works are manifest in those who risk public censure to share their own stories or the stories of parents, children, or friends who have AIDS. God's works can be seen in those who are advocates for people with HIV and AIDS and who give hope. Those who minister to "the least of these," are ministering to Christ. The works of God may be most powerfully manifested in Alicia's coming to the point where she can love and accept herself in the assurance of God's unfailing love.

NOTES

1. Ford Foundation, *REPORT,* Special Report, Part II, "Confronting AIDS" (Summer 1994), p. 14.

2. Robert L. Stivers, et al., *Christian Ethics,* Second Edition, Maryknoll, NY: Orbis Books, 1994, p. 222.

3. Robert L. Stivers, et al., *Christian Ethics,* Maryknoll, NY: Orbis Books, 1989, p. 218.

4. Elena Cabral, "Unmasking an Epidemic: Brazilians Affirm Life in the Face of AIDS," Ford Foundation *REPORT,* (Summer 1994), p. 21.

5. Stivers, *Christian Ethics,* Second Edition, p. 222.

6. James Chin, "The Growing Impact of the HIV/AIDS Pandemic on Children Born to HIV-Infected Women, in Clinics in Perinatology," Volume 21, Number 1 (March 1994), p. 2.

7. David Michaels and Carol Levine, "Estimates of the Number of Motherless Youth Orphaned by AIDS in the United States," *JAMA* 268, Number 24 (December 23/30, 1992): p. 3456.

8. Cabral, "Unmasking an Epidemic," p. 20.

9. A.R.M. Babu, Pacific News Service, *News Notes,* May/June 1995, Volume 20, Number 3, Washington, D.C.: Maryknoll Fathers and Brothers Justice and Peace Office, (1995), p. 3.

10. Chin, "Growing Impact," p. 2.

11. Ibid., p. 8.

12. *Itapecerica da Serra,* São Paulo, Brazil (August 22, 1993).

13. Ford Foundation, "Confronting AIDS," p. 14.

WE WANT TO BE BAPTIZED

Case

When the Reverend Supangat left their living room, Mr. Slamet and his "wife," Suharti, felt strong disappointment. This was the third time they had been informed that they would have to wait for the decision of the next meeting of the session (congregational committee) on their request to be baptized.

Mr. Slamet, who was forty-five years old, and Suharti, forty-one, and their children, Sutini, Martinah, and Sunarto, ages fifteen, twelve, and nine, wanted to be baptized in the Margorejo Church (Reformed), which they had attended for more than a year. Their eldest son, Maryono, seventeen, had been baptized a few months earlier in Gondoharjo Church (Reformed), located near the Christian high school that he attended.

Margorejo Church has around 1,250 adult members and about 960 baptized children. The Margorejo Church members live throughout the city and are divided into fourteen sectors. Each of the sectors has two elders and one deacon or deaconess, who are elected by all members of the congregation to be members of the church session.

The first time Mr. Slamet and Suharti were told that they had to wait for the decision of the church session was more than six months earlier, when they requested to be baptized during a special visit of elders Mr. Gunawan and Mrs. Sumarni and deacon Mr. Marsudi. These three were lay leaders of Sector VII of Margorejo Church. At that time Mr. Gunawan mentioned that a request for baptism must first be discussed at the regular meeting of the session. After the regular meeting of the session where their request was discussed, they were informed that they had to wait for the next meeting of the session, since no decision was made on their request.

The Reverend Supangat tried to explain to Mr. Slamet and Suharti that the session was not able to make the decision because of the information the session had received on the status of their marriage and the status of their children. The Reverend Supangat wanted to be sure that Mr. Slamet and Suharti were legally married, and he wanted to see the marriage certificate. Mr. Slamet and Suharti were both born into a nominally Muslim family and therefore were legally considered Muslims. A certificate of marriage from the government's Religious Office would be adequate proof, even if the marriage had not been duly registered in the Office of the Civil Registration. In a fearful and hesitant way, Mr. Slamet mentioned that he and Suharti were never legally married. He then said that they could not get any official of the local Religious Office to marry them because he and Suharti are siblings, born from the same father and mother. They moved to Yogyakarta from Kebumen where their parents used to live. Both their parents had since died.

Mr. Slamet confided that from the time they were teenagers, he and Suharti were in love. Their parents tried to separate them, sending him to live with his uncle in Sumatra island and Suharti to her grandparents in a village in Central Java, without letting each know where the other was. Their love for each other, however, was so strong that when each finally knew where the other was, they made contact and decided to elope. They had been together for almost twenty years. They came to live in Yogyakarta about fifteen years ago. None of the neighbors knew about their situation.

Mr. Slamet begged the Reverend Supangat to baptize him and his "wife" and their three children so that they could all be saved. He said that he believed in the redemption that Jesus Christ offered. Suharti felt the same way as her "husband." For a very long time they had been yearning for peace of mind and assurance of forgiveness for their sins.

In the next meeting of the session the Reverend Supangat explained the real situation of Mr. Slamet and his family and why there was no marriage certificate. He reminded the session that Maryono, the eldest son who went to a Christian high school, had been baptized by neighboring Gondoharjo Church a few months earlier. Maryono received Christian religious education in his high school and took catechism lessons from the pastor of Gondoharjo Church. Since Mr. Slamet and his family lived near the Margorejo Church and had been attending the Sunday services for about a year, they wanted to be baptized in this church.

Mr. Raharjo, a well-respected elder, argued against baptizing the family. He said that Mr. Slamet and Suharti were not legally married, and baptizing them would imply legalizing their "marriage." "This is not possible since Christian doctrine is against such 'marriages,' and legalizing their union would violate the state law. In the Islamic law, such marriage is not tolerated either. That is why they were not able to be legally married in the first place. No government official would be willing to sanction such a marriage. It is incest and is condemned by all religions and laws."

This opinion was strongly supported by deacon Mr. Susastro and elder Mr. Sampurno. However, elder Mrs. Sumarni felt that baptizing Mr. Slamet and Suharti would help them to live more harmoniously, because they would be under the care of the Christian community, which should be supportive. This opinion was affirmed by two other members of the session. Elder Mr. Gunawan, on the other hand, agreed that while they all should be baptized, Mr. Slamet and Suharti should no longer live as husband and wife. "If we allow them to continue living together," he said, "it will give a bad example to other Christian families."

Elder Mr. Karyo asked the Reverend Supangat what the Bible says about this matter and whether there are any regulations within the Reformed church which prevent the church from baptizing anyone who has confessed to believe in Jesus Christ as Savior.

The Reverend Supangat cautiously answered that he was not sure how nor where in the Bible to find a direct answer or solution to this matter. Neither could he recall what regulations of the church would be applicable to this situation. He said he was not an expert on church regulations or polity, but he would consult the experts from the Theological College. Further, he said he was not sure whether baptizing Mr. Slamet and Suharti would imply legalizing their "marriage." It would be different if they asked for their marriage to be blessed in the church service. They did not ask that. "Is it morally right to ask Slamet to 'divorce' Suharti after they have been living together for twenty years and have four children? Who would take care of the children? What would be the psychological and social impact on the children? Is it humane to 'break down' this happy family in order for them to be baptized?" asked the Reverend Supangat.

After this third regular meeting of the session, the members still did not agree on what to do. Instead they decided to ask a few experts to give them advice and counsel. They wanted to hear the expert opinions of the professors from the Theological College and also to hear advice from a Christian lawyer, especially on the legal aspects of the matter.

NOTE

Although Indonesia has the largest Muslim population in the world, it is not an Islamic country. Islam is not the official or state religion. The Constitution of the Republic of Indonesia is based on *Pancasila* which means "Five Principles." These five principles are: (1) Belief in one supreme God; (2) Just and civilized humanism; (3) Unity of Indonesia; (4) Sovereignty of the people guided by the inner wisdom of unanimity which emanates from the deliberations among representatives; and (5) Social justice for the whole people of Indonesia.

Religious freedom is guaranteed under the constitution. Six religions are officially recognized by the government: Islam; Protestant Christianity; Roman Catholic Christianity; Hindu Dharma (Hinduism); Buddhism; and Confucianism. The majority of the followers of Confucianism, who are mainly ethnic Chinese, are also Buddhists. The Marriage Law of 1974 specifies that the government legally recognizes a marriage if it is officially conducted in a religious ceremony and in accordance with the religious stipulations of one of the above recognized religions.

Teaching Note

I. Goals

A. To deliberate on Christian understanding of baptism and its relation to redemption and forgiveness of sins.

B. To help participants understand the complexity of issues on baptism as they relate to marriage, divorce, and family life in general, especially in a religiously and culturally pluralistic society.

C. To discuss the implications of such issues in pastoral ministry.

II. Background Information

The commentary offers a good deal of background information about the Indonesian setting of the case. The case leader may want to assign selected advance readings or give participants a copy of the "context" section of the commentary along with the case. Some of the most important factors are noted below.

A. Indonesia is a religiously pluralistic society. About 85 percent of the population is Muslim. The Christian population, both Protestant and Roman Catholic, is about 10 percent. The remaining 5 percent are Hindus, Buddhists, Confucianists, and animists.

B. The Javanese Christian churches in Central Java are within the Reformed tradition.

C. Unlike in many Islamic countries, conversion from one religion to another is common in Indonesia. A Muslim can be converted to Christianity and vice versa, or a Hindu can become a Christian, etc.

III. Biblical References for Case Discussion:

A. Along with reading the case, and prior to the case discussion, participants should read the following biblical texts: Matthew 3:1–12 and its parallels (Mark 1:1–5, Luke 3:1–20, John 1:19–28) concerning John the Baptist and his baptism for remission of sins and Matthew 28:19–20 concerning the great commission.

B. Additional biblical references that will be helpful for the discussion are Galatians 2:15–3:15 on justification by faith and Romans 11:25–36 on "All Israel will be saved."

IV. Case Discussion

A. Discuss the context of this case and any factors in the setting which may be particularly relevant to the elders' decision. To what extent, for example, should the minority status of Christians in Indonesia be a factor in the elders' decision? How important is the role of elders in the Reformed tradition?

B. Clarify and post a list of the issues raised by the case. Include in this list the hopes and fears of Mr. Slamet and Suharti. Ask for any points of clarification which are needed.

C. On a separate board or paper post the positions taken by Mrs. Sumarni—to baptize the couple—and of Mr. Raharjo—to refuse to baptize them. Note the reasons given by both elders. Then ask participants to make a straw vote on which position they support. Be sure to note that they may have different reasons from those cited by Mrs. Sumarni and Mr. Raharjo, such as the reasons suggested by Mr. Gunawan, and that they will have an opportunity to share with the group their reasons for their decision. Record the vote. Try to urge all participants to take a position, reminding them that not to decide would in effect be a decision not to baptize Mr. Slamet and Suharti.

Discuss first one and then the other position with the arguments to support them. What are the biblical foundations to support each view? What are the theological, cultural, and personal reasons? What interpretations of the meaning of baptism emerge from this discussion?

D. What steps should the Reverend Supangat take for the church community to come to a decision? Urge participants to be concrete in their suggestions. What should be the pastor's primary goals in any process he adopts?

Commentary

"Come to me, all you who are weary and burdened, and I will give you rest"(Matt. 11:28 NIV). These comforting words of Jesus could very well be the hope and the reason why Mr. Slamet and Suharti wanted to be baptized. The fact that both knew their living together as a married couple was illegal and punishable by law has haunted them throughout their life together. They knew they had done wrong when they decided to live as husband and wife, but apparently they could not help it. Their love for each other was very strong, such that they dared to go against the social and religious taboo. They were willing to take the risks. They must have been aware, finally, that they could never be married legally.

Through Maryono, their eldest son who was baptized in Gondoharjo Church, Mr. Slamet and Suharti learned that in the Christian religion forgiveness of sin is given freely through faith in Jesus Christ and through being baptized in his name. So they began to go to church services regularly. They were finally convinced that they should also be baptized and become Christian in order to receive the forgiveness of their sins and thus attain peace of mind.

THE CONTEXT

Unlike in many other countries, especially in Islamic countries, changing religious affiliation is a common event in Indonesia. The constitution of the republic provides such religious liberty. There are various reasons why people want to change their religious affiliations. One of the more common reasons is marriage. Where two partners are of different religious affiliations, one partner may voluntarily join the other's religion to be in harmony with the spouse. However, some may be coerced to accept the other's religion if the marriage is to continue. Other people are genuinely converted to another religion, after studying or comparing different religious teaching and practices. Yet still others change their religious affiliation because they are dissatisfied with and disenchanted by their own religious teaching and practices.

In Indonesia religious education is compulsory in all schools from kindergarten to the university. Each religious group conducts religious education in the community for its membership. Although Indonesia has a majority Muslim population— approximately 85 percent of about 190 million people—Islam is not a state religion. The Republic of Indonesia is based on *Pancasila* (Five Principles) that underlie the constitution, which in turn guarantees freedom of religion to all its citizens. Indonesians are free to belong to any of the religions recognized by Indonesia: Islam, Protestant Christianity, Roman Catholicism, Hinduism, Buddhism, and Confucianism.

After the Indonesian Communist Party's failed coup d'etat on 30th September/ 1st October, 1965, the Indonesian Parliament passed a law that banned the Communist Party and communism in Indonesia. The law also requires every citizen to belong to any one of the six religious groups recognized by the government. Citizens are free to choose which religious group to join, but they are not free to become atheists or not to belong to a recognized religious group.

Although 85 percent of the population is considered Muslim, only a small percentage devoutly practices Islamic tenets and teaching. The large majority are nominal or statistical Muslims. Mr. Slamet and his family are of such a nominal Muslim group. His eldest son, Maryono, was converted to Christianity after several years of Christian education in his Christian high school.

The church Mr. Slamet, Suharti, and their children attend every Sunday is a traditional Reformed church, which takes the sacraments seriously. Although the church wedding (marriage) is not considered a sacrament, most members and leaders of the church believe in the sanctity of marriage. Many believe that a church wedding is holy and sanctified. Under the marriage law the government recognizes a marriage as legal when it is done in accordance with religious rites. The magistrate only registers the marriage. The marriage certificate is issued by the religious body; in the case of an Islamic wedding, the marriage certificate is issued by the government's Office of Religious Affairs. The marriage is then officially registered in the office of the magistrate.

Ethical and moral issues related to individual or family life are considered very important. As a minority group among the majority Muslim community, Christians are encouraged by the church to show exemplary moral and ethical virtues as a means of witnessing their Christian faith. Deviation from the normally accepted standard of behavior, especially regarding sexual life, is considered to be sinful. Confessing one's sin in front of the whole congregation during a Sunday service is still commonly practiced in churches such as Margorejo, especially if the transgression relates to cases of adultery, premarital sex, or out-of-wedlock pregnancy.

Before accepting adult new members through baptism, Reformed churches usually require converts to take a full course of catechism and allow their private lives to be scrutinized. It is a common practice that members of the church or prospective members who have been regularly attending Sunday services be visited by the pastor or by the elders and the deacon or deaconess. Requests for baptism are usually approved by the session (governing body) of the church, which meets regularly.

THE ISSUES AND THE CONCERNS

The persons in this case have various concerns. Mr. Slamet and Suharti are haunted by the shadow of their relationship which violates a major social and religious taboo. They also know that they broke the law.

They are fearful of the consequences if and when the fact of their being siblings who live together as husband and wife becomes known to the public and the officials. They are constantly afraid that their happy family will be broken up. They have been longing for peace of mind. They now find hope in the Christian religion, which promises forgiveness of sins by grace alone. Forgiveness and peace of mind will be given to them if they believe in Jesus Christ and are baptized into the church. This is what they have understood through attending the Sunday services for more than a year. The issue facing the pastor and his session, however, is whether the church should baptize Mr. Slamet and Suharti, who are not legally married, and their children. If the church baptizes them, would there be any legal implications?

In the Javanese Christian churches in Central Java, the setting of this case, as in many other Reformed churches, the elders are charged with the responsibility of guiding the members to live in accordance with the teaching or the doctrine of the church, with no deviation from accepted dogmas. Elders of the church are given such responsibility to ensure the proper implementation of doctrines and teaching as well as to give guidance in the ethical and moral behavior of the members. It is therefore understandable that Mr. Raharjo, being an elder of the church, is very concerned with this request for baptism. He feels that it is his responsibility to make sure that the church stays on the right path and that all church officers, leaders, and members must respect and obey the church's teaching and regulations as well as the law of the country. He is very concerned with the legal implications of baptizing Mr. Slamet, Suharti, and their children, which he believes would imply that the church accepts their status as husband and wife. He believes that baptism would mean recognizing and thus legalizing their "marriage." And this, Mr. Raharjo fears, would be in violation of the law. Therefore, Mr. Raharjo would never support the baptism.

On the other hand, Mrs. Sumarni, also an elder, is more concerned with Mr. Slamet and his family. She understands the psychological and spiritual burdens they must have, because she also understands the dilemma which confronts them.

She feels that one of the functions of the church as a Christian community is to give support to members and help all families to live harmoniously, peacefully, and happily. By allowing Mr. Slamet and his family to be baptized in the church, Mrs. Sumarni feels that they can become full members and thus receive the support of the whole Christian community.

Elder Mr. Gunawan is concerned with finding a solution to the problem. He feels that a compromise can be reached through some sort of give-and-take principle. The church would baptize the family on the condition that Mr. Slamet first "divorce" Suharti. Thus they would no longer be living in sin. Mr. Gunawan is also concerned about other members of the church. If Mr. Slamet and Suharti remain living as husband and wife, they will not be good examples of Christian living and may negatively influence other members of the church. They would also not be good witnesses to the community at large, and they could become a stumbling block in the relationship of the church to the wider community.

Elder Mr. Karyo is concerned with finding a solution consistent with the Reformed tradition, that is, according to biblical mandate and Reformed Church regulations. He seems to be in favor of baptizing Mr. Slamet and his family unless there is a clear biblical or ecclesial regulation against such baptism. He wants the pastor, the Reverend Supangat to give the answer.

So, the dilemma is faced by the Reverend Supangat, who is concerned both with Mr. Slamet and his family and with the members of his church. The pastor is very cautious. He says he did not receive any request to legalize the marriage or to bless the wedding in the church. Baptizing them does not necessarily accept their status as a married couple. Baptism in Supangat's view is a symbol of reconciliation, the cleansing of sins. Our sins are washed away by the water of baptism so that all may be reconciled with God. Christians are joined in the family of God through baptism. Therefore, he asks: "Is it right to ask Slamet to divorce Suharti—to be separated from each other and from their children in order for them to become reconciled and joined with God?" He feels it is not right to break up a happy family in order to baptize them. And yet he is uncertain whether having them continue to live as family with their children could negatively affect his church. Furthermore, he is unsure about the possible legal implications of such baptism.

If he consulted a lawyer, Supangat would learn that within the Indonesian legal system there is no law or regulation governing the practice of the teachings or doctrines of the church. Doctrines are up to the church, and the state does not interfere. Therefore, the congregation would not be in danger of legal problems if the elders agreed to the baptism, as long as the church does not officially conduct a marriage. Marriage is a social behavior governed by marriage law. Marriage between siblings, which is considered incest, is condemned by law.

PASTORAL STRATEGY

In a very difficult theological case such as this, it is better to have a clear biblical and ecclesial understanding of the sacraments, especially baptism. Baptism in the Bible is a symbol of the cleansing of sins. The baptized are washed by the water of baptism. The baptism that John the Baptist performed was baptism for repentance (Matt. 3:11), that is, for the removal and forgiveness of sins (Acts 2:38), which will enable those being baptized to be reconciled with God. As Peter the Apostle says, "The promise is for you and your children and for all who are far off—for all whom the Lord our God will call" (Acts 2:39 NIV). According to the teaching of the Reformed Church, salvation is given through faith alone. It is given by grace alone in accordance with the Holy Scripture. *Sola fide, sola gratia, sola scriptura.* Does baptism as a sign of forgiveness of sins and as a symbol of the salvation given have anything to do with marriage?

Christians are often confronted with conflicting interests. In the situation facing the leaders of the Margorejo Church, these conflicting interests are maintaining the "purity" of the Church's doctrines and regulations (law) versus meeting the needs of the family, real human beings in need of forgiveness and grace. The situation is a conflict concerning law and grace. Mr. Slamet and Suharti have been living under great strain; they need support, comfort, and assurance of pardon. They have acknowledged their transgressions and plead for mercy and forgiveness.

Nevertheless, there is also a concern about the church's need to stay within the law of the state. The church as a social and religious community should not consciously violate the law. To bless and to condone a marriage of siblings would be a blatant violation of the law and also a violation of biblical law. One question that needs to be answered or clarified is whether baptizing Mr. Slamet and his family would constitute legalizing and accepting his marriage to Suharti. Once this issue is settled, the remaining question is, What is more important: keeping an imperfect family happy and giving them community support or breaking them up for the sake of the morally acceptable way of living?

Questions of both law and grace involve human needs. The human needs are by no means the only needs in this case; those of Mr. Slamet, Suharti, and their children are the primary needs. One must also consider the needs of Mr. Raharjo, Mr. Gunawan, and Mr. Karyo. They need to feel that they are responding properly as they are called to do as elders of the church. Also important are the needs of the Reverend Supangat and Mrs. Sumarni to be supported by colleagues in doing their tasks as they are called to do.

In Galatians 2:15–16 (NIV), the apostle Paul says, "We who are Jews by birth and not 'Gentile sinners' know that a man is not justified by observing the law, but by faith in Jesus Christ. So we, too, have put our faith in Christ Jesus that we may be justified by faith in Christ and not by observing the law, because by observing the law no one will be justified" (also cf. Gal. 3, 7, 9, 14). Jesus has also shown that "the Son of Man came to seek and to save what was lost" (Luke 19:10 NIV). It would be advisable for the Reverend Supangat to ask the session of the church to discuss these biblical resources, to pray together, and then to decide together what should be done.

THE POWER OF TRADITION

Case

The Reverend John, a missionary from Canada, had come to pastor a young congregation of the Epe people in Nigeria. Now he felt helpless and frustrated as he waited for Mr. Nja. An incident that had taken place in the house of Elder Nja was seriously affecting the unity of the young church, which was on the verge of collapse. The pastor was clear that something must be done, but he did not know how to proceed since the case involved tradition.

In the tradition of the Epes, every male child born in the community must be initiated in the Epe's sacred shrine. The people believe that initiation prepares their male children for manhood. Whoever does not initiate his son is not regarded as a man and will not be allowed to vote or be voted for in the council meeting of the village elders. To make matters worse, an uninitiated man will not be allowed to marry, and if he does, his right ear will be cut off, meaning that he has been reduced to the status of a woman.

When Christianity came to the village of the Epe, it was warmly accepted. Many people left their traditional religion and joined Christianity. When the Reverend John came to the village as a missionary pastor, he taught his parishioners the commandment, "You shall not have other gods beside me." Since the traditional initiation of boys involved circumcision and sacrifice to a shrine for spirits, the pastor taught the Christians to refuse initiation for their children. He reminded them of Paul's words, "In Christ we are neither male nor female, circumcised or uncircumcised."

Mr. Nja, a well-known and respected man in the community and also a member of the village ruling council, had accepted Christianity. His charisma as a leader also gained him a position in the church. He was later elected and ordained as an elder commissioner who represented the church in both synod and general assembly meetings. His wife, Ada, became a leader of the women's guild and matron of the young Christian girls in training. Mr. Nja had two sons, Eke and Ewa, aged four and two respectively. As a Christian elder of strong faith, Mr. Nja would not give his sons for initiation. Rather, he had his children baptized in the church.

Mr. Nja's father-in-law, Mr. Eze, one of the members of the village council of elders, was not a Christian. He wanted to have his grandchildren initiated. One day he went to his son-in-law with a jar of palm wine to negotiate for the initiation of Eke, who was four. He reminded Elder Nja of all the implications of not doing so. Elder Nja did not accept the idea and did his best to stop further discussion on the topic.

It happened that the synod meeting and the initiation period coincided. Elder Nja was busy in the church with the Reverend John organizing the meeting. Mr. Eze went to Mr. Nja's home with a group of young boys and took Eke away for initiation. When Elder Nja returned home and heard the news of Eke's initiation, he was so offended that he wanted to take the case to court.

Mr. Eze had the strong support of the village council of elders, who wanted to retain Mr. Eze as their leader and representative at the city council meeting. Furthermore, Mr. Eze's eldest son, brother to Ada, was the only lawyer in the community available to handle the legal case Mr. Nja threatened to bring.

News of Eke's initiation spread among the members of the church; they were not happy about the news. The whole situation began to affect the unity of the church, mostly among those who had refused to give their sons for initiation. Mr. Eze threatened to disown Ada as his daughter if she joined her husband to fight against him. The pressure was too much for Ada, and Elder Nja lost the support of his wife.

Elder Nja then sent a letter to the pastor to help save his dignity and the unity of the church. He threatened to resign from the church and also be absent from the synod meeting if nothing was done about the situation. He arranged to see the pastor at 5 P.M. the same day.

Earlier that same day, the village council had sent a warning to the pastor not to step into the matter. The council told him that if he intervened, they would expel him from the village. While the pastor was still thinking about what to do, he heard a knock on the door and realized that Elder Nja had come for his advice.

Teaching Note

I. Goals for Teaching the Case

A. To understand the necessity of contextualization of the gospel and theology in the process of evangelization at home and abroad.

B. To raise awareness of the danger of an outsider trying to set terms of appropriation of the gospel or striving to become the patriarch of his or her church.

C. To show the importance of appreciating people of other cultures and their cultures and traditions.

D. To show that the gospel, if it is good news, has to be rooted in the internal resources and capacities of a community.

II. Background Information

The discussion leader may wish to refer to the commentary for additional information about the case context. Basic understanding of rites of passage, the tradition of giving palm oil, and the introduction of Western Christianity to non-Western cultures will be particularly useful for an informed discussion of this case.

III. Case Discussion

A. The Actors

There are many actors in this drama. Some have a central role in the case, others a more secondary one. There is also a host of silent stakeholders. The participants need to be aware of them and introduce them into the case discussion to understand the complexity of the situation.

The following actors are most prominent:

The Reverend John

Elder Nja and his wife, Ada

Mr. Eze and his son, Mr. Eze, Jr. (the lawyer)

There are also community actors who are not so visible, but who are still influential in the case. These include members of the church community, in their diversity of interest and age groups, and the village council.

The actors have to be identified and characterized in detail for their profiles and positions in the church and society to emerge clearly. That detailing will reveal societal relationships as well as church relationships, including internal power relationships. The detailing of the church composition and activities will also be important because of the issues of cultural dominance and church dogma. The detailing of the village council, its composition, and its interests is important because of the background pressure the council exerts on some people in the case.

B. Actions and Issues

In bringing together the different actors in this life drama, the facilitator should bring the historical background of the Christian community into focus. That history is a record of the synthesis that kept balance and peace in the parish.

Thereafter the facilitator should recreate the dramatic events in the extended family of Mr. Nja and Mr. Eze. Those events led to the confrontation between the two powerful figures who represent two institutions informed by apparently conflicting ideologies. The participants should discuss how the two institutions in the community, the church and the village council, come into the picture. As the tension between these bodies increases, the family is the first institution to be threatened with disintegration, the church is next, and then the institution of pastoral leadership.

During this discussion, a number of issues will surface. Among the many questions the group can pursue are the following:

What is the role of a missionary as both a carrier of and a representative of a foreign culture and a universal gospel in a foreign culture?

Should a pastor encourage a search toward synthesis as an ongoing exercise among converts to Christianity? Why or why not?

In a situation where that search was not previously encouraged, should it be encouraged or should a dogmatic approach hold sway? What should happen on the side of cultural rigidity?

Who should reopen the dialogue to restore respect for positive aspects of local culture and its synthesis with the best of the gospel in this Nigerian community?

C. Resolution and Resources

Caring for human needs often involves peacemaking. Try to search for a peacemaker or reconciler in this conflict. What kind of person would be acceptable? What would make him or her acceptable?

How should such a person view tradition and culture? How deeply committed a Christian should such a person be and what should characterize his or her commitment, love for people, and dogmatic fervor?

If the Reverend John becomes the peacemaker, what should he do? How does he enter into the conflict in light of the threat of expulsion by the village council?

Can Mr. Nja or his father-in-law, Mr. Eke, become a peacemaker? How are they affected by their own reputations among their followers and admirers?

What theological resources can bring reconciliation in this village and in this church? What cultural resources are important to reconciliation?

Commentary

THE CONTEXT

This case takes place in Nigeria among the Epe. The Epe are one of many Nigerian tribes. Each tribe in Nigeria has its own traditions, culture, and language. In many cases, there are commonalities among the traditions, cultures, and even languages of the various tribes. Each tribe has rites of passage, rituals that introduce every child, male or female, into the different stages of life and lead that child into adulthood and ultimately into death. There are common rituals for male and female children as well as different rituals for each sex. All these rituals are compulsory for all the children in the tribe. Christianity and dominant cultures arrived and disturbed the harmony, as is the case here.

One of the rites of passage is the initiation. Initiation is a tribal school for young boys, and in some cases for girls, who are placed in age groups for cultural education to prepare them for adulthood. The surgical act of circumcision, in which the foreskin of a male child is ceremoniously severed, forms part of this initiation course.

All the villagers in this case study are Epe people and share a common tradition, culture, and language. They lead their lives like people everywhere. They have families, send their children to school, and observe traditional norms and values. The male members of the community periodically attend a village council that organizes, coordinates, and runs the political, social, economic, cultural, and religious affairs of the tribe. During modern times, the village council has a chairman who may not be a chief but who is respected and influential. Such a chairman wields a lot of power among these people, who always strive for harmony and peaceful resolution of tribal matters. The council leader must be exemplary and have a model home in order for his power not to be eroded from the inside.

The Epe experienced an invasion by Christian missionaries in the nineteenth century. The coming of Christianity was both a blessing and a problem, hence its acceptance by some and rejection by others. In some cases, acceptance of Christianity meant the abandonment of some traditional practices and religious beliefs because of incompatibility between Christianity and tradition. It should be remembered that Christianity was encapsulated in a culture that was claimed to be the only normative expression of that faith. In other situations, a synthesis consisting of the best from Christianity, cultural practices, and traditional religion has been arrived at after a long period of trial and error. This does not mean that there is total harmony between the different traditions. Power relations in the village as well as in the church either keep the balance or disturb it.

One of the most important cultural gestures of the Epe is the giving of a jar of palm oil. A traditional practice among many tribes in Nigeria is to give a token of good will to people with whom one wants to conduct business or discuss serious matters. Such a gift, in this case palm oil, shows respect and is normally given by a junior to a senior member of a family or tribe. It is very unusual for the opposite to happen, even among Christians. In this case, the unusual happens. The father-in-law gives palm oil to the son-in-law! This gift shows the seriousness and irregularity of the matter that he has come to discuss. The father-in-law is virtually on his knees before his son-in-law to humbly make his request. He is almost saying, "Please don't refuse." This reversal is very unusual and cannot go unnoticed by the son-in-law. The reversed gesture puts the son-in-law in a very difficult position wherein he is not given any choice. He cannot afford to humiliate his father-in-law who has already humbled himself, a senior who should be receiving not giving palm oil.

THE CONFLICT

Conflict has arisen in a family that includes a powerful, traditional father-in-law and an influential, modern son-in-law, who is also a Christian leader in a local church. This conflict threatens to engulf the entire village and church community if appropriate action is not taken quickly. Only one person, the Reverend John, can and must take that action. He is under considerable pressure from one quarter to speak decisively but under a real threat of expulsion if he does.

The Reverend John, a Canadian missionary, has been put in a difficult position in which he is expected to make a pronouncement or take an action that will either reconcile a powerful man and his son-in-law, heal a family that is being torn asunder, or justify their permanent separation. That same pronouncement or action could guarantee the growth of the church community he has worked so hard to nurture or could usher in its rapid demise. His action may trigger a heated conflict in the church community between males and females, youth and adults.

One can imagine that Christian men who have turned their backs on traditional practices that are seen to be in conflict with the gospel would feel as Mr. Nja does, that no compromise should be made. The resistance to compromise would be strongest with those men who are in powerful positions in the church. Many church leaders are commoners in the village hierarchy and would never otherwise enjoy the status and power they have in the church. Many other men would consider the conflict solely in terms of the interests of the gospel. They would think about liberation from the suspicion, superstition, and fear that haunt many traditionalists. They would think of equality of all believers, male and female, young and old. Forgiveness, an element deeply entrenched in Christian faith, would be uppermost in their minds. During this time they would forget about those instances when culture and the gospel overlap. They would also forget that they, too, are selective about cultural matters and that they have actually been involved in an ongoing process of sifting and re-evaluating cultural practices, accepting some while rejecting others. Most women in the congregation would react differently. Many would react as mothers, imagining the suffering of their sons in a case where the uncompromising rigidity of the Christian faith would exclude their sons from marriage or village leadership. This pain would not be acceptable to them.

As for the youth in the church, great tension would result from this episode. As modern youth who are in touch through radio and perhaps television with other youth in the forefront of change in the world, they would be thinking of going to school and breaking with tradition. These young men and women would not think about the good things in their culture. They would not consider how their culture has harmonized relations in their village and how it has kept peace and regulated assistance to the poor and needy. For them, that culture stands for only one thing: backwardness. They would want to identify Christian faith with modernity and regard it as a catalyst to the future. On the other hand, tradition is strong in the village because it is in the hands of such strong men as Mr. Eze, against whom the youth would feel powerless. Faced with the inevitable penalty for rejecting tradition, they would submit and join the protest of the women of the church. Few, if any, young people would want to face punishment for the sake of faith, not even Christian faith.

This conflict also threatens to polarize the church and the village. Conditions have been created in which church people forget about some good things in African culture, and traditionalists have forgotten or downplay the contribution that the church has brought to Nigeria. What the Reverend John says or does will either ensure his expulsion from Nigeria or his peaceful stay. At a deeper, personal level, the outcome may have great consequences for the Reverend John. It could change his faith and erode its theological foundations irretrievably or reflect an incorrigible theological rigidity which he might later live to regret.

The Reverend John cannot overlook all the possible consequences of his response and its lasting impact. Neither can he exhibit superficiality and opportunism in his response because the matter is as deeply theological as it is cultural. He will have to be very understanding and respectful of the traditions of his congregants as well as very faithful to the truth of the gospel that gives meaning to his sojourn in a Nigerian mission field. Above all, he will have to strive to save the humanity of people and not lose sight of it.

THE DILEMMA

The dilemma that faces the Reverend John is occasioned by Mr. Eze, a wealthy and powerful member of the village council, who wishes to protect his position and remain true to his traditions by circumcising his grandson without the consent of the boy's father. Mr. Nja, the son-in-law, is an educated Christian leader who has decided to part with the traditions of his people in this situation, as have many other people of his generation. He feels that his father-in-law's action is sowing confusion and subverting his own power in the church, where he is highly respected. Mr. Nja also feels deeply humiliated, powerless, and frustrated.

The Reverend John cannot consider only concrete actions and complaints; he must also deal with what both these men have forgotten in the heat of their struggle against each other. He has to deal with their initial politeness to each other and basic respect for each other. He would not forget Mr. Eze's gift of palm oil whereby he demonstrated his respect for his son-in-law.

ISSUES IN THE CASE

This confrontation involves, at a personal level, the two sides of an African family, a son-in-law and his father-in-law. Mr. Nja is angry at Mr. Eze, who subverts Mr. Nja's authority in his own home. On the other hand, Mr. Eze is convinced that he is dealing with a son-in-law who does not want to think about the dire consequences of his rejection of a basic cultural precept as it relates to his own son. Mr. Eze is convinced that a responsible grandfather must intervene in favor of a grandson whose father is selfish and inconsiderate. The Reverend John's intervention has to deal with these personal feelings of family members. As a pastor to one member of the family, he will have to find theological resources that will enable him to reconcile the family. He will have to realize that Mr. Nja's faith is on trial. He could strengthen or weaken it with his reconciling mission. As a pastor operating in the Epe cultural context, the Reverend John will have to acquaint himself with the culture of the Epe which is so dear to Mr. Eze. In attempting a reconciliation, he will have to be seen by Mr. Eze as fully respectful of the Epe culture. He should not ride roughshod over it if reconciliation is to succeed. He should emphasize that Christians must bear one another's burdens and offer them unconditional love.

The confrontation goes beyond the confines of the family, due to both men's community involvement. The circumcision of Mr. Nja's son inevitably places Mr. Nja in a difficult position in the church because of the perceived contradiction between the gospel and this cultural ritual. His visibility as a leader in the church makes unavoidable a heated debate about his role as well as the issue of circumcision for a Christian family. It is possible that some members of the church will concentrate their attention on the church leader, Mr. Nja, while others will concentrate on the issue of the gospel and culture or the gospel and circumcision. However, giving attention to Mr. Nja will not solve the problem of the synthesis between gospel and culture; at best, it will only postpone the problem.

The pastor needs to address the real issue, namely gospel and culture. The solution to that problem will solve the difficult position of Mr. Nja and the foreign missionary and his culture. In dealing with this issue the following questions are pertinent. What is the role of a missionary as a carrier and representative of a foreign culture and as a messenger of a universal gospel in another culture? Should he encourage a continual search for a synthesis or not? Should dogmatic rigidity hold sway?

This conflict offers an opportunity for a review and rethinking of the appropriate approach of a missionary in his or her mission work in a foreign culture. The traditional arrogance and omniscience often displayed by missionaries do not help. The missionary honors the gospel by humility and by being prepared to learn and listen before evangelizing people, especially in a foreign culture. During that period of listening and learning, the missionary will discover that there are convergences and divergences between culture and the gospel and that in some areas, such as concern for the poor and the widows, neighborliness, and an emphasis on community, agreement prevails. The missionary will learn that, in view of this convergence, it would be advisable to encourage continued searching for more such areas. He has to distinguish his own culture from the essence of the gospel and be aware of the temptation to equate his culture with the gospel. He must guard against the tendency to see his own culture as superior and to want to impose it on other people. Evangelization and civilization are neither the same nor equal.

As far as culture is concerned, should the church community ever reject basic traditions without analysis? Or should there be an analytical approach and a search for culture in the earliest Christian communities about which the New Testament teaches? As noted above, this conflict has the potential to explode peace in the Christian community of the Epe. On the other hand, if wisely handled, it also has the potential to open doors for the gospel, deepening its roots among the Epe and leading to a wave of growth for the church.

To achieve the latter, the missionary has to be analytical even in his approach to the gospel. He will soon realize that the gospel, from the earliest days of the church, has always been intertwined with culture. The gospel never rejected culture in toto. Instead, it purified culture and strengthened it and used some elements as its vehicles.

There is another level of the confrontation that will have to be addressed—the tension between two powerful institutions: the church and the village council. Every member of the church owes allegiance to the council as well as to the church community. The village council is the guardian of traditions while the church is the guardian of the teachings of the universal Christian church. Both institutions are deeply concerned with the welfare of every member of the community, Christian and non-Christian. Both are deeply concerned with the plight of the underdog in society. Both emphasize community, mutual assistance, and care. Both institutions aim at achieving a high moral life in the community. Does that common goal not constitute the basis for dialogue and synthesis? On the foundation of that commonality, the two can have a dialogue about the use of power by the secular institution and pervasive mistrust, superstition, and the deep rootedness of vengeance and revenge in many traditional cultures.

THEOLOGICAL ISSUES IN THE CASE

In the ensuing dialogue, many members of the church who stand for a total separation between culture and the gospel will be inclined to emphasize the prohibition of service to two masters (Ex. 20). Those members who would wish to exercise freedom to search for a synthesis will be inclined to argue that the law is made for human beings and not human beings for the law (Mark 2:27). Both groups err by starting with the divergences between the gospel and culture and holding onto these diametrically opposed positions as if they are the essential and only positions of the gospel and culture. What they both miss is the convergence between the two, which is, in fact, what describes the life of all of them. Both groups accept without question parts of culture, such as the giving of palm oil. In this situation it might be helpful for the pastor to build on the common goal of both institutions and emphasize that Jesus came "that you should have life and have it abundantly." The Reverend John should lead the opposing groups in the church in the identification of the many practices wherein the Epe culture and the gospel are not opposed to each other. They can reinforce one another to enhance the quality of the life of the community without threatening the purity of the gospel.

Having taken that step, the Reverend John should then urge both council and church to acknowledge that there are cultural practices that do not enhance the quality of life of every Epe. Instead of asking them to search arbitrarily for such practices, he should get them to accept common criteria to search for the essence of the gospel as well as that of culture. It is here that the redeeming life and death of Jesus come in. Redemptiveness does not only lie in what Jesus has attained for humankind, it also lies in teaching differing parties to differ without denying, threatening, or hurting each other. If both parties can reach a consensus about the criteria, both have to undertake a rigorous critique of culture together with the aim, not of discarding it, but of purifying it to serve as a vehicle for the realization of the Kingdom of God. The parties have to go further and accept that some positive elements of culture help Christians to understand some gospel imperatives. These elements can serve as analytical and critical lenses in reading the scriptures and discerning the essence of the gospel. As a matter of fact, it is in the critical appropriation of both culture and the gospel that the prohibition against serving two masters who are opposed to each other would be valid.

AUTHORS AND CONTRIBUTORS

AUTHORS

Takatso Mofokeng, Professor of Systematic Theology at the University of South Africa in Pretoria. He is the author of *The Crucified among the Crossbearers: Towards a Black Christology,* has written numerous articles on Black Theology, and has strong ties with the anti-apartheid struggle. He is an ordained minister in the Uniting Reformed Church in Southern Africa.

Judo Poerwowidagdo, Executive Secretary for Asia and the Pacific, Ecumenical Theological Education, Unit on Unity and Renewal, World Council of Churches, Geneva. He has taught at and was Principal of the United Theological College Duta Wacana, Yogjakarya, Indonesia, and taught philosophy of language at the Graduate Faculty of Gadjay Mada State University, Yogjakarya. Before joining the World Council of Churches staff, he was President of Duta Wacana Christian University in Yogjakarya.

Henry S. Wilson, Presbyter of the Church of South India and Executive Secretary of the Department of Theology of the World Alliance of Reformed Churches, Geneva. Prior to this appointment, he was the Director of the Board of Theological Education of the Senate of Serampore College (Association of Theological Schools and Institutions in South Asia) and a lecturer at the United Theological College, Bangalore, India. He is the editor of *Human Rights Issues and the Pastoral Ministry: Indian Theological Case Studies.*

Robert A. Evans, Executive Director, Plowshares Institute, Simsbury, Connecticut; Visiting Professor, Center for Conflict Resolution, University of Cape Town, South Africa; and Co-Executive Director of the Association for Case Teaching. He is a Presbyterian pastor and the author and co-author of numerous books including *Christian Theology, The Globalization of Theological Education,* and *Human Rights: A Dialogue between the First and Third Worlds.*

Alice Frazer Evans, Director of Writing and Research, Plowshares Institute, Simsbury, Connecticut; Visiting Scholar, Center for Conflict Resolution, University of Cape Town, South Africa; and Co-Executive Director of the Association for Case Teaching. She is an elder in the Presbyterian Church (USA) and author and co-author of numerous books including *Pedagogies for the Non-Poor* and *Christian Ethics: A Case Method Approach.*

CONTRIBUTORS

Adao Francisco Alexandre, Pastor, Angola.

Stephanie Davage, Pastor, Covenant Presbyterian Church, Wendall, North Carolina, USA.

Lionel Derenoncourt, Associate for International Hunger Concerns, Presbyterian Church (USA), Louisville, Kentucky, USA.

Vuata Saimoni Duvui, Fijian minister of the Uniting Church in Australia, Calvary Presbytery (Aboriginal and Islander Christian Congress), Rockhampton, Queensland, Australia.

Purna Chandra Jena, National Council of Churches in India, Coordinator, Urban Industrial Rural Mission, Orissa, India.

James Joseph, Regional Coordinator, Development Department, Alternativa, Lima, Peru.

Naomi Kowo, Director for Church and Society, Zimbabwe Council of Churches, Harare, Zimbabwe.

Yonasani Kahaibale Lubanga, Rector, Nima parish, Anglican Diocese, Church of the Province of Uganda.

Nazir Masih, Principal, Milan Memorial Senior Secondary School, Dhariwal, Punjab, India.

Samuel Agha Okoro, Minister, The Presbyterian Church in Nigeria.

Paul Roberts, Johnson C. Smith Seminary, Atlanta, Georgia, USA.

Premkumar Soans, Presbyter, Vice President of the Karnataka Southern Diocese, Church of South India.

Elizabeth Wieman, Associate Pastor, Grace Congregational Church, Framingham, Massachusetts, USA.